Lines of Authority

❦ ALSO BY STEVEN N. ZWICKER

Dryden's Political Poetry: The Typology of King and Nation

Politics and Language in Dryden's Poetry: The Arts of Disguise

Politics of Discourse: The Literature and History of Seventeenth-Century England (coeditor)

Lines of Authority

Politics and English Literary Culture,
1649–1689

STEVEN N. ZWICKER

Cornell University Press

ITHACA AND LONDON

An earlier version of Chapter 6 appeared as "Representing the Revolution: Politics and High Culture in 1689," in *The Revolution of 1688–89: Changing Perspectives*, edited by Lois G. Schwoerer (Cambridge: Cambridge University Press, 1992), reprinted by permission. Parts of Chapter 4 appeared in "Virgins and Whores: The Politics of Sexual Misconduct in the 1660s," in *The Political Identity of Andrew Marvell*, edited by Conal Condren and A. D. Cousins (Aldershot, England: Scolar Press, 1990), reprinted by permission.

First published 1993 by Cornell University Press.

International Standard Book Number 0-8014-2070-9
Library of Congress Catalog Card Number 92-33995
Printed in the United States of America
Librarians: Library of Congress cataloging information
appears on the last page of the book.

♾ The paper in this book meets the minimum requirements
of the American National Standard for Information Sciences—
Permanence of Paper for Printed Library Materials, ANSI Z39.48–1984.

❦ For

Laura, Benjamin, Jonathan, and *Aaron*

Contents

Acknowledgments

It is a pleasure to thank colleagues and institutions for the help I have received in writing this book. At Washington University I am indebted to a number of colleagues for friendship and encouragement: to Stanley Elkin, who is a model of the writing life; to Wayne Fields, Joseph Loewenstein, and Charles Newman, whose various work on politics and culture has shaped my understanding of the subject; and especially to Naomi Lebowitz, who has been an ideal audience, attentive to argumentative design, generous with comment, never hesitating to put aside her own work to read these chapters. Among friends in the History Department I am especially grateful to Gerald Izenberg, who has helped with conceptual problems and whose own work on European Romanticism has clarified issues for me in the early modern field; and to Derek Hirst, who has read chapters, provided commentary, supplied information, and opened the field of seventeenth-century British politics for me in invaluable ways. I am grateful as well to Martin Israel, Dean of the Faculty at Washington University, and Edward Wilson, Dean of the Graduate School, for leave time and research support.

I also thank the staffs of the libraries where I have read for this book: the William Andrews Clark Library of the University of California, the Henry E. Huntington Library, the Folger Shakespeare Library, and the Beinecke Library of Yale University. To the National Endowment for the Humanities and to Dr. Martin Ridge, Director of Research at the Huntington Library, I am indebted for the award of a National Endowment for the Humanities–Huntington Library fellowship that allowed me to read at the Huntington during the academic year 1987–1988. I am also indebted to the Huntington for my colleagues during that year, Edward and Lillian Bloom, Barbara Donegan, Richard Helgerson, Cynthia Herrup, Fritz Levy, Stanley Stewart, Seth Weiner, and especially Barbara Harris. At the Folger Library I thank the Steering Committee of the Folger Institute for the History of British Political Thought, John Pocock, Gordon Schochet, Lois Schwoerer, and its executive director, Lena Orlin. In addition, I thank Gordon Schochet for his comments on my reading of Dryden and Locke, and Lois Schwoerer for her help with materials on the Glorious Revolution. My thanks also to Nancy Klein Maguire for assistance with Restoration drama and Nicholas Phillipson for his comments on Chapter 4.

To fellow students of seventeenth-century English culture—Mary Ann Radzinowicz, Michael Seidel, Michael Schoenfeldt, and Gerald MacLean—my thanks for correspondence and conversation. To David Bywaters my appreciation for his scrupulous reading of and incisive comments on the manuscript. I also owe long-standing debts of gratitude to Barbara Lewalski and Allen Mandelbaum for their generosity and encouragement.

Kevin Sharpe took time to read the entire manuscript in the midst of finishing his work on the personal rule of Charles I. His comments throughout have helped me clarify arguments and point connections; he will recognize how often his marginal notes have been folded into the text of this book. I am very grateful for his readings. The book has also benefited from the generous attention of Ann Coiro and Michael Lieb, who read the manuscript for Cornell University Press; my thanks as well to Bernhard Kendler of the Press. And my appreciation to Edith Baras, who has given the whole manuscript her scrupulous attention; every page has benefited from her intelligence.

Finally, and most important, my thanks to my family: especially to Judith; to our children, Laura, Benjamin, Jonathan, and Aaron—best company in our travels; to Jonathan for making the index; and to my mother, Golde Zwicker, who has long appreciated the pleasures and companionship of books. I hope this book expresses a measure of my gratitude.

STEVEN N. ZWICKER

St. Louis, Missouri

Lines of Authority

Introduction

L*ines of Authority* is an essay in literary history and critical reading. I have tried to describe a historical moment in ways that allow us to read its politics and literature together. My theme is partisanship as the grounding of politics and culture, the defining condition, in the middle and later decades of the seventeenth century, not only of political action but of writing and reading. This book is not, however, a narrative of influence but an argument about the role of polemic in the imagination. As cultural historians of various persuasions—classical Marxists, new historicists, cultural materialists—have urged, literary texts at once reflect and enact history. Of course, literature represents politics in a number of ways, and symbolic representation belongs variously to the categories of the political and the aesthetic. Here I have tried to argue the shaping force of politics in literature while addressing the capacities of literature not only to engage the realm of political thought but to engage in political action. Such work blurs the categories of politics and aesthetics. But for those who witnessed on January 30, 1649, the execution of Charles I and the next day contemplated the gestures of aesthetics and eternity on the pages of the *Eikon Basilike*, or reflected on the life of Charles I as a series of representations, could the relations between politics and aesthetics have been stable and distinct? For those who meditated on retreat and sociability in the pastoral shades of *The Compleat Angler* or considered, in the midst of national humiliation and metropolitan calamity, the civic import of innocence and corruption in *The Last Instructions*, the tangled relations between politics and aesthetics must have remained close to the center of their experience.

The borders of this study have been drawn by events in national politics—the execution of one king and the deposing of another—and while such borders help define the terrain and shape approach, they need not restrict the subject, for the traffic between politics and art in this age allows us to see that all the work of the literary imagination is embedded in polemic and contest. In these years ephemera and eternity have important relations, and texts that display the gestures of canonical self-celebration often allow the most complex and illuminating conversations with the local, the partisan, and the political.

In describing these conversations, I have taken the conditions of public life in these years—the harsh and brilliant and often dangerous dynamic of political contests; the libels and hazards of literary partisanship and political faction; the noise of court rumor and innuendo; the lampoons, squibs, and scandals; the turns and counterturns of personal enmity and party invective—as a model for critical reading. Such a model aims to complicate the way we read literature with an apprehension of what it might have been like to compose and consume texts in a world whose social structures, political habits, and intellectual manners were very different from our own. Recent historicist work on the English Renaissance has sharpened our sense of those structures and habits and renewed our appreciation of the social and political energies of its art. It is an irony of literary history that study of the later decades of the seventeenth century—a culture that has always demanded a high level of political literacy—has seemed more often preoccupied with elevating the literary above the political than with discovering the authority of polemic, the ubiquity and force of politics. Perhaps because politics is so deeply and pervasively situated in the literature of the middle and later decades of the seventeenth century—often the circumstance *and* the subject matter of poetry—critics have been drawn to cooler perspectives on this culture: the discounting of partisan temper, the disengagement of literary culture from the harshness of politics. Perhaps, too, critical projects are generational. A radicalized John Milton has begun to displace the loftier and less engaged poet; a polemical Andrew Marvell, partisan and protégé of great men, has in part eclipsed and surely complicated our notion of the poet as detached ironist; and an image of John Locke closeted and plotting with political activists during Exclusion, perhaps involved as well in the Rye House Plot, has tempered our impression of the habits, character, and writing of the political philosopher. Critical work of the past dozen or so years has not only given us new images of poetry, religious prose, and political theory in this age; it has altered our understanding of the traffic between politics and culture and has argued their urgent and constitutive relations.

There remains, however, in some of the theoretical work on politics and Restoration culture what seems not only a generational residue but more enduring sentiments about polemics and aesthetics, notions that concern the freedom of the imagination and the limiting force of politics and patronage. Conceptual issues always frame critical attitudes. Convictions about literature and universality, the capacities of great texts to transcend the topical, the relations between poetry and philosophy—all these determine the ways in which we have read and valued not only the poetry but the lives of Milton and Marvell and their contemporaries. It may be difficult to shift sentiment about literary value, but it should not be difficult to appreciate how deeply lodged were the political impulses of English culture in the years between the civil wars and the Glorious Revolution, how habitual were political aim and polemical suspicion not just among political actors but among those who invented and consumed this culture, and finally how important it is not only to value the universalizing impulses of literary texts but to see how these impulses arise from the friction between partisanship and eternity.

I want to suggest a way of framing this problem not from within or from the relations between literary texts—problems and perspectives that form the content of this book—but from a collusion we might observe between conditions of writing and habits of reading in this world, habits that can help us grasp the experience of polemic not only as the obvious and overt condition of politics but as the circumstance of literature. We do not know enough about how books were read in the past.[1] We have some guidelines in Renaissance literary theory, but critical theory, then as now, often tells us more about the cultural ambitions of writers and their programs of literary defense than about the habits of mind of those who read epics and lyric poems, satires and controversial prose. We have a fairly detailed sense of early education, of literacy and changing literacy rates, of professional training, and of university curricula from these years; but of the actual habits of reading and attitudes toward literature we know considerably less. The one book whose consumption we do know about is, of course, the Bible. This was a book central to English culture across religious divisions and political factions, and it was not simply read but minutely examined for traffic between past and present. Biblical exegesis was a various practice, but in these years the application of sacred narrative, parable, and prophecy was legion. No book was more insistently applied to contemporary experience than the Bible and no redemption more carefully monitored than the history of the Jews: English politics was experienced as sacred history. But my point is less the sacral convictions of puritan or, less often stressed, royalist politics than the deeply felt habits of exegesis and application and their steady presence far beyond the reading of Scripture. Allegory and application were central to the experience of Scripture. They were also modes of reading the secular past: the poetry of Virgil, Horace, and Lucan; the annals and histories of Livy and Tacitus. Allegory and application were temperamental and intellectual impulses, trained and cultivated by the deep convictions of Protestant exegesis, yet honored far beyond the reach of sacred narrative. They proved capable of expansion and evolution into other and allied impulses and habits: ways of reading the signs and symbols of the natural world, of cultivating emblems, decoding politics, penetrating myth and mysteries, and reading the present. The impulse to decode nature and culture is one of the enduring traditions of Western intellectual training, but in these years the rich varieties of allegory formed more than a venerable tradition. They comprised important convictions about spiritual life and sophisticated methods of reading texts and history; they embraced variously the providentialism of puritan historiography, the civic cares of royalist romance, the contemplative gestures of pastoral, and the puzzles, ironies, and innuendos of Restoration court satire.

But to look beyond the habits of biblical exegesis to allegory and application in lyric and epic contexts, to read shadows of subtexts within texts, is no simple task. There are no sure methods of tracking the habits of reading, though there are occasional hints and serendipitous occasions. The Osborn Collection in the Beinecke Library provides one such occasion: a copy of *Paradise Lost* that might allow us to glance at a world responsive to political allegory and polemical innuendo, a place where literature was consumed as politics. This *Paradise Lost* was issued in 1678, and though it cannot boast the plates that would make Tonson's 1688 edition so intriguing, it does have a marginal note or two in the hand of its owner, one Francis Atterbury, friend of Swift and sometime bishop of Rochester. We do not know when Atterbury held this book in his hands, but on page 31 of this copy we can watch him reading Milton—"He ended frowning, and his look denounced / Desperate revenge, and battle dangerous / To less than gods" (2.106–8)—and noting in a careful hand at the margin: "This probably ye picture of some great man in Milton's time."[2] Atterbury's "probably" may seem an equivocating gesture, but the very casualness with which the assumption is made (and made without certain knowledge of the particulars) opens for us a world where the enterprise of literature is understood as political, where Milton's courts and kings and angels are signs of the poet's engagement with politics in a debauched and fallen world. And here we might recall Dryden reading the fifth book of the *Aeneid:*

> Neither were the great Roman Families which flourish'd in his time, less oblig'd by [Virgil] than the Emperour. Your Lordship [John Sheffield, earl of Mulgrave] knows with what Address he makes mention of them, as Captains of Ships, or Leaders in the War; and even some of Italian Extraction are not forgotten. These are the single Stars which are sprinkled through the *Aeneis:* But there are whole Constellations of them in the Fifth Book. And I could not but take notice, when I Translated it, of some Favourite Families to which he gives the Victory, and awards the Prizes, in the Person of his Heroe, at the Funeral Games which were Celebrated in Honour of Anchises. I, Insist not on their Names: But am pleas'd to find the Memmii amongst them, deriv'd from Mnestheus, because Lucretius Dedicates to one of that Family, a Branch of which destroy'd Corinth. I likewise either found or form'd an Image to my self of the contrary kind; that those who lost the Prizes, were such as had disoblig'd the Poet, or were in disgrace with Augustus, or Enemies to Mecenas: And this was the Poetical Revenge he took.[3]

Without naming, or perhaps even knowing, all the names, Dryden was convinced that those who had crossed the poet or were his patron's enemies had been written into the eternity of Virgil's poem. Of course, this is one poet judging of another, and Dryden had his partisan uses for Virgil as Atterbury had his political suspicions of Milton; but for the moment Dryden is a reader among readers, and if we are lucky we will find others. There are in fact collections of state poems and satirical squibs as well as lyrics and allegories, polemical pamphlets, and works of political theory that are so annotated. We can open Narcissus Luttrell's copy of *The Conspiracy of Aeneas & Antenor* (1682) and see the court identities that Luttrell discovered in Troy, or read

Elijah Fenton's annotations to Edmund Waller's poems, or contemporary annotations to Samuel Garth's *Dispensary;* or we can consider how *The Duke of Guise,* Dryden's vindictive Exclusion Crisis drama, was read in the wake of the Glorious Revolution, or how James Tyrrell's Exclusionist tract, *Patriarcha Non Monarcha,* was read in the late 1690s.[4]

But the most famous instance of the annotated poem from these years is *Absalom and Achitophel.* Indeed, here annotation became something of a cottage industry; several manuscript keys were devised, and a printed key was marketed. But any number of contemporary copies have notes written along the margins, and these look less like study than pleasure, though we ought not to underestimate the meaning of such pleasures in thinking about the passions of reading and writing in these years:

> To name great men is malice grossly shown
> (As if they could not by their crimes be known)
> For what fool knew not, when you nam'd a bear,
> Without a comment Pembroke was meant there?
> When we say fool then all men must agree
> To name Villiers would be tautology.
> Who to the sin of pride does lay most claim:
> Need we say Tollemache, Arp, or Heveningham?
> With these before the wits have had a bout;
> I'll pick up some the poets have left out,
> And yet not name the men, but sing their faults;
> For so wise Satyr makes his sharp assaults.[5]

In his copy of the anonymous *Satyr Unmuzzled* (1680) Pope supplied some of the names of those whose faults had been sung.[6] Not all the names written in the margins of contemporary copies agree, nor can every fault be unlocked, every allegory opened, or parallel drawn to discover the ghost of seventeenth-century politics inhabiting these allegories and innuendos. Some problems resist solution: neither Dryden's contemporaries nor modern scholars have discovered whom the poet had in mind when he wrote of Amnon's murder in *Absalom and Achitophel.* That puzzles remain in the parallels drawn by seventeenth-century writers and in the applications made of their allegories and analogies seems less to suggest flaws of the system than its richness and variety, the energy and daring with which polemic informed the uses of culture.

These allegories and applications were no naïve if impassioned entertainment; Algernon Sidney feared to run on the "dark and slippery places" of allegory as Judge Jeffreys prepared applications of Sidney's writings.[7] Accused of "compass[ing]" and "imagin[ing]" the death of the king, Sidney understood the stakes in this game, the consequences of a king's court sharpening its critical talents on his prose:

> When nothing of particular application unto time, place, or person, could be found in it (as hath ever been done by those who endeavoured to raise insurrections) all was supplied by innuendos.
>
> Whatsoever is said of the expulsion of Tarquin; the insurrection against Nero; the slaughter of Caligula, or Domitian; the translation of the crown of France from Merovens's race unto Pepin; and from his descendants unto Hugh Capet, and the like, applied by innuendo unto the king.[8]

The image of Judge Jeffreys acting as the crown's agent of judicial vengeance while performing as its chief literary critic ought to remind us that allegory and application were hardly matters of dispassionate exegetical choice. The hunting of allegories did not always run to dark and slippery places, but we would do well to imagine books and readers in a world haunted by coercion and fear; rent by religion and politics; wary, in the aftermath of civil war, of the directions in which jealousies and fears might drive a commonweal.

The chapters that follow conjure an image of this world and address a literature in which politics insisted on the right to inhabit the imagination, a literature of contest, of passion and polemical intrigue. In such a world polemic was a condition of writing, and not only for those who were willing to acknowledge the drives of partisanship; polemic engulfed the literary and tempered all the idioms of culture. I describe the character of polemic at moments of crisis—the regicide, the Anglo-Dutch wars and the Great Fire of London, Exclusion, and the Glorious Revolution—but I also let polemic emerge through the juxtaposing of contemporary texts, a series of contiguities that might reveal the rhetorics, structures, and poetics of contest. Such juxtapositions allow the cross-examination and contestation of literary matters while disclosing the social and political idioms within the literary.

I begin with an obvious pair of texts, Charles I's *Eikon Basilike* and Milton's *Eikonoklastes:* their relations illustrate how deeply aestheticized politics had become in the immediate aftermath of civil war and the regicide. But other and less obvious contiguities reveal the depth and character of contestation in this world. Locke's *Two Treatises of Government* has often been read within the genealogy of political thought, but *Absalom and Achitophel,* a text brilliantly self-conscious in its display and defusing of the idioms of Exclusion, might disclose Locke's stance and style more fully than either *Patriarcha* or the political tracts and treatises contemporary with Locke's text. *The Compleat Angler* is, of course, the classic text of georgic retreat; but Walton's cool providentialism and uses of poetry and nostalgia may seem less than irenic when read against Marvell's *First Anniversary,* a poem of tireless literary programmatics, a panegyric that welds lyric fragments into political prophecy. And perhaps the celebrations of abundance and sexual delight that figure so prominently in the first years of the Restoration, what we might call the politics of pleasure, allow us to bring together some of the disparate masterpieces of that season of wonders which opened with the Anglo-Dutch wars and came to include a series of apocalyptic prophecies as well as some rather startling evidence, in the form of fire, plague, and financial ruin, that the end of the world might indeed be at hand. In that world Dryden's *Annus Mirabilis* speaks clearly enough to Marvell's *Last Instructions,* but these poems might be induced to conversation and contestation not only with each other but with *Paradise Lost,* a poem published in that same season of wonders but rarely imagined to participate in the politics of pleasure. In another crisis, a revolution that for some of Dryden's contemporaries seemed like a gift of providence, indeed a Glorious Revolution, the ejected laureate set about composing *Don Sebastian,* a tragedy on the demise of the Portuguese empire. If we surround that lofty work with contemporary pamphlets and panegyrics, materials that its author would have held beneath his well-practiced contempt, we discover programs and slogans that provide a bracing and elucidating context for the Jacobite sentiments and nonjuring convictions of Dryden's tragedy. The light from these antinomies can seem distant and various, but it illumines the passions and energies and arts of these texts, and the worlds where they were first imagined and which they came to haunt and inhabit.

1 Poetics

My theme is the polemicization of English literary culture between the outbreak of the civil wars and the Glorious Revolution. These were years in which the relations between literature and politics were powerful, various, and combustible. Even to isolate literary culture within a historical narrative is to indulge an analytical convenience, for the polemicization of the literary is properly part of the history of the polemicization of an entire society at all levels of discourse: the commonplace and the recondite, the lay and the professional, the popular and the elite. This was a nation entangled by polemic, splintered by religious dissent, riven by partisanship.[1] The years between the two revolutions form a distinct phase of English literary culture; the shared experience of the politics and polemics of civil war had an effect on the program of literature and on the literary imagination, on literary languages, modes, and forms, that is, on all aspects of literary culture. The civil wars displayed the full implications of contest and confrontation, what it meant to stir public opinion, to deploy oratory and eloquence, to indulge verbal savagery and violence. And the memory of that lamented translation from language to arms remained vivid and potent throughout the rest of the century. Civil war was an event that changed the conditions of public utterance, that distinguished the culture of these years from what had come before and from what was to follow when the wars had finally passed beyond living memory.

We need hardly remind ourselves at this point in our reading of Renaissance culture just how intimately were the literary texts of the late sixteenth and earlier seventeenth centuries concerned with the political. The meditations of Sir Philip Sidney and Edmund Spenser on the politics of the Elizabethan commonweal, their own programs and ambitions, the role of writers within courtly factions, their attachment to aristocratic patrons, the visions of the ideal polity conjured in epic, romance, and masque as well as the denunciations of plays and playgoers—such expressions of the civic cares of Renaissance literary culture have been mapped with increasing sophistication over the last decade.[2] We have now not only a politicized but a radicalized and topicalized Shakespeare; and such genres as lyric and romance, which had seemed least likely to yield political argument, have been skillfully brought to bear witness on how the refined, at points rarefied, aesthetic genres reveal the political character of their culture.[3] And yet, however impassioned advocacy and criticism became within Jacobean and Caroline culture,[4] the experience of the 1640s marked so profound a change in the conduct, armory, and psychology of public discourse that the very frame within which literature was conceived and seen to function underwent an irreversible change.

With the raising of arms in civil combat the verbal stakes had been altered. Literature assumed increasing importance both as a site for and as a way of giving shape and authority to the conduct of polemical argument: to moral triumphalism, to the expression of political resistance, to the assertion of political elevation and authority, to the articulation not simply of criticism within the commonweal but of alternative social and political orders. Through the second half of this century aesthetic forms and modes were claimed, contested, and deployed for explosive and highly articulate polemical purpose. Polemic stirs vividly in broadside and ballad,[5] but with the coming of civil war it became a pervasive condition of literary production and reception. We have become familiar with certain parts of this history, with the progress of polemic within particular genres; but I want to argue that the polemicization of culture in these years left nothing untouched. The rise of polemic can be charted in every quarter of the literary: within the personal lives of writers and in professional careers;[6] in the development of older modes and the creation of new literary idioms;[7] in editing and translation projects;[8] in republication;[9] in the production, circulation, and reception of texts;[10] and in the regulation of licensing and publishing.[11] These topics recur in the chapters that follow, but we might begin this inquiry by looking at a group of texts that have traditionally been treated as the exclusive preserve of the literary: texts of literary theory, defense, and apology.[12]

The analysis of literary problems in this age was conducted in a variety of locations: within literary works themselves, through parody, in theatrical prologues and epilogues, and in those prefaces and dedications that accompanied so many literary texts.[13] The whole matter of poetics, from formal treatise, to dedication, to lyric poem, forms an important index of the polemical in this culture. I want first, however, to recover polemic from within formal texts, since literary theory has often seemed the special preserve of aesthetics, a territory whose history and whose ostensible topics have led us to examine the aesthetic as distinguished from the political. The recovery of polemic from within poetics allows us to see that the two are bound together and to observe not simply the incursion of the topical into the aesthetic but the fundamental and pervasive force of polemic within the whole of this literary culture.

Poetics traditionally remarks the regulatory function of literature, and students of poetics have long been familiar with this theme: in Plato, in Aristotle, in Horace, and throughout Renaissance defenses. My interests here are both larger and more specific, for poetics might be read not only from the outside as a way of estimating how a culture at a particular historical moment reflects on the social utility of literature, but from the inside as a register of the polemical character of the culture.[14] Considering literary theory as a locale within which to watch the rise of polemic necessarily displaces some of the familiar narratives of theory. I am concerned with traditional topics—the debate between poetry and history, the much-worried term *wit*, its rise and meaning—not as evidence of changing literary taste, but as a function of the polemical character of post–civil war literary culture, where taste itself could declare political allegiance, where "Wit and Fool, are Consequents of Whig and Tory."[15]

In disclosing the political argument of literary theory, I want to examine its terms within a group of theoretical texts composed during the century's most volatile years. I also want to consider these terms in other settings to suggest the contestative atmosphere of writing itself: how theory is played out in the actual behavior of genres, modes, and languages; how a polemicized muse reflects the hold of the polemical over the literary and how the literary, in turn, transforms the armory of partisan argument. That interplay determines the particular energy and brilliance of literary and political culture in the later seventeenth century. The dominance of polemic in this culture may set our teeth on edge; it certainly contributed to the ferocious literary manners of the late seventeenth century, to its preoccupation with the obscene and the scandalous. But polemic had as well a bracing and complicating effect on low and high culture and on the traffic between, on the acts of incorporation, allusion, and commentary— what we have come to know as intertextuality. Politics would not be denied in this culture, and the ways in which partisanship engulfed the literary and conditioned its creation and reception afford a spectacle we can ignore only if we would abstract the literary from the conditions with which it was preoccupied and in which it was powerfully, if at times hastily, and with various kinds of interest composed and received.[16]

❦

Although Sir Philip Sidney wrote *The Defence of Poesy* more than half a century before the English civil wars, we might begin with the *Defence* because it proved for the whole of the English Renaissance the formative statement of the problems of literary theory.[17] The *Defence* can also be used as shorthand for the situation of poetics and of poetry itself before the civil wars. Whatever role the *Defence* may have played in Sidney's career, and however important the circulation of such a text was in his personal maneuvering within the court,[18] the *Defence* itself was a bid to restore poetry to intellectual eminence. Sidney's overriding concern is not the alignment of poetry with a faction within the commonweal, but the position of poetry among the intellectual disciplines. The crisis that the *Defence* addresses is a general crisis in the authority of poetry; although Sidney allows the significance of literature in the state—the social bearing of pastoral, the regulatory function of tragedy—the center of the *Defence*, the lesson that it most energetically argues, is the intellectual dignity of poetry. The set pieces on this theme are subtle and brilliant, and they were recognized as such by generations of defenders of the domain of poetry.[19] But what is most interesting about the status of this theme in its successive appearances in defenses and apologies after Sidney is the progressive marginalization of the problem, how token the defense of the intellectual dignity of poetry comes to seem by the middle of the seventeenth century. Nor is it simply a matter of per-

spective, a case of the angle or field of vision changing as the fragmentation of political, social, and religious authority displaces the
question of literary authority, one set of crises taking precedence over
another.

Sidney's impassioned concern for the intellectual dignity of poetry
is marginalized for two reasons: the success of *The Defence of Poesy*
and, more especially, the brilliant literary performance of Sidney and
his contemporaries and heirs. Spenser, Marlowe, Nashe, Shakespeare,
Donne, and Jonson more than solved the problem of poetry's position
among the intellectual disciplines. The distinctive intellectual contribution of late Elizabethan and Jacobean England is neither philosophy
nor history, though both were practiced by powerful individuals with
powerful intellects, but rather poetry itself. Sidney and his peers elevated the station of the poet, but it was the political crisis of the mid-
seventeenth century that transformed the role of poetry and its position among the culture's modes of discourse. All the major writers
at midcentury—Milton, Marvell, Dryden, Rochester, Davenant, Cowley, Waller—were both political actors and writers. By the time Milton,
Marvell, and Dryden came to invoke the muse, no one was complaining that England was a hard stepmother to poets. The problems that
needed to be addressed and resolved in apologies and defenses concerned the proper alignment of the muses, the role of poetry in
defense of program and prerogative, the triumphs of prophecy and
providence, the defiance of misconceived authority; but the capacity
of poetry to argue such concerns and to command an audience in
doing so was undoubted. Not only did poetry take on a full range of
political and partisan issues, but it did so in forms that stood fully
within the lines of public discourse.

Sidney's *Defence* occupies a very different space. While passionately
believing in the civic and moral capacity of poetry, Sidney took as his
task the elevating of poetry into public view, clearing a space for poetry
among the modes of public discourse in order to give substance to
the acknowledged social nature of literature. To observe that pastoral
utters "the misery of people under hard lords" (229), or that tragedy
"maketh kings fear to be tyrants" (230), is to argue wishful platitudes
in a defense that begins by confessing that poetry in our time is "the
laughing-stock of children" (212). By the middle of the next century
literary theory is much concerned with the social and political action
that poetry is capable of performing, and such arguments are neither
the idle and elevating platitudes nor the wishful echoes of Plato and

Aristotle that they seem to be in the *Defence*. If one has simultaneously to rescue poetry from low esteem and argue its power to shake tyrants, its authority—both political and social—is rather compromised by the twinned procedure. When Milton prefaced *Samson Agonistes* in 1671 with an epigraph from Aristotle's *Poetics* and with remarks intending to "vindicate tragedy from the small esteem, or rather infamy, which in the account of many it undergoes at this day,"[20] he aimed not to vindicate the whole of literature but to dignify this particular tragedy, to suggest the gravity of his own style, the nobility of blank verse unfettered by slavish rhyme now brought into vogue by the heroic drama.[21] The political force of tragedy, Milton took for granted; the preface is ringed with a combativeness that has everything to do with the polemical thrust of his own work and very little to do with rescuing the public dignity of literature. By the 1670s the civic space that literature might be seen to occupy had long been settled. Warfare over its occupation grew bold in the later decades of this century; but partisan literary conflict provided its own bitter, and at points eloquent, testimony to the importance of literary stakes within the political culture. Literary skirmishes and firefights, and indeed major battles, were conducted not only by those who determined the course of literary culture, but also, and as savagely, by those who determined the course of the state.

Sidney's program for the elevation of poetry turns on the contest he poses between poetry and history on the one hand and poetry and philosophy on the other. That contest argues poetry's superiority to history and philosophy both as a mode of efficacious knowledge and as persuasive expression. Knowledge and expression are not entirely separate in Sidney's argument, but the contexts are differently weighted. Against history, Sidney's argument is concerned with intellectual authority. Belittling veracity, slighting information as knowledge, and attacking the sources of historical narrative, Sidney undercuts history's disciplinary authority and vindicates the priority of poetry as knowledge: its religious origins, its power as divination, its oracular nature. Against historical particularity and partiality, against the moral inferiority of an intellectual mode that is "bound to tell things as things were" and "captived to the truth of a foolish world" (224, 225), Sidney would pose poetry's capacity to idealize, the intellectual generosity of a mode of knowledge that does not grasp at partials and particulars but conjures "the general reason of things" (221). Of course, the same argument cannot be made against philosophy. In that colloquy Sidney must reverse tack, arguing poetry's traffic with worldly particulars and thereby its expressive powers: "The philosopher, setting down with thorny arguments the bare rule, is so hard of utterance and so misty to be conceived" (221) that philosophical counsel is an inhibited performance; better the moving picture, the colors of poetry, the counsel of Homer and Virgil, the perfectly imagined figures of literature than the abstractions of philosophy. The ideal state recognizes the power of poetry to build cities and tame the beast, to move men and stones; this is the state according to Marvell's account in *The First Anniversary*, where Amphion is legislator and lyric poet and Cromwell's laureate winds his horn to kings that chase the beast. Here the poet is counselor to the king, the ruler is patron of art and learning: "Alexanders, Caesars, Scipios, all favourers of poets" (240); Elizabethan England is a hard stepmother to the muse.

Whatever role the *Defence* may have played in Sidney's career, the burden of its literary argument is literature; Sidney's client is poetry. The effort is to get literature onto equal footing with the other intellectual arts, to identify poetry as a separate realm of knowledge. First, the *Defence* concedes, space must be cleared between philosophy and history; hence Sidney's effort to argue the priority of literature to philosophy and history, though the argument concedes that it is rather more the visibility of poetry than its priority that the apologist aims to establish. Sidney would have his audience reminded of poetry's origins, its luminous history, its oracular power. But the body of the *Defence*, brilliant though it is, makes another story clear and manifests humbler aims: Sidney's desire rather more elementally to define a space for modern verse. Sidney cannot assume, as would Marvell and Milton, Waller, Cowley, or Dryden, the authority of modern verse. When the poet is secure in that knowledge, it is not the independence of poetry from history or philosophy that he seeks but rather its alliance with other authoritative modes. Milton exalts poetry, but his drive is never to seek its independence from philosophy or prophecy; Dryden and Sprat conjured the power of verse not in distinction to history but in league with it;[22] Marvell discovered the public muse in the dialectic between poetry and history. Whatever new burdens polemic and division imposed on poets, there is by midcentury little defensiveness about the authority of literature itself. The role of the poet in English political culture between the civil wars and the Glorious Revolution had never been so esteemed. Indeed, the later seventeenth century comprises an unusual moment for literature when poetry was swept to the center of politics; writers found that engagement intoxicating if dangerous business. A century later even poets conceived of poetry at the margins of political culture.[23] In 1649 it was a poet whom the new republic chose to combat the most effective piece of royalist polemic yet produced, itself an exercise in autobiographical fantasy mixed with prayers, verse, psalms, literary allusions, and historical narratives. And Milton paid his own ironic tribute to the civic force of the literary imagination by attempting to quash the deluding and seductive whole of the *Eikon Basilike* as a mere piece of poetry.

Part of the reason for the movement of literature to the center of political culture must be sought in the remarkable performance of literature itself. But this centering was also determined by the absorption of literature into polemic, by its role in something we might call public opinion.[24] The pulpit remained crucial to the moral argument of politics, but now all the armory of print culture was brought irrevocably into play: printed texts and not only sermons but single-sheet broadsides, prints, newsletters, pamphlets, tracts, treatises, confutations, animadversions, contestations, riddles, libels, scandals, squibs, lampoons, allegories, reflections, advices, confessions.[25] As the temperature of political contestation rose, so much the greater became the role of printed texts within the commonweal, or so at least such political historians and theorists as Clarendon and Hobbes believed.

It is not only the amount of printing that rose at moments of political crisis, but quite naturally its adversarial and contestative character as well. Words finally grew so sharp that, according to the civil war's most considered historian, contestation could no longer be confined to the printed page: "First words of great contempt, and then (those words commonly finding a return of equal scorn) blows, were fastened upon some of the most pragmatical of the crew."[26] Nor was verbal contestation limited to works identifying themselves as contestative, though there is a notable rise in works that were willing to be so designated. Indeed, after 1640 a vocabulary develops that is specifically intended for contest; the word *animadversion,* for example, changes meaning in the middle of this century, acquiring the contestative force with which we are now familiar,[27] and "animadversion" is only one instance. The literature collected in what is known as the Thomason Tracts, the outpourings from the press at moments when the licensing laws lapsed,[28] the amount of unlicensed printing,[29] the rate of anonymous publications,[30] and the large number of commonplace books and manuscript collections and anthologies that we can date from these years[31]—all give some notion of both how literate and how contestative English culture was by the middle of the seventeenth century. Indeed, the amount of print, its simple heft, is itself a lesson not only in the verbalization but in the textualization of mid-seventeenth-century English culture. Sidney lamented that England was a hard stepmother to poets in the 1580s; no one was making that complaint by the middle of the next century. When William Davenant published his *Preface* to *Gondibert* in 1650, he had, as a royalist, much to complain of, but the neglect of poetry was not one of his themes.[32]

In 1650, in Paris, Davenant took the unusual step of publishing a lengthy and sophisticated *Preface* to his verse epic *Gondibert,* a work as yet unpublished and incomplete. Clearly, such a *Preface* was intended to do something other than introduce *Gondibert,* and it was work far different from what Sidney had performed in the *Defence.* Yet in discussing the relations among history, narrative, and poetry, Davenant not only announced Sidney's position in the lineage of his *Preface,* but underscored Sidney's dignifying presence by praising the generalizing power and elevation of verse and echoing Sidney's slighting reference to austere history with its "bond" to truth. Nevertheless, the concerns of the *Preface* are very different from those of the *Defence.* While the conjuring of eloquence and elevation, the positioning of the *Preface* fully within the domain of poetics, is deliberate, the burden of Davenant's argument is not the rivalry of poetry with history, not the vindication of literature from low esteem, but the politics of culture. Whether Davenant felt that poetics was a necessary refuge from within which to make such an argument, or that poetics provided not only cover but also topics, texts, and pretexts for a politicized discussion of literary culture, the force of his arguments and the edge of his language are very political indeed. The *Preface* is not only the first of what becomes an important variant in the history of poetics; it is also a significant example of how politics and polemics can be folded into the argument of poetry. For Davenant directs our attention to a number of important topics: precedence, innovation, and authority; the character of the multitude and the court; the role of retirement and solitude; the quality of honor, fame, and reputation; and most especially, the nature of inspiration and the rise of wit. All these issues argue the importance of the *Preface* not just to the history of literary theory but to the history of political argument. Perhaps literary theory itself should be situated in the history of political engagement.

How else are we to understand the force of Davenant's defense of his choice of story for *Gondibert*?

> These were partly the reasons why I chose a Story of such persons as profess'd Christian Religion; but I ought to have been most enclin'd to it, because the Principles of our Religion conduce more to explicable vertue, to plain demonstrative justice, and even to Honor (if Vertue, the Mother of Honour, be voluntary and active in the dark, so as she need not Laws to compel her, nor look for witnesses to proclaim her), then any other Religion that e're assembled men to Divine Worship. For that of the Jews doth still consist in a sullen separation of themselves from the rest of humane flesh, which is a fantastical pride of their own cleaness, and an uncivil disdain of the imagined contagiousness of others; and at this day, their cantonizing in Tribes, the shyness of allyance with neighbours, deserves not the terme of mutual love, but rather seems a bestial melancholy of herding in their own Walks.... But Christian Religion hath the innocence of Village neighbourhood, and did anciently in its politicks rather promote the interest of Mankinde then of States, and rather of all States then of one.... Such is Christian Religion in the precepts, and was once so in the practise. But I resolv'd my Poem should represent those of a former age, perceiving 'tis with the servants of Christ as with other servants under temporal power, who with all cleanness, and even with officious diligence, perform their duty in their Masters sight, but still as he grows longer absent become more slothful, unclean, and false. And this who ever compares the present with the Primitive times may too palpably discern.[33]

The burden of this passage, with its defense of Christianity and antiquity and its hostile social history of the Jews, is neither the dignity of the past nor the moral superiority of Christian history, but the sullenness, the pride, the melancholy herding of cantonizing puritanism. It also argues the innocence of the Anglican confession and the nobility of a defeated court, the charity of its politics and the generosity of its precepts and practices. Davenant was not the first writer to allegorize puritanism under the veil of Jewish history, an allegory that has a brilliant future in the Restoration; but the economy and fluency of that accommodation are notable. The aesthetic program that Davenant creates for *Gondibert*—his praise of antiquity, his denigration of innovation, his celebration of the innocence and generosity of the Christian religion—folds literary apologetics into polemical argument. Davenant's passage conjures a courtly, an aristocratic, and an elevated Christian past. It is from such a culture that Davenant would take his story in *Gondibert*, and it is such a culture against which he poses the image of sullen and herding puritanism.

Nor does this incident stand alone. The *Preface* begins with an allusion to the debate between ancients and moderns that already suggests the allegorical urgency of the text:

> I will ... begin with Homer, who though he seems to me standing upon the Poets famous hill, like the eminent Sea-mark by which they have in former ages steer'd, and though he ought not to be removed from that eminence ... yet some (sharply observing how his successors have proceeded no farther then a perfection of imitating him) say that, as Sea-marks are chiefly useful to Coasters, and serve not those who have the ambition of Discoverers, that love to sail in untry'd Seas, so he hath rather prov'd a Guide for those whose satisfy'd Wit will not venture beyond the track of others, then to them who affect a new and remote way of thinking, who esteem it a deficiency and meaness of minde to stay and depend upon the authority of example. (2:1–2)

Innovation and *authority* are key terms in literary theory and never more so than in Renaissance poetics; Davenant invokes the past to announce an allegiance with authority, his skepticism of new and remote ways of thinking. Had this piece of innovation stood in a text that did not so thoroughly allegorize poetics, we would have less reason to put political pressure on the aesthetic. But within the *Preface* and particularly as Davenant develops his argument about the politics of a courtly society and the function of culture, there can be no doubt that the invocation of ancient ways is a tribute to both the literary and the political past, the first volley in a campaign not only to allegorize politics as culture but to see them as concomitant. The heroic and generous past is the appropriate subject for epic and a model of that society which Davenant and his companions re-created in exile and in the imagination, in poetry and in poetics. *Heroism* and *antiquity*, like *ambition* and *innovation*, are richly suggestive terms in 1650.

Other key terms in the *Preface* complicate and deepen the political argument of Davenant's work. Listen, for example, to Davenant on the court as a school for morality:

The most effectual Schools of Morality are Courts and Camps: yet towards the first the people are unquiet through envie, and towards the other through fear, and always jealous of both for Injustice, which is the naturall scandal cast upon authority and great force. They look upon the outward glory or blaze of Courts, as wilde Beasts in dark nights stare on their Hunters Torches; but though the expences of Courts, whereby they shine, is that consuming glory in which the people think their liberty is wasted,—for wealth is their liberty, and lov'd by them even to jealousie, being themselves a courser sort of Princes, apter to take then to pay,— yet Courts . . . are not the Schools where men are bred to oppression, but the Temples where sometimes Oppressors take sanctuary, a safety which our reason must allow them. . . . Who can imagine less then a necessity of oppressing the people, since they are never willing either to buy their Peace or to pay for Warr? (2:12–13)

The passage is a brilliant composite of social theory, political defense, nostalgia, and irony. Davenant begins with a conventional literary topic, the court as a school for politeness, but the passage quickly and transparently turns to politics, the undeserving mob, a fickle people who neither defend their superiors nor pay for war. The most affecting and vivid image is also the most polemically revealing: the multitude "look upon the outward glory or blaze of Courts, as wilde Beasts in dark nights stare on their Hunters Torches" (2:12). It may be that Davenant discloses more than he intends by this imagery; the sentence elevates the court and argues the interdependence of court and high culture; it also deprecates the multitude and argues the distance, antipathy, and danger of that gulf between court and country. This is an image of national culture that is not so much hierarchical as exclusive; for Davenant, literature is not the moralizing, moving teacher of the many, but the preserve of the few who possess either "prerogative of blood" or "greatnesse of minde" (2:14). The brutal herds have no capacity to participate in a commonweal of culture; the multitude can only envy and stare in dumb amazement at the brilliance, color, and splendor of aristocratic display. It is not surprising that a royalist in exile contemplating the publication of a heroic romance shortly after the execution of the king might hold such opinions of the many and the few; what needs observing is how thoroughly politics informs this aesthetic inquiry, how far polemical urgency can be felt in the images of court culture as in the domain of literature. The *Preface* is an example not of aesthetic language covering a polemical position but of an intellectual structure in which aesthetics argues a polity.

Nowhere in this essay is the politics of culture more passionately argued than in the attack on inspiration and the concomitant celebration of wit. Both inspiration and wit are crucial features of seventeenth-century aesthetics, and the *Preface,* appearing in 1650, marks the courtly position at a moment of crisis and change. The argument begins by acknowledging the ancient bond between poetry and prophecy, but Davenant is quick to contrast past and present. In the present, inspiration is a cover for fury, a mask for anger and jealousy, a device of the clergy to achieve dominion in the state. Religion, which should conserve the polity, now inspires rebellion:

> Some upbraid the want of extempory fury, or rather inspiration, a dangerous word which many have of late successfully us'd; and inspiration is a spiritual Fitt, deriv'd from the ancient Ethnick Poets, who then, as they were Priests, were Statesmen too, and probably lov'd dominion; and as their well dissembling of inspiration begot them reverence then equall to that which was paid to Laws, so these who now profess the same fury may perhaps by such authentick example pretend authority over the people. (2:25)

The doubling of poetry and prophecy is a central argument in poetic defenses; Sidney offers a classic iteration: "David in his Psalms; Solomon in his Song of Songs, . . . Moses and Deborah in their Hymns . . . Orpheus, Amphion, Homer in his Hymns, and many other, both Greeks and Romans" (217). For Sidney, prophecy and poetic fury are conjoined as sources of literary authority; it is the force of divine rhapsody that elevates the poet above philosopher and historian. By the time Davenant composed his *Preface,* inspiration had become deeply politicized, and Davenant wished both to distance his aesthetic theory from inspiration as "a spiritual Fitt" and to deprecate the politics and aesthetics of inspired composition. Inspiration, which Davenant neatly attaches to "the ancient Ethnick Poets," links the earlier attack on "sullen separation" and "fantastical pride" to the widespread claims of inspiration by which prophetic politics justified the triumph of the saints. Indeed, Davenant's whole address to inspiration, his degrading of visionary poetics and devaluing of revelation as an instance of political and social radicalism, could not have been understood in 1650 apart from its attack on militant puritanism with what

Davenant regards as its spiritual arrogance and false claims of sanctity. Though divines are ordained "to temper the rage of humane power ... and they are sent hither as Liegers from God, to conserve in stedfast motion the slippery joints of Government, and to perswade an amity in divided Nations" (2:33), the elevation of religion over the state—a history Davenant subtly suggests is attendant on the Protestant Reformation—is the cause of revolt and disquiet.

Davenant aims, however, at a more complex assertion. He derides inspiration as the device of priestcraft, a collocation no one will handle more brilliantly than Dryden, and then defines his own aesthetic program with wit as the counterforce to inspiration, the very center and substance of poetry, its defining intellectual and aesthetic principle:

> Having describ'd the outward frame, the large rooms ... and now the furniture, it were orderly to let you examine the matter of which that furniture is made.... I shall not give you the trouble of inquiring what is, but tell you of what I design'd, their substance, which is, Wit: And Wit is the laborious and the lucky resultances of thought, having towards its excellence, as we say of the strokes of Painting, as well a happinesse as care. It is a Webb consisting of the subt'lest threds; and like that of the Spider is considerately woven out of our selves; for a Spider may be said to consider, not only respecting his solemnesse and tacit posture (like a grave Scout in ambush for his Enemy), but because all things done are either from consideration or chance, and the works of Chance are accomplishments of an instant, having commonly a dissimilitude, but hers are the works of time, and have their contextures alike.
>
> Wit is not only the luck and labour, but also the dexterity of thought, rounding the world, like the Sun, with unimaginable motion, and bringing swiftly home to the memory universall surveys. It is the Souls Powder, which when supprest, as forbidden from flying upward, blows up the restraint.... It is in Divines, Humility, Exemplarinesse, and Moderation; in Statesmen, Gravity, Vigilance, Benigne Complacency ...; in Leaders of Armies, Valor, Painfulness, Temperance, Bounty, Dexterity in punishing and rewarding, and a sacred Certitude of promise. It is in Poets a full comprehension of all recited in all these, and an ability to bring those comprehensions into action. (2:20–21)

In Davenant's rhapsody, wit is transformed from intellectual propriety into the defining quality of all proper intellectual and spiritual activity: it combines reason and instinct; it is at once luck and labor, dexterity and application, design and memory. Davenant has moved wit to the center of his politicized aeṣthetic, for he aims to displace inspiration as the defining intellectual and spiritual property not only of poetry but of divinity as well. This is a major piece of aesthetic legislation, and it is eagerly taken up by Hobbes, who must have recognized the force and application of Davenant's account of wit.[34]

Both men saw in this term a convenient and elastic alternative to the politics and poetics of inspiration; and in the effort to realign the defining intellectual terms of poetry, neither Davenant and Hobbes nor, later, Dryden saw the need to distinguish poetry from philosophy or history. They recognized how useful the alignment with both disciplines might prove for an art of poetry that is vigilant, measured, comprehensive, and proportionate. Though Davenant has been read as the precursor of English neoclassicism, I suspect that nothing could have been less on his mind than the translation of French aesthetic rules to English literary property. Davenant and Hobbes may have fostered neoclassicism,[35] but they aimed beyond aesthetics, arguing broadly from aesthetics to the social, spiritual, and political realms. They offered an account of poetry and society that would serve as an antidote to piety and inspiration. They did not choose aesthetics simply as convenient or safe ground, though it was both of those; they began there because out of the aesthetic they could spin an alternative vision of society and of human nature that might carry with it the authority of the aesthetic. It marks a very long road to have taken from Sidney when, in the early 1650s, the aesthetic might be the foundation of the political. This is not to say that politics found itself everywhere confessing the primacy of the aesthetic—quite obviously, the political was fully able to construct arguments in a variety of idioms—but that the aesthetic could play a significant role in articulating the political, that they occupied contiguous and at times continuous territories. When Hobbes opens his *Answer* to Davenant, he begins with an account of man and society that politicizes all writing. What the *Preface* and *Answer* announce is the signal victory of Sidney's program to move the poet to the center of civic colloquy.

Hobbes's response to Davenant came very quickly indeed; in fact, it was published together with Davenant's *Preface* in the Paris edition of 1650. *Gondibert* was not to join the *Preface* and *Answer* until 1651, and then in an incomplete state. There was already in Davenant's *Preface* sufficient material for Hobbes to answer. Hobbes begins his work with a political geography of mankind that predicts the familiar social scheme of literary genres: epic takes the court as its subject;

satire and comedy find their subjects in the city; and pastoral discovers the country. Like Davenant, Hobbes makes an explicitly political theory of genres: for the court he discovers the propriety of heroic elevation; for the city, the fitness of satire; for the country, the neutralizing pastoral. This much is familiar; the argument becomes rather more interesting when Hobbes takes up the problem of inspiration. Like Davenant, he begins the account of inspiration by twinning the arts of poetry and prophecy; then, like Davenant, he describes the degrading of prophecy into discord, tumult, and zeal:

> For my part, I neither subscribe to their accusation, nor yet condemn that Heathen custom otherwise then as accessary to their false Religion. For their Poets were their Divines, had the name of Prophets; Exercised amongst the People a kinde of spiritual Authority, would be thought to speak by a divine spirit, have their works which they writ in Verse (the divine stile) pass for the word of God and not of man, and to be hearkened to with reverence. Do not our Divines (excepting the stile) do the same, and by us that are of the same Religion cannot justly be reprehended for it? Besides, in the use of the spiritual calling of Divines, there is danger sometimes to be feared from want of skill, such as is reported of unskilful Conjurers, that mistaking the rites and cerimonious points of their art, call up such spirits as they cannot at their pleasure allay again, by whom storms are raised that overthrow buildings and are the cause of miserable wracks at sea. Unskilful Divines do often times the like: For when they call unseasonably for Zeal there appears a Spirit of Cruelty; and by the like error, instead of Truth they raise Discord; instead of Wisdom, Fraud; instead of Reformation, Tumult; and Controversie instead of Religion.[36]

Hobbes's analysis does not have quite the elasticity of Davenant's account, but it is every bit as thorough and, in its pacing, rather more polemical. The paragraph begins with an ambling account of divinity among the ancients; when Hobbes directs his gaze at his own time, he tightens the pace, abbreviates the periods, and piles accusation on accusation, rushing to the conclusion that the ancient arts of prophecy and poetry have been irreversibly degraded into discord, fraud, and tumult. The politics of religious inspiration and the aesthetics of such piety are equally derided:

> But why a Christian should think it an ornament to his Poem, either to profane the true God or invoke a false one, I can imagin no cause but

a reasonless imitation of Custom, of a foolish custome, by which a man,
enabled to speak wisely from the principles of nature and his own meditation, loves rather to be thought to speak by inspiration, like a Bagpipe.
(2:59)

In place of inspiration, Hobbes supplies the program of judgment
and fancy, the twin faces of Davenant's capacious "wit." Judgment is
the source of structure; fancy, the source of ornament in poetry. The
aesthetic is cool, reasoned, and alert. In attacking inspiration, Hobbes
aims at political and aesthetic targets. The argument is not exactly an
allegory of the political, but something we might again call, as in
Davenant's *Preface,* the politics of culture. With judgment and fancy
Hobbes associates the aesthetics of discrete order, perfect registration,
what is "beautiful or defensible in building, or marvellous in Engines
and Instruments of motion" (2:60). Judgment and fancy are the foundations of European civilization: "Whatsoever distinguisheth the civility of Europe from the Barbarity of the American savages, is the
workmanship of Fancy but guided by the Precepts of true Philosophy"
(2:60). Like Davenant, Hobbes discovers judgment and fancy to be
the basis for all intellectual labor, the very foundation of art, society,
and political culture. The affinity with Davenant is so close that it
sounds like a concerted program. But it is more than aesthetics that
Hobbes and Davenant have in mind when they use this language; it
is a political, social, and cultural stance that would replace the fury
of zeal and the destructiveness and moral absolutism of divine politics
with propriety, reason, and nature.

The language of prefaces and defenses of poetry is fundamentally
aesthetic, and their ostensible territory, literature; but under the pressure of civil war, defeat, and exile, the most urgent business for aesthetics as well as for political theory and philosophy was the restoration
of the state. Celestial harmony was an ancient and honored figure of
speech for the ordered universe; in it the links between art and politics,
between the muses and statecraft, were apprehended. The program
of *Gondibert* itself was the restoration of amity and community in a
divided state, and Hobbes makes the apprehension of that moral the
source of his approval of structure and fable: "But when I considered
that also the actions of men, which singly are inconsiderable, after
many conjunctures grow at last either into one great protecting power
or into two destroying factions, I could not but approve the structure
of your Poem, which ought to be no other then such as an imitation

of humane life requireth" (2:61). Hobbes's *Answer to Davenant* contains a politics of invention and a politics of reception. It is difficult to imagine an aesthetic program more exactly responsive to the circumstance of royalist exiles in 1650 than that devised by Davenant and Hobbes. Although the program may have ended up in our histories of literary criticism as the opening act in the formation of English neoclassicism, what Davenant and Hobbes sought was something more urgent than aesthetic regulation: they were calling for the reformation of the politics and the poetics of inspiration.

It is one thing to raise such a flag in exile and among friends, to denounce "extemporary fury" from the comfortable distance of Paris, but the Paris edition was followed in 1651 by a London edition that included Davenant's *Preface*, Hobbes's *Answer*, and the first three books of *Gondibert*. Perhaps the prefaces, once attached to the body of the poem, had a less inflammatory air, a clearer literary identity. When Abraham Cowley issued a London edition of his *Poems* in 1656, his own preface, an important document in our history of poetics, proceeds quite circumspectly. Cowley was an intimate of the Hobbes-Davenant circle in Paris and an author of commendatory verse to both. Not only was his association with the exiled court well known, but he was suspected of being a secret agent of that court, a spy and an informer.[37] Neither the neutralizing, casual reference to "my return lately into England"[38] with which the preface begins nor the cautious aside to "the late unhappy War" (2:78) tells the whole story of his exile and repatriation. As the preface acknowledges—indeed, openly argues—an issue of the *Poems* in 1656 could not be solely a literary act; publication is first an effort to redeem what Cowley regards as his low reputation. During what Cowley refers to as "the time of my absence" (2:77), a pirated edition of a work entitled *The Iron Age, i.e., The Foure Ages of England* had been issued under his name. He professes bewilderment at the publication of "another Mans" work under his name (2:77); he alludes to injury; the language contends malice, power, and destruction. This vocabulary seems slightly overloaded for protecting a literary reputation; but something more than literary manners is at stake, for *The Iron Age* includes a powerful invective against puritanism called, in its original 1642 edition, *A satyre against Separatists, or, the conviction of chamber-preachers, and other schismatickes contrary to the discipline of this our protestant profession.* The 1642 issue was signed *A.C.*, printed twice in that year, and then issued in 1648 with Cowley's name printed on the title page.

Without naming the offensive satire, the 1656 preface to *Poems* attempts to distance the author from that work. The denial of the pirated edition of *The Iron Age* is the first step in this argument; the preface situates the poet and his poetry in a highly politicized geography; this is a suspected royalist agent returning to Cromwell's London and declaring innocence of motive. He is aware of the divisive and inflammatory atmosphere that surrounds publication, and he not only attempts to deny the *Satire Against Separatists,* but is ready more broadly to edit his work to exclude whatever might be construed as dangerous:

> We ought not, sure, to begin our selves to revive the remembrance of those times and actions for which we have received a General Amnestie as a favor from the Victor. The truth is, neither We nor They ought by the Representation of Places and Images to make a kind of Artificial Memory of those things wherein we are all bound to desire, like Themistocles, the Art of Oblivion.... The Names of Party and Titles of Division, which are sometimes in effect the whole quarrel, should be extinguished and forbidden in peace under the notion of Acts of Hostility. And I would have it accounted no less unlawful to rip up old wounds then to give new ones; which has made me not onely abstain from printing any things of this kinde, but to burn the very copies, and inflict a severer punishment on them my self then perhaps the most rigid Officer of State would have thought that they deserved. (2:84)

Cowley had to perform another act of political editing after 1660 when he reissued the *Poems* and suppressed this passage from the preface. The confession of political editing, like Cowley's entire preface, argues the civic force of the literary; to suppress and cast away in times of civic strife is to acknowledge how political is the enterprise of culture, how inflammatory is the "War of the Pen" (2:83), how powerful is the obligation that "Tongue as well as Hand . . . serve and assist the side" (2:83) in which a man is engaged. Pagan fables, Cowley argues, make an important contribution to the state by strengthening "the authority of Law with the terrors of Conscience, and expectation of certain rewards and unavoidable punishments" (2:89). Poetry in the cold climate of civil war and republican triumph is a sensitive register for the state. The whole of the first part of Cowley's preface makes us aware of how sensitive and contested was the publication of verse in the late 1640s and 1650s. Having corrected his "literary" reputation by the publication of *Poems* in 1656, Cowley vows to make himself "absolutely dead in a Poetical capacity," and resolves "at present... never to exercise any more that faculty" (2:79–80).

The preface argues first how thoroughly implicated in politics is poetry, but Cowley also makes a contribution to the aesthetic program of the literary. And here, like Davenant and Hobbes before him, he celebrates the estate of wit: "Wit and Reason" are the soul of poetry (2:84), "Wit and Eloquence" its best fortification (2:88). Cowley's miscellany opens with an ode that celebrates wit as a reflection of divinity; but he declines the concomitant address to enthusiasm. Such an attack on "extempory" inspiration would have been too bold for the repatriated exile in 1656; further, Cowley had his own design on poetic rhapsody. The third section of the miscellany consisted of Cowley's Pindaric odes; as his prefatory remarks suggest, with these odes Cowley meant to claim more than elevation and erudition: "The digressions are many and sudden.... The Figures are unusual and bold.... The Numbers are various and irregular" (2:86). The program is not exactly poetic furor, and Cowley declines the conjunction of prophecy and poetry; but the prefatory account implies a poetics of inspiration that Cowley wished to claim for the miscellany, and especially for the fourth and longest part of the book, the *Davideis*.

Cowley's preface announces the *Davideis* as an epic project designed after the pattern of "our Master Virgil" (2:86). Of paramount importance to the program of *Poems*, the *Davideis* not only is the most exalted and extended part of the book; it lodges a royalist counterclaim on the central book of puritan religious and political culture: the Old Testament. As the *Eikon Basilike* had shown, David was crucial to the celebration of persecuted monarchy,[39] and no figure, either classical or scriptural, was more prominent in Restoration panegyrics and sermons than King David. In the *Davideis* Cowley is not writing polemic in the fashion of his other incomplete epic, *The Civil War* (a work that he claims to have destroyed in the interests of harmony and ecumenical politics [2:83]), but is concerned with sovereignty and prerogative, obedience and loyalty, privilege and power. The poetics is exalted but not frenzied; the pattern is Virgil as well as II Samuel. In the preface and in the body of *Poems*, Cowley reclaims the sacred, elevates wit, redefines the territory a royalist might hold as his own. As with Davenant and Hobbes, wit is central to Cowley's literary program; but more daringly, Cowley claims a sacred poetics. His syncretism has a less well defined polemical edge than the poetics of Davenant and Hobbes, but we ought not to lose sight of the different circumstance in which he promulgated his poetics and republished his miscellany. Anyone opening the volume in 1656 and noting the pieces on Lord Falkland, on Charles I's return from Scotland, on the bishop of Lincoln, to Davenant, and on Crashaw could not have doubted Cowley's royalism. The program of the volume both acknowledges the power of politics in the ordering of the literary and reinforces the royalist poetics of wit, but it would also assimilate some of the poetics of inspiration and the authority of Scripture to its own literary and cultural cause and to the poetics of wit.[40] As the *Eikon Basilike* had demonstrated in 1649 and as the Restoration panegyrics would make abundantly clear in 1660, those who celebrated monarchy were not willing to allow the politics of the saints to exclude them from the precincts of sacred authority. Indeed, they wished not only to reenter these precincts but to reclaim their texts and symbols and thereby to regulate the politics of enthusiasm.

Cowley's suppressed verse continued to play a role in polemic through the rest of the century. Some of the poems that had been omitted from the 1656 volume were reprinted by Cowley himself in 1660, and after his death they continued to circulate and reappear. The *Satire Against Separatists* was reissued in 1675, 1678, 1680, and 1705; *The Puritan and the Papist,* a furiously polemical attack first published in 1643, was suppressed and denied by Cowley in the 1656 edition and then republished during the Exclusion Crisis in *Wit and Loyalty Reviv'd* (1682).[41] The volume carries a preface, "The Publisher to the Reader," itself an interesting document in the history of literary polemicization. There the publisher defends republication by authenticating the satire as Cowley's, claiming to discern the author's "masterly Hand" visible in the art of this satire: "There want not the like bold strokes and life touches in the Style that evidently betray whose Originals they are."[42] But the publisher has a larger argument than the restoration of authorship; the publication of Cowley, Berkenhead, and Butler aims to revive in the aftermath of the Popish Plot and Exclusion the memory of civil war, to argue the analogy between dissent and rebellion, and to suggest, as did so many Tory polemicists, that '41 was come again. Having revived his cavaliers and argued the politics of folly and inspiration, the publisher widens the social and cultural implications of his argument:

I cannot think it any reproach to Mr. Cowly for him to walk abroad into the world in good company; the other two Gentlemen being, both of them celebrated Wits, and of the Loyal party engag'd, in the same interest, and active in the same Cause with himself. And it is no new thing for Wits and Cavaliers, to find out one another and associat together. Indeed they were men whose Mirth was so innocent, whose Wit so regular, and whose Conversation so entertaining and agreeable as I cannot but persuade my self, that they themselves would have made choice of no other Company when they were Living.[43]

The conflation of wit and loyalty, of social innocence and art: such is the program of royalist polemic fresh from the years of exile, and it is repeated and elaborated in the years that lie between civil war and Exclusion. In this anthologized collection of attacks on puritanism and dissent, the offices of culture, sociability, wit, and loyalty are insistently commingled. The 1682 edition of the satires makes bold and explicit the program of wit, politics, and high culture. There is, moreover, an additional argument, a vision of society within which the politics of wit is inevitably found, for conjoined with wit are innocence, mirth, high spirits, and high sociability. The social argument that underpins politics and culture forms its own net of associations throughout the 1650s, the 1660s, and beyond. Together with wit and loyalty we find among the defeated royalists in the 1650s not exactly the embrace of carnal pleasure—that was yet to come—but invocations of sack, ale, of conviviality and community: the union of low and high culture, the linking of maypoles and taverns, claret and verse in a vision of innocent hierarchy.

As the Restoration panegyrics would make clear, the return of monarchy could be argued as a restoration not only of political forms but of "culture" in our sense of the word; and the royalist conjoining of arts and empire forms a significant cultural claim in the decades to come. The panegyrics offer one field for examining the triumph of wit, but cultural politics can still be tracked through aesthetic theory. The defenses of poetry in the 1660s continue to provide a field for polemical assertion, and I want to follow my theme into two other theoretical texts, the preface to *Annus Mirabilis* and the conclusion to the *History of the Royal Society*. Dryden's preface and poem were published in 1667; they mark a new stage for literary apologetics as polemic, for they reveal how, within the restored commonweal, aesthetics can be transformed from fugitive argument into partisan program, though Dryden's calculated ease can make his polemical argument difficult, at first glance, to observe. The partisan and apologetic argument of the preface to *Annus Mirabilis* is not made with the kind of insistence that we find in Davenant and Hobbes, nor was Dryden writing under the pressure of defeat and exile, though he was navigating in his own difficult and partisan circumstances. In his adaptation of the quatrain from *Gondibert*, Dryden openly acknowledges Davenant; rather more significantly, Davenant's discussion of wit and the political freight of that word seem to be on Dryden's mind as he begins to handle a term that is at the center of his definition of poetry in the mid-1660s.

Directly following the praise of an age that takes pleasure in the best of kings, an age in which the praise of virtuous men will not excite the jealousy of a bad or degenerate prince, Dryden goes on to define the central tenet of poetry:

> The composition of all Poems is or ought to be of wit, and wit in the Poet, or wit writing, (if you will give me leave to use a School distinction) is no other then the faculty of imagination in the writer, which, like a nimble Spaniel, beats over and ranges through the field of Memory.... Wit written, is that which is well defin'd, the happy result of thought, or product of that imagination. But to proceed from wit in the general notion of it, to the proper wit of an Heroick or Historical Poem, I judge it chiefly to consist in the delightful imaging of persons, actions, passions, or things.[44]

I am here concerned not with the elasticity of, or indeed the contradictions embodied in, the definition,[45] but rather with Dryden's choice of the term *wit* to define his stance as poet of the court's cause in this year of "wonders." *Annus Mirabilis* aims to raise the spirits and fortunes of a beleaguered king and court. In that project, Dryden does not simply align himself with Davenant and Hobbes on wit; he produces his own triumphant account: the composition of all poems is or ought to be of wit. There is nothing hesitant or equivocal about the poetics of wit in this preface: "Wit written, is that which is well defin'd, the happy result of thought." What exactly Dryden had in mind with this capacious definition is less important than the certainty with which he staked his claim to this language. Wit is the idiom of thought and reason, the soul of the imagination; but Dryden's "imagination" is not the instrument of poetic furor, possession, and divinity: this is "imag-

ination" defined by propriety and reason. Dryden defines wit to include liveliness, speed, and variety; but he also aligns wit with history
and rationality. If we follow out all the suggestions of the language,
the word seems to function not as a definitional or analytical tool, but
as a cultural sign; its boundaries are indeterminate, for wit is emblem
and masthead.

Wit is a term that appears only once in that other famous poem of
1667, *Paradise Lost,* where we should not be surprised to find it associated with fallen intellect, with sleights, deceits, and fraud, "as from
[a wily snake's] wit and native subtlety" (9.93). Milton understood quite
well the politics of wit; the term had accrued important polemical
associations in the 1650s and 1660s, and when Dryden chose to begin
his defense of the court and to project his own ambitions he knew
exactly what language would convey his cultural politics. That it is
difficult to fix the definition of a term both slippery and capacious
seems to me very much part of its quality as cultural and polemical
marker. Sharper definition would have rendered the term less useful;
the very elasticity of the word determined its longevity in the politics
of culture. Dryden's various and brilliant handling of wit contributed
to its continuing polemical liveliness: "Wit and Fool, are Consequents
of Whig and Tory," he wryly observed in the preface to *Absalom and
Achitophel.* Nor had the polemics of wit been exhausted by the close
of the Exclusion Crisis. We ought to recognize, however, that over
the course of the late seventeenth century, wit gathered increasing
strength as an aesthetic idiom. Perhaps as the threat of canting religion
declined, the aesthetic bearing of wit became more highly concentrated. Of course, the career of wit from the polemical to the aesthetic
realm was hardly a continuous evolution over these decades, nor was
it the only term to make this transit; and in the Exclusion Crisis, when
conjuring the ghost of inspiration served obvious Tory aims, the polemical force of wit might be allowed full play. But by that moment
in the eighteenth century when sectarian enthusiasm could be diag-
nosed as pathology rather than rebellion,[46] the idioms of wit and
inspiration had come to occupy a realm rather different from the one
they contested in the 1650s.

The poetics and politics of wit were given one additional turn in
the 1660s in the *History of the Royal Society of London,* where Thomas
Sprat argued the alliance of monarchy, right reason, and empirical
science. That confluence of issues and interests comes late in the
History, just before Sprat closes the work with a catalog of all those

"eminent men of all Qualities: who have ingag'd to bestow their labors, on a design so public, and so free from all suspicion of mean, or private Interest," a brace of names that includes nearly every aristocrat, courtier, and politician attached to the early Restoration court.[47] In the lengthy anatomy that Sprat hangs on the *History* as an account of the "benefit of Experiments . . . to the Wits, and Writers of this, and all future Ages" (413), he examines the conditions of wit in various historical and intellectual modes. The wit of fables and ancient religion is "well-nigh consum'd" (414); the "Works of Nature" now provide "one of the best and most fruitful Soils for the growth of Wit" (415). Hence the unsurprising alliance between wit as intellectual property and the experimental work promoted by the Royal Society. Moreover, Sprat carefully allies experimental science and civil obedience; where right reason reigns—both in the works of nature and in civil society— there we can expect intellectual authority and political moderation. Sprat puts into direct opposition natural philosophy, which "take[s] away all sharpness and violence about [the] Civil" (429), and the "fury of Enthusiasm" (428), sedition, and pride. Experimental knowledge is the antidote to superstition, vanity, and fancy; it corrects transgressions of the law and contempt for civil authority.

Sprat conjoins wit and science in contest with sedition and inspiration; like Cowley, whose *Ode to the Royal Society* stands with the dedication to Charles II at the very portals to the *History*, Sprat would claim both the sovereignty of wit and the propriety of reverent scripturalism. Their motives in reclaiming Scripture may have differed— Cowley would provide a loyal and royal poetics for his *Davideis*, while Sprat is rather more fearful in his scripturalism, perhaps intent on deflecting charges of atheism by aligning the Royal Society with Christian reverence—but the public gestures are similar. Neither Sprat nor Cowley would forfeit the language of Scripture to sectarianism and dissent. Royalists had long insisted on the propriety of their scripturalism, and the daring analogies that they drew between the execution of Charles I and the Crucifixion suggested just how far they were willing to extend the scriptural sanctity of the Stuart cause. But Sprat's alliance of wit, science, religion, and civil history remarks a broader, more powerful syncretism. The conclusion of the *History of the Royal Society* is something of a manifesto of royalist and Restoration causes and cultures. The similarity of its interests to those that Dryden addresses in the preface to *Annus Mirabilis*, like the mingling of scriptural, civic, and scientific idioms in Dryden's poem, argues, if not a common orchestration of the themes of the restored court, certainly a coherent perception of where the court's interests lie and how they might be conjoined and identified. And in those interests, the language of wit played a significant role.

Nor should it surprise us that the idioms of wit and loyalty remain forcefully joined at least until the Glorious Revolution, or that Stuart, and then Jacobite, loyalty and the offices of culture should be brought together after 1688,[48] or echoed again in Pope's nostalgic twinning of the politics and culture of the Stuart cause. The mingling of wit and loyalty was not simply a continuous way of organizing the alliance of politics and culture; it also reflects the continuing authority of literature within the culture, its capacity to carry polemical weight, and the sensitivity of writers to those needs and potentials. Zeal, blasphemy, disloyalty, and dullness: political crisis sharpened the familiar royalist litany, but its history is long and nearly continuous from the 1640s onward. So too, efforts to define a poetics of godliness and reform, and, after the Restoration, to discover a dissenting muse, to clear literary space for loyalty and opposition, drew the steady concern of writers like Marvell and Milton and disclosed how satire might function on behalf of the politics of moral probity.

Literary theory and apologetics of the 1650s and 1660s give us some sense of how political argument came to organize the literary program of exiled royalists and returning cavaliers. A reading of the defenses, for example, not only argues the polemical role of wit and history; it also suggests how complete was the integration of politics and culture, how responsive were aesthetic distinctions and discriminations to political programs, how resourceful in the cause of politics was aesthetics. But to suggest that aesthetics was simply commandeered by politics is to argue the primacy of one discourse over the other. The traffic between politics and culture went in both directions; cultural texts not only expressed but shaped political interests. Both high politics and high culture were organized by social, economic, religious, and ideological pressures; they argued in each other's languages, and they understood each other's idioms, because they derived from shared impulses. Their integration is nowhere more brilliant and obvious than in the work and careers of Marvell, Milton, and Dryden. But the case can be made with texts of less brilliance and novelty, for polemical urgency was a fact of life not simply for the most responsive of writers or the most visible and vocal elements of the polity, but to its utmost reaches.

The story we have followed in the theoretical writings of Davenant, Hobbes, Cowley, Dryden, and Sprat is one thread of a broader discourse. Its lineaments can be discerned at many sites: in occasional poems, in university anthologies, in translations, in the creation of new dramatic idioms and the restaging and refurbishing of older theatrical forms, in heroic poetry, and, of course, in satire and lampoon. The verse collections issued in the 1650s and 1660s became vehicles themselves for polemical argument. Such volumes as *Parnassus Biceps* (1655), *Wits Interpreter* (1655), *Poesis Rediviva* (1655), *Sportive Wit* (1656), *Choyce Drollery* (1656), *Naps upon Parnassus* (1658), *Wit Restor'd* (1658), *The Rump, Or a Collection of Songs and Ballads* (1660), and *An Antidote Against Melancholy* (1661) reflect a steady concern with the fortunes of mirth and monarchy. At times this interest is expressed rather directly in prefatory remarks, but it occurs as well in these works' mixture of idioms, themes, and genres, and their use of previously published materials; in their panegyrics to living and epigraphs to fallen royalists; in their squibs on presbyters, Jesuits, and Protestants; in their invocations of classical poets; and perhaps most of all in their articulation of good fellowship, high spirits, and social innocence, that collaboration of the rites and conviviality of drink.

Lyric invocations of sack and ale might seem marginal gestures within this complex polemical structure, but they offer a sustained cultural argument, nostalgically linking cavalier with cavalier, peasant with aristocrat, and challenging the politics and aesthetics of godly inspiration, sobriety, and moral triumphalism. The literary form of the argument is often fragmentary, but that ought not to obscure its force or the degree to which it engages and contests the social, political, and aesthetic culture of puritanism. Drink acts as a leveler of social barriers and as a preservative of social and political values, and not only through nostalgia. For quite consistently the lyrics both posit images and evocations of communality, fellowship, and high spirits, and draw into specific contest the values of what they argue as the dominant political culture: the culture of zeal and plots, of suspicion and separation, of religious, social, and political fragmentation. Moreover, the politics and aesthetics of conviviality play an equally important and equally polemicized role after the Restoration, when sensuality is a pressure point for both the celebration and the denunciation of court culture.

In 1660 subjects may have been warned against distinction, cautioned against the use of harsh words and divisive labels, but wishful gestures could not neutralize the powerful shock of polemic that had braced this culture in the 1640s and 1650s. Although a unitary hopefulness is clear in the early 1660s, other currents are also visible. Vindictiveness, self-justification, and triumphalism guaranteed that the rifts in national culture opened by the wars would not be easily resolved in a return to older forms in 1660. Indeed, for all the appeals to, and the genuine efforts at, moderation, the forces of polemic would not be moderated in the decades to come; the alignment of weaponry and wit in the Exclusion Crisis[49] and the vigorous career of libel, invective, and slander in the 1680s and 1690s add yet another dimension to the polemic force of literary culture.[50] Stephen College was executed undoubtedly as an example and warning, but it was not incidental to the spectacle that *A Raree Show* was written in verse.[51]

Of course, the royalist exaltation of lyric high spirits did not go unchallenged; godliness, plain speech, and plain manners have themselves a long and complex history as a critique and repudiation of courtly indulgence, sensuality, and extravagance. Moreover, the polemical explosion of the 1640s and 1650s drew sermon and pamphlet literature into the warfare over manners, mores, and poetics. The indulgence of ceremony and drink; the pleasures of dancing, singing, and maypoling; the raising of spirits—all had met with a stream of puritan criticism, as had, of course, the theater, that cultural institution transformed by puritan argument into a most potent image of court culture. The closing of the theaters for nearly twenty years together with the charges leveled against indulgence and liberality formed an important polemical position through the 1640s and 1650s, and these themes remained vivid through the rest of the century.[52] The critique of drunkenness, whoring, idolatry, and sensuality—a complete armory of moral condemnation—was given vigorous life by the events and institutions of the mid-1660s, when dissent against the center found a powerful satiric voice. Echoes of the confrontation between piety and luxury continue to be heard in the Exclusion Crisis, in the polemic against Catholic monarchy during James's reign, and in the panegyrics welcoming Dutch William, perhaps also in the literature of moral reformation that emerges in the 1690s.[53] Nor do variations on these themes cease to be spun when the living memory of those events of civil conflict that began first to polarize and polemicize the nation in the 1640s has finally disappeared. But the nostalgic recovery of civil war polemic in the eighteenth century takes us to precincts beyond the borders of this inquiry. It is to those texts in which polemic lives its most vivid and complex life that I now turn.

2 The King's Head and the
Politics of Literary Property:
The *Eikon Basilike* and *Eikonoklastes*

Of the many companion pieces, animadversions, and contestations published in the seventeenth century, none has achieved
more lasting fame than the *Eikon Basilike* and *Eikonoklastes*.[1] The king's
book was issued on the day after his execution; within the year it had
gone through thirty-five London editions,[2] a success beyond the
scheming and imagining of its creators.[3] Milton's book was issued in
two separate states in 1649, revised and enlarged in 1650, translated
into Latin and French,[4] formally answered in 1651 by the *Eikon
Aklastos,* and sufficiently notorious by 1660 to be confiscated and publicly burned;[5] but it was no match for the *Eikon Basilike*. What the king
could not do alive, he more than achieved through martyrdom, in
literary mythology, and on the pages of the *Eikon Basilike*. In his person
he had compromised the royalist cause; in death he provided a sudden
and dramatic focus for the claims and affections of his party. The
Eikon Basilike was a personal testament, a monument to the king's
piety, to the tenderness of his conscience and purity of his spirit, to
the innocence of his motives and the elevation of his mind; but it was
also a public vindication of the king's constitutionalism and an assertion of his reverence for custom and law. It instantly became the holy
book of royalist politics; there was no missing the integrity of its effects.
Milton's grasp of its iconic position was prescient, though "iconic"
hardly does justice to the breadth of the book's strategies, to its assertion, simultaneously, of art and truth. At every turn Milton challenged the *Eikon Basilike:* he derided its principal, ridiculed its style,
denounced and refuted its politics; he posed documentary evidence

[37]

against Charles's anecdotes and chronicles, declarations and histories against the king's fancies and fictions.

The contestative force of *Eikonoklastes* is obvious, written not only into the lockstep of Milton's "point by point" (*E,* 568) refutation of the *Eikon Basilike* but into the language of his preface with its gauntlets, antagonisms, and challenges; and, throughout, in the abrasive cross-examining of the king, the personal sniping, the ridiculing of the king's domestic affections, the mocking of his piety, and the confuting of his scripturalism.[6] Such contestative work, fierce and encyclopedic though it may have been, was of course hardly singular. *Eikonoklastes* was published eight months after the *Eikon Basilike,* but the king's book had already been answered in the *Eikon Alethine,* itself promptly challenged by the *Eikon e Piste.* Moreover, the *Eikon Basilike,* the book at the center of this turbulence, was itself fully engaged, delicately maneuvered into contest, poised to "confute and revenge all those black and false scandals" cast on the king (*EB,* 87). The king's book was intended as well to appropriate the pieties and providences, the spiritual searchings and convictions of sin that had long been property of the "Saints." Not least important, the *Eikon Basilike* exploited the rich and elevating associations of this king with aesthetic culture, with theater, poetry, and portraiture. It is difficult entirely to gauge the contestative character of either the *Eikon Basilike* or *Eikonoklastes* through the terms they set down for each other; they were but two points in a whirlwind of publication and controversy, both responsive to a network of themes and associations that stretched far beyond their immediate occasion. But the dialectic between the books helps to define the contest over the character of Charles's kingship and the events that precipitated the destruction of monarchy. The books also serve an emblematic function for us, characterizing a moment, a set of conditions, and a number of the ways in which polemic inflected an entire verbal culture: its social, its religious, and most particularly its literary idioms.

The frontispiece to the *Eikon Basilike* made obvious Milton's need to address the aesthetic as well as the political and spiritual bodies of the king.[7] The aesthetic body was not, however, confined to visual imagery. Milton was aware, even by the summer of 1649, of the flood of writing that issued from the king's book, replicating its political and aesthetic claims in sermons and prayers, psalters and meditations; in allegories, pastorals, and dream visions; in laments, epitaphs, and elegies; in verse histories and tragedies on the incomparable martyrdom of Charles I.[8] The king's book may not have been conceived as "literature," but it excited an astonishing quantity and variety of literary production.[9] Milton understood that to combat the book and its legacy he would need to deny its capacity as literature and its imaginative authority; but in a more complex and what must have been for Milton more difficult move, he aimed altogether to deny the authority of the aesthetic within political discourse. The association of the king's person with learning and aristocratic refinement, with poetry, drama, and visual culture, forced Milton to trivialize the artistic forms and genres most closely identified with Charles I. Milton dismisses the *Eikon Basilike* for its pathos and poetical strains; he ridicules the king as a "more diligent reader of Poets, then of Politicians" (*E*, 406); but finally and most daringly, he quashes the whole book as a "peece of Poetrie" (*E*, 406). This could not have been an easy gesture for Milton; that he was willing to make it suggests how central were the materials of culture to the articulation of authority in 1649.

It comes as no surprise that Charles I should have been closely associated with the cultivation and properties of literary art or that such association would be exploited in social, ethical, and political terms both in the *Eikon Basilike* and in *Eikonoklastes*. Recent work on the Caroline court has shown us how extensive was its patronage system, how deeply allied were the effects of art with the person of the king.[10] The magnificent if closeted Caroline masques have long been understood to express the taste and ideology of Charles's court and of the king himself,[11] but the association of the person of the king with high culture reached beyond the privacy and privilege of court drama. It was promulgated through rituals and progresses, through paintings, engravings, and the creation of royal collections,[12] through royal patronage of poetry and the theater;[13] and it was explosively evidenced in such acts as the destruction of the queen's altarpiece by parliamentary forces and the dispersal of the king's picture collection.[14] The social, theological, even financial character of such events complicates our understanding of the transactions among the materials of art, social identity, and religious ideology in the Caroline period,[15] but however we refine the argument, we must reckon with the broad and powerful association of Charles I with the genres and effects of high culture throughout the whole of his reign.

The force of that association was clearly expressed in William Marshall's frontispiece to the *Eikon Basilike*,[16] in the arrangement and articulation of the materials of Charles's narratives and prayers, and in the highly figured language and elegantly balanced periods of the king's prose. It must also have been calculated in the commemorative aspirations of the *Eikon Basilike*, for the book was intended to transmute the king into an aesthetic object.[17] Such a strategy was crucial to the polemic of the *Eikon Basilike* and to the myriad of royalist elegies that gloried in the very body of the martyred king transformed into literature—recorded, published, and dispersed through elegies and epitaphs that used all the strategies of rhetoric and art to resurrect the body of the king as an everlasting monument in the hearts of true believers.[18] That verse should have the power to transform the body into art is the classic consolation of epitaph and elegy: "here doth lye / BEN. IONSON his best piece of poetrie" is only the most obvious example.[19] The topos achieved special meaning in the commemorative literature on Charles I because its force was at once consolatory and polemical. The body of the king and the institution of monarchy may have been destroyed,[20] but the political personality of the king and the cause of his party would be rendered immortal through the good offices of the *Eikon Basilike*, that "best Colossus,"[21] that "stately building of Meditations, Consultations, Essayes, Debates, and Devotions,"[22] that "Monument of richer metall than all the Tombs of Brasse or Marble erected to the honour of his Predecessors; which no Inscription whatsoever, though in Letters of Gold, and engraven with a pen of Diamonds, can be able to parallel."[23]

In resurrecting that body, the king's elegists ransacked history and myth; they proposed analogies and metaphors to express the inexpressible, "the transcendencie of this horrid work of darknesse, this masterpiece of Hell."[24] Although some doubted that a parallel could be discovered or a language found—"where the Theme's ineffable, the way / To speake it is, Not to know what to say"[25]—the attempt to fashion idioms for imagining and regretting the death of the king drove the elegists in two directions: toward sacred rhetoric and toward secular literary genres. Samson and Job—those favorite puritan types of Christic patience and fortitude—as well as Jonah and Josiah offered parallels and occasions for comprehending the king; and the modeling of Charles's prayers after David's Psalms underscored the figural significance of all the Old Testament material within this armory;[26] but the overwhelming sacred parallel for the king's suffering was the Savior's Passion. In 1619, and with a striking and prophetic irony, James I had dedicated his *Meditation upon S. Matthew* to Prince Charles:

One day reading privately to my selfe the passion of Christ in the end of S. Mathews Gospel, I lighted upon that part, where the governours souldiers mocked our Savior, with putting the ornaments of a King upon him; which appeared to me to be so punctually set downe, that my head hammered upon it divers times after, and specially the croune of thornes which never went out of my mind, remembring the thorny cares, which a King (if he have a care of his office) must be subiect unto, as (God knows) I daily and nightly feele in mine owne person. Whereupon I apprehended that it would be a good paterne to put inheritors to Kingdoms in mind of their calling, by the forme of their inauguration; and so resolved to borrow some hours from my rest, to write a short Meditation upon it...and I thought you the fittest person to whom I could dedicate it.[27]

Now, in the days and months following the king's execution, sermons and poems argued the utter conformity of Charles with Christ, hunting the divine parallels and sacred analogies through their lives and passions.[28] The king's book itself appropriated Christ's language and the form and figural sanctity of David's Psalms to set definitive commemorative terms. The frontispiece inaugurated this argument, but the text was a network of Christic allusions and parallels. The king's story, a monarch "Publiquely Murdered by His Calvino-Judaicall Subjects,"[29] discovered all the elements of Christ's Passion:

This is a parricide so heinous, so horrible, that it cannot be paralleled by all the murthers that ever were committed since the world began, but onely in the murther of Christ. And indeed the providence of God gave me first occasion to institute this parallel: for that day that our gracious Soveraigne was murthered, being the 30. of January, a day for ever to be noted with a black coale, as his Majesty was at divine service, before he was led forth unto the scaffold, the Chapter that was read unto him, was the seven and twentieth of St. Matthews gospell, which containes the passion of Christ; and that Chapter was read not by choise but by the direction of the rubrick, it being the lesson appointed for that day, so that we could not but conceive, that the murther then to be acted, was like unto that which in the chapter is described.[30]

The analogy proved almost inescapable.

Sacred history was not, however, the only text for comprehending the death of the king. The genres of literary art and particularly the

idiom of the theater provided rich materials for imagining and regretting the martyrdom of Charles I. The theater allowed the com-
bining of moral commonplaces with more pointed aesthetic and
political associations; it provided ways of underscoring and lamenting
puritan rebellion as political and aesthetic barbarity.[31] In the "Prologue to the Gentry" to *The Famous Tragedie of King Charles I* (1649),
Jacobean and Caroline dramatists—Jonson, Shakespeare, Davenant,
Suckling, Beaumont, Fletcher, and Shirley—are allied with king and
court as writers "loathed, by the Monsters of the times."[32] Theater
itself is celebrated as a mirror "wherein Mens actions are reflected to
their own view. Which, perhaps, is the true cause, that some, privy
to the Uglinesse of their own guilt, have issued out Warrants, for the
breaking all those Looking-glasses; lest their deformities recoyl, and
become an eye-sore to themselves."[33] The execution turned the entire
nation into a stage: for some, "the last Act though most bloody, proved
the best"; for others, the king's death was but "the first act of that
tragicall woe, which is to be presented upon the Theater of This
Kingdome, likely to continue longer then the now living Spectators."[34]
Whitehall was the playhouse, the scaffold a stage, the king's demise
an incomparable tragedy, and the horrified spectators an audience to
this theater of death.[35] The most exquisite variations wrought on the
execution as theater were played out in the *Horatian Ode,* where Marvell balances the capacity of the metaphor to distance the execution
against its ability to expose the violence of the scene:

> That thence the Royal Actor born
> The Tragick Scaffold might adorn:
>   While round the armed Bands
>   Did clap their bloody hands.
> He nothing common did or mean
> Upon that memorable Scene.[36]

The figure is handled with uncommon analytical power, but the materials themselves are so commonplace that we need to appreciate in
Marvell's delicate assay of their conventionality not only his sensitivity
to the ambiguities of the topos but also his baffling of its partisanship.

    Elegy uses art to control pathos, but theatrical metaphors do more
than offer solace through comprehending distance. Those figures
were intimate with the king's personal effects and with the mythos of
power and authority that had developed around his kingship; they

argued the fitness of literary art, the cogency of the theater, and the propriety of tragedy to compass the betrayal and execution of the king.[37] The metaphor of the stage, the transfiguration of the body, the elevation of the *Eikon Basilike* into divine rhetoric: all the harmonies of literary culture converged in royalist polemic on the occasion of the king's execution. They formed an arsenal the force of whose weaponry was not lost on defenders of the shattered cause of royalism. That the king's party had, for the present, no other field of battle was true, and yet out of aesthetic idioms a defensive position was created that allied the cause of kingship with the harmonies of art and challenged the legitimacy of the republic by regretting the regicide as an inhuman barbarity perpetrated on the civic and aesthetic bodies of the commonwealth.

In situating the *Eikon Basilike* within these streams of contestative rhetoric, we must further remember that it was not only the elevated reaches of literary art that were brought into the eddies of political controversy: songs, ballads, and broadsides argued similar themes. Indeed, language itself had come to seem dangerously charged, inextricably tangled into political contest. Slurs and calumnies were claimed; tumults and noise were raised; railing and cursing, scandals and aspersions were everywhere apprehended. Political debate in this century had often been angry and tumultuous, but never more so than in the years of civil war when language itself had achieved combative status. The tongue was a weapon as teeth grew out of that "unruly member...or rather in the tongue, tongue-teeth, bitter words, and sharpe reproaches."[38] The 1649 Act against Unlicensed and Scandalous Books paid its own tribute to the "divers Scandalous, Seditious and Libellous Pamphlets, Papers and Books [which] are daily contrived, printed, vended and dispersed," and to those who "Make, Write, Print, Publish, Sell or Utter, or cause to be Made, Printed or Uttered, any scandalous or Libellous Books, Pamphlets, Papers or Pictures whatsoever."[39] Despite the licensing act, and perhaps because swords had been laid aside, the force of words seemed ever more ominous: "mouth Granadoes"[40] displaced muskets, "troops of valiant Verse" were drummed up from the ancient languages,[41] and type fonts marched in military formation.[42] The king himself observed that words were now weapons, that "foul and false aspersions were secret engines" (*EB*, 84), and the teeth of his enemies "spears and arrows, their tongue a sharp sword" (*EB*, 93). It was in such a context— indeed, in recognition of the extraordinary force of printed language and of the spiritual and political authority of its more dignified forms and modes—that the *Eikon Basilike* was conceived; and it was, of course, to address that authority and to contest the "publishing, dispersing, commending, and almost adoring [of] it" (*E*, 340) that *Eikonoklastes* was contrived.

Not all was image and metaphor. The king's political case was laid out in the *Eikon Basilike* as a series of historical vignettes that enabled Charles to present his own reading of the critical episodes in the raveling of the state and the unfolding of his tragedy. He begins, if not at the beginning, then with the first of a chronological series of events. On November 3, 1640, the king called what was to be known as the Long Parliament, a demonstration, he suggests, of his devotion to the immemorial institutions of English law and governance. The chapters that follow take up contiguous events: Strafford's impeachment, attainder, and execution on May 12, 1641; the attempt to arrest the Five Members of the House of Commons on January 4, 1642; the king's flight from Westminster on January 10, 1642. But chronology in this history soon collapses.[43] The king's "retirement" from London is followed by a chapter on Henrietta Maria's "departure" from England in July 1644; the attempt to arrest the Five Members on January 4, 1642, is separated from the narrative surrounding the Triennial Bill, passed and signed on February 16, 1641; and the chapter on the Nineteen Propositions, which were presented to the king on June 2, 1642, is followed by reflections on the Irish rebellion that broke out in October 1641. Later sequences are similarly disrupted; chapters on general themes are mixed into narrative sequences, and chronology is abandoned for a series of reflections on "Jealousies . . . and Scandals" (*EB*, 84), "Church Government" (*EB*, 101), and "The Reformations of the Times" (*EB*, 123). Toward the end of the book historical narrative is restored with a sequence of chapters on Charles's flight to the Scots, his imprisonment at Holmby, the escape to the Isle of Wight, and "Meditations upon Death"; the whole is brought to a close with meditation and prayer.

Historical narrative is clearly a secondary effect in the *Eikon Basilike*. The loose chronology of the book allows the king to heighten the themes most important to his political argument and most flattering to his self-portraiture. The casual use of historical sequence also enables Charles to suggest, through telescoping and reordering of the narrative progression, not simply cause and effect as he chose to compound them but, more important, the sense of collusion and

conspiracy that pervades royalist readings of the inexplicable com-
bustion of civil war. The play on sequence further allows the subor-
dination of events to personality. National conflagrations are but leaves
from the king's diary, and affect—tenderness of conscience, personal
honor, domestic sentiment—is magnified over the destiny of the commonwealth, the fate of reformed religion, and the lives of combatants.
In his defense of the trial and execution of the king, John Cook plays
on exactly this egotism and literary self-absorption: "He was no more
affected with a List that was brought in to Oxford of Five or six
thousand slain at Edgehill, then to read one of Ben: Johnsons Tragedies."[44] Perhaps the king could only have comprehended the 1640s
through such intense personalization, but Milton struggles throughout *Eikonoklastes* not only to "correct" the king's narratives but to
enlarge their frame, to allow history, political theory, and ideology
their proper role in narrating the destruction of monarchy and the
creation of a republic. Although Milton discredits and defames the
person of the king, he wants at the same time to depersonalize the
king's struggle so that civil war might be elevated into history, a realm
distant from the mixed and trivial genres—the fancies, allusions, and
forgeries—of the *Eikon Basilike*.

Much of Milton's effort at contestation is directed into rewriting
the narratives of the *Eikon Basilike*; he chose to answer them fully,
often "point by point" (*E*, 568), complaining of the length of the
"endless work to walk side by side with the Verbosity" of the king's
book (*E*, 433). *Eikonoklastes* is, however, substantially longer than the
work it answers, and that bulk is comprised of the documentary cases
with which Milton confutes the king's narratives. But the poet understood that the authority of the *Eikon Basilike* lay not in the book's self-
serving narratives, but in its pathos and affect. It was something other
than false narrative that endangered the republic, and both Milton's
unease over and his struggle within the realm of the aesthetic are
evident in his engagement with the *Eikon Basilike* as literary art, with
its mixed genres and modes, its metaphors and allusions, its borrow-
ings and adaptations, and finally with the meaning of authorship and
the consequent relations between literary and political integrity. These
are issues already vivid in the preface to *Eikonoklastes*.

I have suggested the psychological difficulty that Milton faced in
choosing to combat the *Eikon Basilike* by debasing the book's estate as
poetry. The discomfort is apparent in his opening sentences.[45] The
tactic was forced on Milton by the affective power of the *Eikon Basilike*

and by the stress on the literary genres to which the events of 1649 had repeatedly been conformed:

> To descant on the misfortunes of a person fall'n from so high a dignity ... is neither of it self a thing commendable, nor the intention of this discours. Neither was it fond ambition, or the vanity to get a Name, present, or with Posterity, by writing against a King: I never was so thirsty after Fame, nor so destitute of other hopes and means, better and more certaine to attaine it. For Kings have gain'd glorious Titles from thir Favourers by writing against privat men.... I shall make no scruple... to take up this Gauntlet, though a Kings, in the behalf of Libertie, and the Common-wealth. (*E*, 337–38)

However we parse his motives—and Milton complicates our reading of his ambitions in *Eikonoklastes* by insisting on his reluctant authorship, his coolness toward a project that was "assign'd" rather than "chos'n or affected," the "irksom labour" involved in its composition, and his seeming indifference to its completion, evidenced, he tells us, by his "finishing it so leasurely, in the midst of other imployments and diversions" (*E*, 339)—the opening words announce more the aesthetic than the political concerns and force of his work. "To descant" is to sing variations on a fixed theme, to produce intricate harmonies on a set piece; perhaps the verb is wholly ironic—there is surely nothing lyric about *Eikonoklastes*—though the notion of theme and variations fits the conduct of Milton's book well enough. With or without the ironies of descanting, the phrase "misfortunes of a person fall'n from so high a dignity" announces literary matter, tragic forms and themes. Personal and authorial issues preoccupy Milton in the preface to his work, and it is in competition with Charles I as author that Milton feels most endangered. As a writer, Milton claims "better and more certaine" means of achieving fame; he has concerns over the care and industry with which his work will be read and judged. These competitive and overtly literary issues are the terms that drive the opening of Milton's book. Though surely Milton understood that in the case of the king's book, it would be impossible to separate the literary from the political meaning of authorship, that the literary authority of the *Eikon Basilike* derived not only from its fancies and allusions but from the political identity of its purported author. Milton does not openly admit this perplexity of authorship and authority; for him their separation and the subsequent vulnerability that he exposes in the king's literary manners would seem to allow an easier subversion of political authority. But the intimacy of the king's political and literary identity in the form of the *Eikon Basilike* is clearly the point of Milton's accusations of plagiarism, and just as clearly the source of what Milton insists on as literary anxiety at the opening of his book. As for the overtly political challenge that Milton means to pose, it is only at the close of the first paragraph that he allows his political themes: liberty and the commonwealth.

Of course, Milton's attention is not devoted only to the literary origins of his animadversion. He raises other literary issues: the genres of the king's book, its rhetorical and aesthetic authority, and the identity of the book as a "Masking Scene" replete with "Emblems and devices begg'd from the old Pageantry of some Twelf-nights entertainment at Whitehall" (*E*, 342–43). Ridicule is often the intent of the language when Milton turns to the aesthetic properties of the *Eikon Basilike*—the tone patronizing and contemptuous—but the conjuring of masque and pageantry not only acknowledges Charles's association with the theater, it confesses the political authority of such idioms. For what concerns Milton here is the book's affective power, its capacity to carry the king's words and arms. Milton's apprehension is obvious in the analogy he proposes between the distribution of the *Eikon Basilike* and the uses of Caesar's will, which

> wrought more in that Vulgar audience to the avenging of his death, then all the art he could ever use, to win thir favor in his life-time. And how much their intent, who publish'd these overlate Apologies and Meditations of the dead King, drives to the same end of stirring up the people to bring him that honour, that affection, and by consequence, that revenge to his dead Corps, which hee himself living could never gain to his Person, it appears both by the conceited portraiture before his Book, drawn out to the full measure of a Masking Scene, and sett there to catch fools and silly gazers, and by those Latin words after the end, *Vota dabunt quae Bella negarunt;* intimating, That what hee could not compass by Warr, he should atchieve by his Meditations. (*E*, 342)

Milton debases the trappings of the *Eikon Basilike;* he ridicules those responsive to the book's blandishments; he claims, moreover, that his own work is based on reason, but his language betrays a desire to intimidate and a fear that the arts of the king's book will be difficult to contest.

In part, Milton attempts to control the affective power of the *Eikon Basilike* by embarrassing or, perhaps more accurately, humiliating and denouncing its audience; but the issue of reception allows him to intertwine intellectual and social abuse. The notion of a vulgar audience enables Milton to move seamlessly between the two. At first, vulgarity seems to have only a literal meaning, for Milton refers to the Latin motto that appears at the close of the *Eikon Basilike* in the same breath with which he dismisses the king's "conceited portraiture," materials to "catch fools and silly gazers" (*E*, 342). The audience is vulgar in a linguistic sense, incompetent to decode visual conceits or the Latin motto, language over which Milton intends to exercise his full intellectual rights.[46]

Linguistic vulgarity has a clear intellectual charge, but Milton broadens the term into a social argument that echoes and inverts, perhaps as well mocks, the conventional royalist charges against the Elect. Those who adore the king's book are "exorbitant and excessive in all thir motions" (*E*, 343); they are "the mad multitude" (*E*, 345) who exhibit the "boistrous folly and superstition that possesses and hurries on the vulgar sort" (*E*, 348), that "miserable, credulous, deluded... creature... which is call'd the Vulgar" (*E*, 426). They are "imbastardiz'd from the ancient nobleness of thir Ancestors," and now with a "besotted and degenerate baseness of spirit,... are ready to fall flatt and give adoration to the Image and Memory of this Man" (*E*, 344). Nor are the vulgar to be found only among the king's most naïve admirers, who "dote upon his deformities... [and] live and dye in such a strook'n blindness, as next to that of Sodom hath not happ'nd to any sort of men more gross" (*E*, 341–42). The clergy belong to the same vicious class, "corrupted and beleper'd... with a worse infection then Gehezi's.... For never such holy things as he means, were giv'n to more Swine, nor the Churches Bread more to Dogs, then when it fed ambitious, irreligious and dumb Prelats" (*E*, 497). The king's followers are scared up from the "cold and dark provinces of ignorance and leudness" (*E*, 529), formed from the "ragged Infantrie of Stewes and Brothels; the spawn and shiprack of Taverns and Dicing Houses" (*E*, 380–81). The court itself is composed of the "most corrupted sort of men; and Court Ladies, not the best of Women; who when they grow to that insolence as to appeare active in State affaires, are the certain sign of a dissolute, degenerat, and pusillanimous Common-wealth" (*E*, 370). The whole is a "dissolute rabble... both hees and shees, if there were any Males among them" (*E*, 455), made up of thousands of "blaspheming Cavaliers . . . whose mouthes let fly Oaths and Curses by the voley . . . and [whose] Carouses [are] drunk to the confusion of all things good or holy" (*E*, 452). Milton complicates the notion of the vulgar here by compounding ignorance and folly with sexual license, indecency, and effeminacy. The whole argument is fulfilled at the close of *Eikonoklastes*, where Milton unfolds a tirade against the "inconstant, irrational, and Image-doting rabble." And now vulgarity—intellectual, moral, and social—is compounded with political baseness as Milton denounces the "credulous and hapless herd, begott'n to servility, and inchanted with these popular institutes of Tyranny, subscrib'd with a new device of the Kings Picture at his praiers, [who] hold out both thir eares with such delight and ravishment to be stigmatiz'd and board through in witness of thir own voluntary and beloved baseness" (*E*, 601).

Conjuring a fit audience among the intellectual elite—"few perhaps, but those few, such of value and substantial worth, as truth and wisdom, not respecting numbers and bigg names, have bin ever wont in all ages to be contented with" (*E*, 339–40)—is not, of course, work singular to *Eikonoklastes,* but it assumes an important contestative force here. Milton's language allows him to engage the social argument of the *Eikon Basilike,* to combat the elevation of king and court, their condemning of sectaries and schismatics as social rabble, and their derogation of political activism as the ingratitude of the barbarous hordes. The *Eikon Basilike* makes a pointed and sustained connection between high culture and cultivation; Charles is the perfect gentleman, a man of tender conscience, of mitigation and restraint, now thrown on the mercies of a rapacious crowd stirred by calumny, savage in its hatred and fury. What can such a king do but regret the "confluence and clamors of the vulgar" (*EB,* 14) as a personal affront? But tumults and social disorder—the "menacing, reproaching, shaking, yea, and assaulting some members of both Houses"—shock "the very foundations of all" (*EB,* 14). The failure to revere authority is a scandal to hierarchy, a threat to the legal foundations of the state, and an affront to God: "Nor doth anything portend more God's displeasure against a nation than when He suffers the confluence and clamors of the vulgar to pass all boundaries of laws and reverence to authority" (*EB,* 14). The king's book poses the "savage rudeness" (*EB,* 27) of the opposition against Charles's mildness and moderation. The emphasis is, of course, on politics, but throughout, the *Eikon Basilike* mingles political, social, and aesthetic values: "As swine are to gardens and orderly plantations, so are tumults to Parliaments and plebeian concourses to public counsels, turning all into disorders and sordid confusions" (*EB*, 18).

In part, the king compounds social and aesthetic elevation through style; Charles's poise and moderation as perfect gentleman are echoed in the balance and elevation of his manner.[47] The verbal art of the *Eikon Basilike* allows prose to make the man: the rhetoric of moderation and the balance of carefully weighted periods argue refinement of manner, and more purposefully, they express the king's deliberative intelligence. Charles's moderation is a bulwark against faction and partiality (*EB*, 3), his prose a hedge against intolerance, zeal, and popular heats. More, however, was at stake; for social rebellion and political betrayal—the "exquisite methods of cunning and cruelty" (*EB*, 131)—are also conceived as cultural barbarism. The destruction of monarchy spelled the decay of learning and the demise of the verbal and visual arts. Milton countered the politics of such an argument by deploring the foolish imagery, the aesthetic confusions, and the plagiaries of the king's book. But the aesthetic case was too important to Milton's work in *Eikonoklastes* for him to rely solely on abuse. The dialectic that he proposes is not between sublime and trivial art but between truth and lies, reason and deceit. Milton would tear the veil from the king's shows and pretenses as he "speak[s] home the plain truth" (*E*, 341). The political suspicion of art has, of course, ancient roots, but it is given an urgent contemporary turn in *Eikonoklastes* because of the associations between courtliness and poetry and because of the reception of the king's book in the months following his execution. The association of visual imagery with superstition was long-standing in a country where religious reform had more than once inspired iconoclastic violence (*E*, 343). Yet despite popular iconoclasm this was a nation, Keith Thomas reminds us, where segments of the populace were still addicted to such images and to the nostalgic lore associated with the power of images.[48] The attack on the theater had been given recent legislative authority;[49] but the generic arguments that Milton launched against the *Eikon Basilike*, his ridicule of the impropriety of lyric and romance forms, and the charge of aesthetic disproportion and triviality lend a particular urgency to his work as literary critic. Just as the king denounces oppositional language by dismissing it as railing and cursing, and condemns nonconformity for the modes of its piety—its "affectations, emptiness, impertinency, rudeness, confusions, flatness, levity, obscurity, vain and ridiculous repetitions" (*EB*, 97)—so Milton has urgent work to perform as literary critic in *Eikonoklastes*.

That work has two main foundations: the genres, literary sources, and decorum of the king's book, and its literary integrity. In Milton's exposition of these issues, he frequently mixes questions of decorum and originality, but I want to begin with the more purely aesthetic matters that Milton trails before his reader in the preface. Here he first raises the matter of the book's patchwork mixture of genres and devices when he glosses the aim of those who published the *Eikon Basilike*. By those devices they intended "stirring up the people to bring him that honour, that affection, and by consequence, that revenge to his dead Corps, which hee himself living could never gain to his Person" (*E*, 342). The "conceited portraiture" (*E*, 342) of the frontispiece and the Latin motto that closes the book are devices intended to "befool the people" (*E*, 343) and transform the king into martyr and saint. They reveal, however, not the king's saintliness but the "loose and negligent curiosity of those who took upon them to adorn the setting out of this Book," loose and negligent because "quaint Emblems" and "devices begg'd from ... some Twelf-nights entertainment at Whitehall" are inappropriate materials with which "to make a Saint or Martyr" of the king (*E*, 343). The pagan and polluted sources of such materials, their trivial and secular character, the failure of discretion and decorum in their display—the self-conscious affecting of "a civil kinde of Idolatry" (*E*, 343)—argue generic and aesthetic indiscretion as moral corruption, variations on that "Court-fucus" with which the king "washes over ... the worst and foulest of his actions" (*E*, 347). It was surely Milton's conviction that politics, aesthetics, and morals are always bound together; it was also, at least in part, to his argumentative advantage in *Eikonoklastes* to make that case. He had to dispute the king's handling of history and politics; but it was aesthetics to which Milton brought his most familiar, his most intimate, and in some ways his most authoritative hand. Aesthetics offered him not only familiar territory but a way to strike at moral probity and undermine the powerful affective charge that the *Eikon Basilike* so clearly carried. Decorum and decency as aesthetic matters allowed Milton to ridicule Anglican claims to spiritual propriety and decorum; but most important, the issue of aesthetic propriety allowed him repeatedly to locate the king's book within those damaging environs of the aesthetic, the realms of fancy and fiction.

At various points in his pursuit of the *Eikon Basilike* Milton raises the issue of decorum, and always to drive the moral and political argument of his own work. He belabors Charles for comparing the earl of Strafford to the sun, a metaphor "which in all figurative use, and significance beares allusion to a King, not to a Subject" (*E*, 372). He denounces the tyranny of the Book of Common Prayer as a "Pinfold of sett words" (*E*, 505) and regrets the way in which prelates have compounded Scripture "with many mixtures of thir own, and which is worse, without salt" (*E*, 505). The important issue is the set form of the liturgy, but the tail that Milton attaches to this charge allows him to administer an aesthetic rebuke, to regret the tasteless admixture of holy words and prelatical invention. The most serious play on the issue of generic admixture comes, however, as Milton begins to unfold the problem of the king's plagiarism.

Milton first lays out the matter of the theft from Sidney by charging the king with spiritual indiscretion. Instead of using Anglican devotional materials, the king has seized on a pagan prayer to offer in his moment of most solemn devotion, a choice that heaps ridicule and derision on his own clergy and party. The mingling of pagan and Christian devotion also offends God, and Milton has God join him in the distaste for plagiarism and mixed genres:

> And sure it was the hand of God to let them fal & be tak'n in such a foolish trapp, as hath exposd them to all derision; if for nothing els, to throw contempt and disgrace in the sight of all men upon this his Idoliz'd Book . . . thereby testifying how little he accepted them from those who thought no better of the living God then of a buzzard Idol, fitt to be so servd and worshipt in reversion, with the polluted orts and refuse of Arcadia's and Romances, without being able to discern the affront rather then the worship of such an ethnic Prayer. (*E*, 364)

There is no missing the contempt in this language, but it is more than the charge of literary trash—mixed leftovers, scraps from the dinner table of fable and romance—that brightens Milton's attention here. "Orts and refuse" allows him to deplore both the king's taste and his failure of decorum in mixing literary kinds and spiritual occasions. The same issues engage Milton when he enlarges the attack on the generic indiscretion of a king who

> might gather up the rest God knows from whence; one perhaps out of the French Astraea, another out of the Spanish Diana; Amadis and Pal-

merin could hardly scape him. Such a person we may be sure had it not in him to make a prayer of his own, or at least would excuse himself the paines and cost of his invention, so long as such sweet rapsodies of Heathenism and Knighterrantry could yeild him prayers. (E, 366–67)

Part of the aim of the literary genealogy is to associate Charles with heathen characters and foreign texts—romances from Roman Catholic France and Spain—and to regret the decline of English taste into idleness and superstition;[50] but the passage does more, for the whole matter of the imagination is here brought under censure. What Milton argues is a dichotomy between spiritual rigor and fancy, between the upright heart and pure and the luxury of literary invention. It is difficult to gauge how far Milton is handling and indeed exciting a popular suspicion of the imagination and how far he is being handled by his own psychological affinity with such suspicion. But without needing to determine exactly what here is under and what is out of Milton's control, the armory of suspicion is made to trivialize the king's spiritual personality, to suggest an unholy alliance between rhapsody and prayer—the very charge leveled against enthusiasm and so long used to demean nonconforming religion—and finally to condemn the whole of the king's book as mere poetry. The *Eikon Basilike* may have begun as tragedy—"To descant on the misfortunes of a person fall'n from so high a dignity"—but the book clearly ends as comedy or rather farce because of the mixed generic character of the whole. Milton returns to the politics of mixed genre in the preface to *Samson Agonistes,* which offers a similar attack on the mixture of kinds and levels of writing in order to contest the fitness of another contemporary and courtly literary idiom. The literary contest in which Milton engages in 1671 is rather different from the battle he had joined in 1649. But the keenness with which he grasps the polemical value of generic questions is worth observing; it suggests not only his sustained sensitivity to the politics of literary choice, but its enduring importance for the conduct of polemic.

The richest polemical issue within the aesthetic and the most central attack on the literary authority of the *Eikon Basilike,* and hence on its authority as the written word, come in Milton's "discovery" of the king's plagiarism from Sidney's *Arcadia.* The accusation is delivered in the very first chapter of *Eikonoklastes;* toward its close, Milton turns from the political arguments of Charles's narrative to its devotional matter, "model'd into the form of a privat Psalter. Which they who so much admire, either for the matter or the manner, may as well admire the Arch-Bishops late Breviary, and many other as good Manuals, and Handmaids of Devotion, the lip-work of every Prelatical Liturgist, clapt together, and quilted out of Scripture phrase" (*E*, 360). At first Milton seems content to question the devotional matter of the *Eikon Basilike* by suggesting its dependence on Scripture and the liturgy: the verses are "clapt together, and quilted out of Scripture phrase"; this piety seems more like needlework than prayer. But devaluing the psalter does not end with questions over its originality, questions that Milton has already hinted at when he intimates that the *Eikon Basilike* is the product of some "secret Coadjutor" (*E*, 346)[51] or when he deprecates the king's providentialism: "These petty glosses and conceits on the high and secret judgements of God, besides the boldness of unwarrantable commenting, are so weake and shallow, and so like the quibbl's of a Court Sermon, that we may safely reck'n them either fetcht from such a pattern, or that the hand of some houshold preist foisted them in" (*E*, 430).[52] Milton has other business to conduct with the psalter. He is clearly attracted to the issue of piety as a cover for tyranny, and he traces a short history of such sophistry: Aristotle in his *Politics* discloses such practices; both ancient and modern history abound in examples. Milton then discovers another such instance in Shakespeare, whom he cites to provide an example with which the king should be especially familiar:

> I shall not instance an abstruse Author, wherein the King might be less conversant, but one whom wee well know was the Closet Companion of these his solitudes, William Shakespeare; who introduces the Person of Richard the third, speaking in as high a strain of pietie, and mortification, as is utterd in any passage of this Book; and sometimes to the same sense and purpose with some words in this place, *I intended*, saith he, *not onely to oblige my Freinds but mine enemies*. The like saith Richard, Act 2. Scen. 1. (*E*, 361)[53]

The passage is extremely interesting for the train of associations and arguments it sets in motion. Here Milton extends the question of authorship raised in the remarks on the king's devotions "clapt together, and quilted out of Scripture phrase"; but the argument goes further, for Milton suggests that Shakespeare is not only the king's closet companion in his solitude but indeed the "author" of the king's stance and language. The passage raises the issue of plagiarism in a literal and somewhat grander figurative way, for in addition to questioning the king's authorship of his own language, it throws into relief the relations between literary and political integrity and in turn the whole matter of authority. The fact that the king plagiarizes from the drama implies a kind of double plagiary in which the king takes language written for another and contrives to make it his own. Milton uses the conventional associations of the king and theater—associations he had already excited with references to the king's masquing scenes, his love of pageantry, the "licentious remissness of his Sundays Theater" (E, 358) with its suggestions of triviality—and further complicates the resonance of theater by suggesting that Charles is the author neither of his own actions nor of his own language, a mere actor borrowing language written for another character.[54] The polemic is sharp and economical: it argues theatricality as falsehood and associates the king with a striking example of a monarch who masked tyranny with piety. The passage also underscores the importance of literary capacity to Milton's conception of political authority, for by subverting the king's authorship, Milton aims to deny not only the king's intellectual and ethical capacities but more fundamentally his political integrity. And the king's capacity as author was to prove a crucial issue in the afterlife of the *Eikon Basilike*. It was not only the book's immediate audience that grasped the political implications of authorship; the debate over Charles's responsibility for his own text was stirred repeatedly after the Glorious Revolution as partisan crises over political legitimacy and authority revived the uses and memory of the civil war and its principals. In that context, the encounter between the *Eikon Basilike* and *Eikonoklastes*, and particularly the issue of authorship, had a remarkably vivid polemical life.[55]

Nor was Milton quite finished with the issue of the king's plagiarism, for he next produces an instance of plagiarism that he uses to invade the very heart of the king's civic and religious authority. Now Milton discovers the king's theft of Pamela's prayer and Charles's use of that prayer for his own final devotions. As we have seen, this detection allows Milton to disclose a long train of abuses: deceit, the degrading of Christianity and defiling of the Anglican communion, a general contempt for religion, and—not least interesting—the violation of intellectual property rights. The passage also reveals Milton arguing at close range about the politics of literary form in a moment of political crisis. The issues of intellectual property rights and the politics of literary form are in fact separate matters, though they are strung together in such a way as to form something like a frontal assault on the king's intellectual, political, and moral capacity: "But this King, not content with that which, although in a thing holy, is no holy theft, to attribute to his own making other mens whole Prayers, hath as it were unhallow'd, and unchrist'nd the very duty of prayer it self, by borrowing to a Christian use Prayers offer'd to a Heathen God" (*E*, 362).

First, Milton seems troubled by a wholly aesthetic matter, the propriety of mixed genres, a failure of taste that approaches spiritual carelessness. Indeed, the accusation does not begin with plagiarism at all since Milton admits that the use of other men's whole prayers is not really a "holy theft."[56] But when he returns to the question of appropriating other men's words, the charges are altered, and what before was "borrowing" now becomes "a Prayer stol'n word for word from the mouth of a Heathen fiction praying to a heathen God" (*E*, 362). He raises the ante on the issue of both propriety and property. The source is disclosed as "the vain amatorious Poem of Sr Philip Sidneys Arcadia; a book in that kind full of worth and witt, but among religious thoughts, and duties not worthy to be nam'd; nor to be read at any time without good caution; much less in time of trouble and affliction to be a Christians Prayer-Book" (*E*, 362–63). With each repetition—and Milton goes on at some length—the charges are rendered more profound as Milton contends that "the King among all his Preistery, and all those numberles volumes of thir theological distillations,... was forc'd to robb Sr. Philip and his Captive Shepherdess of thir Heathen orisons, to supply in any fashion his miserable indigence" (*E*, 366). What Milton discovers here is only in part a problem of theft, though theft itself is made into an especially difficult issue in this passage. The other matter that he discloses is connected back to the problem of literary kind and mixed genre.

The literary matter that Milton finds in his detection of the theft from Sidney is twofold. Following on the accusation of plagiarism from Shakespeare's *Richard III*, Milton discovers an even worse plagiary, the theft of an entire prayer, word for word, which the king has passed off as his own. But Milton is not now content with the accusation of mere deceit; he forces the issue here to bear on the king's invasion of Sidney's property rights: the theft was "a trespass also more then usual against human right, which commands that every Author should have the property of his own work reservd to him after death as well as living. Many Princes have bin rigorous in laying taxes on thir Subjects by the head, but of any King heertofore that made a levy upon thir witt, and seisd it as his own legitimat, I have not whom beside to instance" (*E*, 364–65). That the use of Pamela's prayer should be taken in the direction of property rights has an interesting bearing on the history of intellectual property as it was conceived in relation to real property and on the political debate over rights. The argument allows Milton to arraign the king on charges of invading property rights, a violation of English legal tradition that had come up before, and most explosively, in the Ship-Money Case. The charge conforms the issue of plagiarism to the long tug-of-war between king and Parliament over the king's capacity to collect taxes. The politics of the argument compounds the charges of intellectual plunder with complaints against the king's invasion of real property. Five years earlier Milton had addressed the issues of originality and intellectual property rights in *Areopagitica;* that impassioned defense of intellectual liberty provides one of the contexts for his discussion of intellectual property in 1649. But his return to these issues in *Eikonoklastes* also signals the powerful status as political and literary property that the king's book had enjoyed from the moment of its publication. Milton aims to deny the rights of the king to a property that has been so effectively claimed on his behalf. His last will and testament, the holy book of his person and politics, Milton would deny altogether as property belonging to the king.

Milton rings one further and final variation on the theme of plagiarism. In handling the theft from Sidney, Milton argues in legal and political terms; the theft of intellectual property excites memories of the long train of property violations. But the last variation spiritualizes plagiarism. Milton replies to Charles's chapter on his "surprisal" at Holmby by accusing the king of forging the manuscript of God's providences. The king reads the disturbances and confusions that followed his removal from Holmby House as sure signs of God's judgment: "I see vengeance pursues and overtakes (as the mice and rats are said to have done a bishop in Germany) them that thought to have escaped and fortified themselves most impregnably against it, both by their multitude and compliance. Whom the laws cannot, God will punish by their own crimes and hands" (*EB*, 155). Milton had earlier ridiculed the king's readings of signs and portents; here he gives the ridicule a literary turn that allows him to link the king's providentialism with his earlier thefts and intellectual improprieties and at the same time to debase the king's providentialism as literary fancy, mere imagination. "No evil," Milton writes,

> can befall the Parlament or Citty, but he positively interprets it a judgement upon them for his sake; as if the very manuscript of Gods judgements had bin deliverd to his custody and exposition. But his reading declares it well to be a fals copy which he uses; dispensing oft'n to his own bad deeds and successes the testimony of Divine favour, and to the good deeds and successes of other men, Divine wrath and vengeance. But to counterfet the hand of God is the boldest of all Forgery: And he, who without warrant but his own fantastic surmise, takes upon him perpetually to unfold the secret and unsearchable Mysteries of high Providence, is likely for the most part to mistake and slander them. (*E*, 563–64)

The argument proceeds by steps as Milton carefully shades his accusations. At first the king's providentialism seems to be an exegetical matter, a problem of presumption and misreading; the king acts as if "the very manuscript of Gods judgements had bin deliverd to his custody and exposition." The literary metaphor allows Milton to emphasize providentialism as interpretation, territory in which he is happy to challenge the king. The metaphor also allows Milton to transform spiritual into intellectual error, for the king's exegetical presumption next becomes a manuscript problem: the king mistakes the meaning of the events following his removal from Holmby House because he is reading "a fals copy" of God's providences. The "fals copy" then turns out to be the king's own fantastic surmise of God's mysteries; Charles's providentialism is an imitation, a "counterfet," and finally "the boldest of all Forgery." It is one thing to steal from your own divines, another to take Shakespeare's language or the prayer that Sidney composed for a heathen princess. This instance has now become the most outrageous of the king's forgeries; for such providentialism is but a mockery of true spiritual reading, a surmise of fancy, a slander of the "unsearchable Mysteries of high Providence." The issue of spiritual presumption accounts for part of the pressure that Milton puts on this "boldest of all Forgery"; but surely part also derives from Milton's efforts to reclaim puritan providentialism, to recover a stance and prophetic style that the *Eikon Basilike* had skillfully made over as the king's own.

The literary turn of Milton's argument allows him to drive the political in the direction of fancy and the imagination. Once he locates the king's politics or his piety within an aesthetic frame, he is free to discredit the civic and spiritual matter of the king's book as deceit, mere poetry. Though he can ridicule its aesthetic affectations, Milton cannot deny the aesthetic to the *Eikon Basilike:* that much the reception and re-creations of the king's book had made absolutely clear to the poet turned controversialist. What Milton is then forced to do is to politicize aesthetics, to turn the aesthetic into an accusation, to render inspiration suspect, to insist not on the intimacy of poetry with history but on their utter disjunction. So much had controversy demanded of Milton in 1649; at what cost he took this rhetorical posture we can only wonder, and though we have the republication of the early poetry in the 1645 volume and a handful of sonnets from the 1650s, it is worth speculating not on the distinctions between the life of politics and the life of poetry (these surely were one, and not only for Milton), but on the kinds of psychological—or was it merely rhetorical?— denial that contestation had demanded of Milton when he took up the gauntlet of the king's book.[57] In the 1660s, when Milton was no longer in a position to act the prose controversialist for the good old cause, he embraced the deepest work of the imagination, not to deny polemic or history or veracity but more fully to unite controversy and the imagination.

3 Hunting and Angling:
The Compleat Angler and
The First Anniversary

The *Eikon Basilike* and *Eikonoklastes* provide an example of the most directed form of colloquy and contest, a struggle of politics and style, the instance of one text not simply answering but repudiating and exploding another. Such contest demonstrates the polemicizing force of the civil wars and some of the ways in which polemic took on stylized expression in their immediate aftermath. But direct colloquy was not the only model for verbal contest. The powerful currents released by the wars polemicized a broad range of texts and subjects; reading the 1650s with an awareness of those currents allows us to see a variety of discourse absorbed in and directed by the quest for literary authority and authentication.

Walton's *Compleat Angler* and Marvell's *First Anniversary* were composed with the aim neither of contesting nor of responding to one another.[1] Initially, they seem so disparate a pair as wholly to deny colloquy. One is a casual, often-revised meditation on the pleasures of angling, a text that has its roots in georgic and pastoral and takes its form from the dialogue of instruction.[2] The other is a formal panegyric on a very public occasion. *The First Anniversary* sought to give definition and authority to the Cromwellian protectorate, to delineate the role of its "laureate," and to condemn and deny voice to critics of the regime.[3] *The Compleat Angler* gave classic expression to the culture of sequestered royalism;[4] *The First Anniversary* articulated a militant and triumphant puritanism. Reading them together not only allows a cross-examination of literary matters; it opens both texts to social and political inquiry, and it helps fix their literary modes and manners within the political culture of the 1650s. More was involved

[60]

in literary polemic and in the politicization of the literary than direct contestation; *The Compleat Angler* and *The First Anniversary* suggest how broad and how fine the definition and demonstration of polemic could become.

✌

I want to consider *The Compleat Angler* and *The First Anniversary* as stable and highly stylized versions of cultures in sharp opposition;[5] yet these works also disclose the conditions of writers contending with polarization, attentive to the force and authority of literary culture, aware of the applications to which literary manners could be turned. In such an enterprise, Marvell was a paradigm of self-consciousness; he had made a career out of dialectic and self-definition;[6] and it is no surprise to find him reflecting on the public force of poetry and poetics in *The First Anniversary*. Walton had composed but two of the *Lives* before *The Compleat Angler,* and he gives little overt sense of a writer contending with the meaning of authorship in political terms; and yet, for all the casualness of the text, *The Compleat Angler* is a work hardly innocent of self-definition. Its loose and seemingly spontaneous anthologizing of themes, motifs, stances, and literary gestures forms a social and a political argument more self-conscious and more contestative than has often been allowed. Pastoral is a rich and various mode in the English Renaissance, and yet *The Compleat Angler* is a singular work in that tradition; no English pastoral has taken anything like its hold on the literate imagination. Initially, that authority must be located in the expression the work gave to a broad political community, to the vision of a society coherent, communal, recreative, and nostalgic—a forceful, an articulate, and, in 1653, a timely symbol.

We do not know if Marvell or Walton read each other's work: little of Marvell's poetry was in print before 1681, and Walton was not among the intimates to whom Marvell showed work in manuscript. Nor is there evidence that Marvell read the early editions of *The Compleat Angler;* his pastoral and georgic masterpiece, *Upon Appleton House,* was already complete by the fall of 1651.[7] Nevertheless, I want to begin with a figure that links the two writers in a nearly biographical way and allows us to thread *The Compleat Angler* and *The First Anniversary* together through *Upon Appleton House*. Lurking in the shadows of that great poem is the recreative angler—a reflexive, self-conscious, and extravagant version of Walton's Piscator. Marvell's angler is a symbol for play, an emblem of the higher idleness, the imagination loosed from moral and social restraint. In the poem's last stanza the narrator, glancing from the high ground of the estate to the river Denton, sees a group of fishermen step from the river onto the shore, an allegory for him of the double life: contemplation and history. The fishermen move with ease between the two; the instrument of their amphibiousness is an overturned canoe, at once shell and vessel, perhaps too a figure of this poem that enabled Marvell casually to move between the worlds of pastoral and prophecy.

By the close of *Upon Appleton House,* Marvell's angler has acquired a number of associations: leisure, ease, retreat, poetry itself. Without overreading the brilliant and enigmatic close, we might see in the final stanza the poet's own unsteady balance between lyric and prophecy. In the narrator's progress, the angler is a climactic figure, reprising the poem's earlier figures of retreat and play, but now fixed within the urgent landscape of the 1650s, posed against both the Lord General and the redemptive child. Though Mary Fairfax is neither an articulate nor a self-conscious actor, her reform of nature has an apocalyptic purposiveness. She provides steady and sharp contrast to the poet as angler, the two figures forming a dialectic that raises questions about human nature and conduct, about the possibilities of reform, and about the appropriate posture of mankind within a world disordered by war and revolution. At the poem's close, the angler is watchful and ironic, alert to the tensions between contemplative ease and the hope of reformation. He is aware of both poles of the dialectic and of the ways in which they complement and qualify each other. Marvell is both angler and contemplator of angling, a lyric poet haunted by the voices of prophecy and history. The paths out of his poem lead to different places: in one direction lies piscatory leisure; in the other waits the angel of the apocalypse.

To suggest that contention and authority, rhetorical calculation and method, are part of the scheme of Walton's pastoral runs counter to the declarations of the book itself. Dedication and preface confess only pleasure and diversion; not only does Walton deny ambition and design, the very character of the book—its stance and symbols, its literary mode, its overt argument—suggests nothing so much as distance from the business of contest, though in the 1650s the identity of pastoral with courtly argument allowed the further complication of an already rich set of social and literary associations. But Walton's book begins by advising patron and reader of its very lack of authority, the defects of its learning, the impossibility of instruction in its own subject. This manual of advice lacks practical application, for angling is an art "not to be taught by words" (60). Toward the end of the preface Walton hints that the book may have a slightly larger public life, perhaps later impressions and editions, "for slight books have been in this Age observed to have that fortune" (60), though the correction of faults and defects is at odds with the insistence on authorial innocence and signals a rhetorical ambition somewhat higher than Walton admits.

Moreover, we are familiar with the gestures of modesty that often frame literary works; self-deprecation and the confession of artless composition belong to the rhetoric of dedication and preface. There is something of this convention in Walton's remarks: an author away from books; sheets spun out of idleness, without design or claims to authority. So Sidney remarks at the beginning of the *Defence;* so Dryden will claim as he opens *Of Dramatick Poesie.* But Walton also makes good on at least part of the prefatory work. *The Compleat Angler* is in fact loosely organized and, if not wholly without method, casual in its formal disposition. It seems more reflective than programmatic, a moral and philosophical meditation rather than a manual of instruction whose technical learning, as students of the book have discovered, is almost entirely secondhand.[8] The book is, moreover, genuinely hard to classify. It is a dialogue of instruction, and perhaps as well a georgic meditation, a verse anthology, or an exercise in natural history. But *The Compleat Angler* does not wholly belong to the tradition either of pastoral eclogue or of instructional manual. One reader has suggested Menippean satire with its intermixture of genres and materials, yet nothing in this book's moral and philosophical program conjures the tradition of Varro or Petronius.[9] Indeed, its very looseness of mode— the mixture of genres and kinds, the play of manual against anthology, and the combination of lyric and didactic measures—offered Walton space for work that could not wholly be contained by one genre or mode.[10] Like the verse anthologies that appeared in the mid-1650s with their mixture of literary kinds, *The Compleat Angler* uses generic ambivalence for work that is only in part casual and recreative.

Without suggesting that contestation was the principal aim of a work that so studiously condemns strife, I want to argue that *The Compleat Angler* has commemorative and contentious designs that go quite beyond Walton's proffered description of the book. It is a work, even in its first and simplest edition, absorbed by questions of authority and authentication, attentive to mythmaking and cultural nostalgia, to images of social order and discrimination. The book consists in part of descriptive pleasure, but it is also laced with gestures of piety and deference toward a community of learning, spiritual authority, and art. Walton aims to occupy space within a contentious world, to proclaim innocence and simplicity, but also to insist that true liberty of the spirit follows from a particular moral, social, and political stance. His book is a lament for social harmony destroyed by jealousies and fears; it is an act of self-definition and consolation for the exiled and sequestered community of Stuart loyalists.[11] To occupy such a space in 1653 and again in 1655 took caution and art; both are in evidence in this digressive text.

The Compleat Angler proved to be remarkably popular. Produced in five editions during Walton's life, it went through more than three hundred separate editions and reprintings in the following three hundred years. Next to the Bible, *The Compleat Angler* is the most often reprinted work in English.[12] Its enormous popularity in the late eighteenth and nineteenth centuries springs from its pious and nostalgic evocation of a Jacobean golden world; the book became an icon of contentment for successive generations. But the soft focus of nostalgia was only part of its initial meaning, for its social and political argument was both sharper and perceived more clearly in the 1650s than it would be in later generations. The dedicatory verse, which prefaced the 1655 edition, indicates that resonance:

> Since 'tis become a common fate, that we
> Must in this world or Fish or Fishers be;
> And all neutralitie herin's deny'd,
> 'Tis not my fault that I am not supply'd
> With those three grand essentials of your Art,
> Luck, Skill and Patience.
>
> (434)

The rest of Alexander Brome's verse suggests, with practically no cover, his ardent royalism; he condemns those "King-riders," business and care, and conflates stoicism and royalism. "Thy mind's thy Kingdom, and content's thy Crown" is a sentiment and consolation common to cavalier lyrics of exile and defeat, where pastoral and stoic gestures equate retreat with moral elevation and allegiance to a hapless political cause.[13] Nor is the reminiscence of the king's stance in the *Eikon Basilike* without strategic force, for the royal martyr and his cavaliers shared not only a political fate but a moral style and literary stance as well. What is particularly interesting about Brome's commendation is its insistence not simply on a polity divided but on the polemicization of emblems and symbols and of reception itself: "Since 'tis become a common fate, that we / Must in this world or Fish or Fishers be . . . all neutralitie herin's deny'd." What Brome sees is a palimpsest on which innocent signs have been rewritten and rendered contentious by a world gone mad with strife. There is no neutral space for a work of amity and innocence like *The Compleat Angler* to occupy. Writing itself is polemicized by war and revolution, the classical canon rendered suspect, the Bible contested by and divided between parties.[14] It is such a world in which Walton's book was written and first received. After the Restoration, when the contentious dimensions of Walton's book were elided by its encomiastic and commemorative measures, Brome's argument about polarization was not reprinted.

Not that Brome saw contention where there was none, that he suggested partisanship and polemicization without cause. For mixed with Walton's modest demurs, embedded within the evocation of rural conviviality and sociability, are sharper notes. Walton juxtaposes mirth and its discontents:

> In writing of it, I have made a recreation, of a recreation; and that it might prove so to thee in the reading, and not to read dull, and tediously, I have in severall places mixt some innocent Mirth; of which, if thou be a severe, sowr complexioned man, then I here disallow thee to be a competent Judg. For Divines say, there are offences given; and offences taken, but not given. And I am the willinger to justifie this innocent Mirth, because the whole discourse is a kind of picture of my owne disposition. (59)

Besides covering the author with rhetorical innocence, the passage reminds us of the way Brome had first polemicized reception. The world into which Walton releases his book is beset with dangers of misreading; Walton's "Mirth" is innocent, but precision, censure, and suspicion misjudge rhetorical innocence.[15] The author situates his work, if not in defiance of censure, then surely with an awareness of the ways in which censure creates contestation.[16] He compounds authorship with recreation (59), contrasts sociability and trust with suspicion, and advises candor and innocence for the reception of his work: "If [the reader] bring not candor to the reading of this Discourse, he shall both injure me, and possibly himself too by too many Criticisms" (60).

The same awareness recurs in the opening chapter when Viator says, "I am sorry you are an Angler: for I have heard many grave, serious men pitie, and many pleasant men scoffe at Anglers" (64). To such contest, Piscator replies:

> There are many men that are by others taken to be serious grave men, which we contemn and pitie; men of sowre complexions; money-getting-men, that spend all their time first in getting, and next in anxious care to keep it: men that are condemn'd to be rich, and always discontented, or busie. For these poor-rich-men, wee Anglers pitie them; and stand in no need to borrow their thoughts to think our selves happie: For (trust me, Sir) we enjoy a contentednesse above the reach of such dispositions. (64)

While claiming elevation and quoting Montaigne and Solomon, Walton also challenges puritan contentiousness;[17] scoffing forms a significant subject in this chapter, where the language combines resistance and apology.

Although there are occasional and oblique glances at strife, contention, and legalism, the most overt expressions of contest occur in the opening pages of *The Compleat Angler*. Once Walton has begun to spin out his angling pleasures, the work is not determined by a program of direct contestation; it argues more obliquely through a fabric of deference and piety, through the evocation of Anglican quietism, through the celebration of rural conviviality and obeisance toward authority and antiquity.[18] Walton's citations from learned authors; the quiltwork of poetry, song, and ballad; the emblems of social harmony and wholeness; and those rather complicated strands of inference, symbol, and allusion create for *The Compleat Angler* a social and political argument while preserving the impression that the text is above contention.

Of course, pastoral traditionally reserves the right of complaint while arguing from the position of seclusion and retreat.[19] The moral geography of country life allows a suspicion of power, a contempt for politics, and ethical elevation—traditions and postures that those in exile and retreat found welcome and consoling. The appeal of this text, both to its immediate audiences in the mid-1650s and to a slightly later generation in the 1660s and 1670s, must then be explained by its plasticity, its constitutive ambiguities, its capacity both to engage in moral contest and to decline such contest on the high road to quietism and retreat. The book rebuked the triumphant puritanism of the 1650s; it sanctioned seclusion and retirement as moral elevation; it engaged, without direct argument, those who in the 1650s had come into power and property.[20] Once the old order, or at least a semblance of that order and its symbols and ceremonies, had been restored, *The Compleat Angler* could gradually be released into the happy category of icon of piety, eclogue of nostalgia.[21] From a bibliographical and political perspective, it is interesting to note that this very popular text, issued in five editions during Walton's life and reprinted 386 times between 1653 and 1970, was not republished at all between 1676 and 1750. After the Restoration the first two generations of its readership surely understood both its contentious and commemorative arguments; but the text must have seemed difficult to repolemicize in the 1680s. The contest over Exclusion, the fury of anti-Catholicism, the crisis of James II's rule, and the rage of party in the 1690s excited a polemical atmosphere hardly suited to the soft focus of *The Compleat Angler*. Jacobites might well have taken comfort from its evocation of old ways, its piety and deference; in his dedication of *Don Sebastian* to the earl of Leicester, Dryden glances affectingly at the garden of Leicester House, twinning themes of retirement from the political fray with the consolations of Roman poetry and philosophy.[22] But it was not until the later eighteenth century that *The Compleat Angler* was released into its life of purely recreative nostalgia.

❧

Part of the appeal of *The Compleat Angler* came, then, from its articulation of social values and its apparent superiority to contention and wrangling. That articulation, though prefaced with disclaimers and surrounded by gestures of artlessness and innocence, is in fact a careful assemblage of stances and tags, of allusions and innuendos, of symbols and ceremoniousness, of balladry and poetry. The assemblage argues, in a loose and accretive way, for the virtue and innocence of an entire social order from king and court to milkmaid and rural poor. The social inclusiveness of *The Compleat Angler* is, of course, a fiction; like most pastoral, this green world lacks the middle. Walton presents a version of social hierarchy whose point of nostalgic reference is rural Jacobean England, but the careful details and the

mixed literary character of the whole mitigate partiality and sentimentality. The generic peculiarity of the work, with its mingling of
piety, pastoralism, and pedagogy, allowed Walton to create, with increasing complexity as he added to the work throughout his life, an
art of assemblage.

The constituents of this assembly fall into three broad categories:
social materials, literary and cultural relations, and natural lore. My
own order for these categories reverses the overt priorities of the text;
by far the greatest attention in this work is devoted to nature. Social
relations seem, if not incidental to the business of the book, certainly
of a secondary order of importance, as does the world of letters and
learning. But the core of purely descriptive materials, the catalog of
fish and their habits, could hardly have formed the crux of contest.
The naturalist materials of *The Compleat Angler* are the occasion of the
book rather than the center of its argument. Moreover, that argument
is not simply the product of my present focus; for Walton and for his
first readers, the contestative matter was as important as the piscatory
catalog. The description of fish was not so much Walton's passion as
itself an assemblage of other men's learning on the subject. Angling
must have held some personal significance for Walton, but he understood as well that the occasion of his book was not coincidental with
its meaning.

The frame of *The Compleat Angler* is a fishing trip with tutorial, the
dialogue its primary formal device. The dialogue matches two figures,
one master and the other deferential novice, to be initiated into the
mysteries of an art. These two, Piscator and Viator, are occasionally
joined by other rural figures—Peter and Coridon, a milkmaid and
her mother, an innkeeper and hostess—to form a casual but coherent
rural grouping. The community is extended by citation and reference
to include contemporaries or near contemporaries of the master: Sir
Abraham Williams and Dr. Alexander Nowel; literary figures both
cited and quoted—among them Donne, Herbert, Sir Henry Wotton,
and Du Bartas, a poet whom James I had admired and translated;
and authorities of nature and the spirit—Bacon, Gesner, and Pliny,
Christ and the apostles, Moses, Aaron, and David. At its fullest extension, the community of Walton's book is composed of its speakers,
their contemporaries, and the figures of literary, intellectual, and
spiritual authority quoted to define, illustrate, and underpin its learning, its moralizing, and what we might call its philosophy. From the
social composition and the relations among the figures and their uses

of one another, we might extrapolate an argument about the role of tradition and authority and the relations among kinds of learning: the connection between what we might call folk culture and learned culture.[23] From such an extrapolation we learn as well of the bonds uniting types of social figures and kinds of authority.

The book arranges these materials to form an argument about society and articulates the vision through the language of conviviality, deference, and social innocence. The grouping is on casual and familiar terms, figures who, while nearly strangers to one another, are not estranged. The language of social relations contrasts coherence and conviviality with instability and estrangement—jealousies and fears, to use the formula that runs like a bright thread through so much of the writing of these decades. The social experience of *The Compleat Angler* stands as a foil to suspicion and dissent,[24] to the fragmentation of an idealized Anglican community of manners and beliefs, of ancient, traditional, and coherent relations among social classes and among members of an organic community.

The social relations figured in *The Compleat Angler* form, of course, a political argument, a repudiation of "puritan" community and social values. The sociability of *The Compleat Angler* is both casual and traditional and is everywhere hedged about by convivial pleasure; indeed, the dominant image of sociability in this book is ale and good fellowship.[25] The language conveys a notion of how men should take pleasure in one another's company and of the sanctity and ceremoniousness of such pleasure. The sociability of the alehouse,[26] the exchange of songs, the shared meals—all convey the color and texture of the social relations while insinuating a polemical argument. The book is a response to suspicion, mortification, and denial: it not only asserts community but gives play to the pleasures of the senses and to the ceremonies of song and drink, which together forge social bonds between master and student and among men and women of different classes and character.[27] The bonds of society within the ideal community are local and traditional, spiritual and temperamental, rather than commercial or national, ideological or visionary. When Viator admits that he has "always look'd upon Anglers as . . . simple men," Piscator praises "that simplicity that was usually found in the Primitive Christians, who were (as most Anglers are) quiet men, and followed peace; men that were too wise to sell their consciences to buy riches for vexation . . . men that lived in those times when there were fewer Lawyers" (66–67). They are men of spiritual profession, masters of "an Ancient and laudable Art" (67). Throughout, angling is twinned with art and conflated with antiquity. Social bonds among anglers link men of similar temperament and spirit, communities that revive the social innocence of primitive Christianity. They have been outpaced by commerce and litigation; art, patience, and reverence for antiquity are the marks of the fraternity of anglers: angling "is as ancient as Deucalions Floud . . . Belus . . . was the Inventer of it . . . Seth, one of the Sons of Adam, taught it to his sons, and . . . by them it was derived to Posterity" (68).

Walton's argument is, of course, quite traditional for the literature of pastoral retreat.[28] The landscape by the riverside not only allows philosophical ease but intimates that mysterious approximation of divinity we achieve through contemplation: "The nearer we Mortals come to God by way of imitation, the more happy we are: And that God injoyes himself only by Contemplation. . . . The very sitting by the Rivers side, is not only the fittest place for, but will invite the Anglers to Contemplation" (69–70). Just such a scene, though isolate and hedged with doubt and self-reflexive irony, Marvell had imagined toward the close of *Upon Appleton House.* Indeed, who more searchingly than Marvell had explored the contemplative implications of pastoral? Walton uses this material in a less guarded manner, but the poet had acknowledged the spiritual possibilities that Walton here embraces.

The social community of *The Compleat Angler* includes pastoral figures, contemporary acquaintances of Walton, and, at furthest extension, those masters of literary art, nature, and the human spirit who compose the second set of materials within the work: the matter of authority. The occasion of the book itself is an act of authority, an initiation into the mysteries of an art that combines folk wisdom, the craft of the guild, and natural philosophy. Among the ancients, angling was regarded as an exalted intellectual activity, a discipline akin to music and mathematics; for Walton's contemporaries, angling is a branch of natural philosophy, and chief among his authorities are Pliny and Aristotle from the ancients, Bacon and Gesner among the moderns. Walton's text is casually crossed by citations from these and other naturalists, citations meant not only to dignify the text but to indicate the character of its art and the constituents of its wisdom.

The function of literary texts within the work is similar, though slightly more complex. The names of Donne and Herbert lend not only the piety of the Anglican communion to the lore of natural philosophy but also the authority of art itself to this art. Part of that authority is refinement and elevation, particularly those verses from Donne, Herbert, and Du Bartas that address the natural world; but the argument of poetry is polemically more complex than that of natural philosophy. Whereas the Stuart court did not have exclusive authority over ancient or natural philosophy, the identity of the Caroline court not simply with the patronage of art but with its character and effects was very broad indeed, and particularly so in those genres that Walton chose to anthologize in *The Compleat Angler*. The argument of poetry is, then, the argument of cultural authority acquired and dispersed through the patronage and practice of its arts. To cite Donne and Herbert is to conjure piety and elevation and to attach to a pastoral text and to natural philosophy the mystery of an art that Walton would twin with angling. The book offers an image of a community of anglers and of a community of texts. To cast the subject matter of the book into the forms of sonnet and song is itself to make an argument about the identity and authority of the culture that practices and celebrates this art of angling.

Moreover, while poetry conveys refinement and social elevation, *The Compleat Angler* enlarges the role of song, mixing ballad and sonnet with the more intricate stanzas of Du Bartas and Donne. The catholicity of literary forms offers an analogy between literary sociability and the mixture of social orders within the angling community. Baronets and divines, rural and rustic types, all are bound together by the study of quiet and by the contemplative art of angling; the "culture" that art embraces is learned and elevated but also rural and traditional. The juxtaposition of Du Bartas and folk ballad is an assertion of the binding powers of the angler's art and of the community that this art embraces and exemplifies. The embedding and anthologizing character of *The Compleat Angler* has one further effect: in addition to claiming lyric forms and gestures for its own and identifying the refinement and elevation of poetry with angling, the book acts in a quieter way as the preservative of a culture under stress and restriction. The iconoclasm of parliamentary troops casting down church statuary and destroying stained-glass windows, like the attack on universities and university learning in 1653,[29] argues the repressive vigor we associate with militant and triumphant puritanism. Under such duress the impulse to bind together the remnants of a once-coherent culture must have been powerful, and we ought to recognize the simultaneously preservative and polemical significance of Walton's text.

But the argument of culture is yet broader, for the learning of this manual is at once natural, humane, and spiritual. In this last category belong the citations from ethical texts and spiritual authorities that combine to form the culture of pious Anglicanism. The punning appropriation of *angle* from *anglican* has long been noted; it is suggested by scriptural citation—Jesus transforming his fishermen into fishers of men—articulated in the iconography of Christian spiritual texts,[30] and argued directly from Scripture. While *The Compleat Angler* suggests a culture of sociability, it is careful to temper conviviality with the wisdom of moderation and to balance high spirits with professions of piety. If the book is engaging in a contest over social and cultural vision, it is also careful to delineate its profession of spiritual values. The stress on quiet, on communal dignity, on meekness and humility is not simply an assertion of character; it is also a repudiation of spiritual fanaticism and religious frenzy, of the sanctimonious and the censorious. Mildness and humility are angling virtues; angling is the craft and fraternity of virtue and patience (67–68). Scripture was the book of puritan triumphalism in the 1650s, but *The Compleat Angler* would enter its own claims on the social and spiritual politics of that book. Rather than sanctifying apocalyptic social disruption, the scripturalism of *The Compleat Angler* argues the virtues of patience and piety; the Psalms of David are an emblem of the harmonies of this profession. Prophets and patriarchs conjure the authority of the Old Testament and the purity of primitive Christianity for this angler.

The discourse of nature constitutes the largest element of Walton's book: in the scenes of rural serenity, in the bits of naturalist lore scattered through the text, and in the recipes and formulas that comprise the instructional materials of the book as fishing manual. These might seem the least likely to carry polemical argument, and in fact they are the noncontroverted center of the book.[31] But the materials of nature and the angler's relation to those materials have their own polemical meaning. At its broadest, the harmonics of the pastoral world, its complete integration of nature and society, is itself a demonstration of the sanctity conjured by Walton. But there is a more pointed argument about the sanctity of country life in the assertion of wholesomeness and harmony. Walton's characters know how to use nature, to live in intimacy and harmony with its terms, to honor the reciprocity between use and needs in a way that sharply contrasts with landholding and urban power.[32] This is the conventional opposition of country and city, one of pastoral's most familiar themes, but for a royalist to play such a theme with variations in the 1650s— and it runs through a number of cavalier lyrics—was to enter into a controversial mode.

There is, however, one further way of disclosing the argument of nature in *The Compleat Angler,* and that lies in the seasonal certainty that governs this world: "Everything is beautifull in his season" (116). Cycles and seasons frame the book; its schemes are cyclical rather than linear, recurrent rather than progressive. The countryside partakes of the long, familiar rhythms of nature, rhythms that hold its wisdom and its discourse with antiquity. Moreover, the cyclical and the seasonal are sharply at odds with the millenarian time of puritan eschatology. *The Compleat Angler* is an affirmation of recurrence and antiquity; millenarian vision is apocalyptic, transformative. Walton's book reaffirms ancient wisdom, passed between generations through folk custom and song; the social visionary is intent on breaking old patterns so that the ancient ways can be transformed into new orders.

Walton's seasons and cycles do not exactly form a critique of the apocalyptic, but they reaffirm the rhythms of traditional wisdom. And those rhythms stand out in sharp relief against the rhythms of millenarian time, rhythms that Marvell captures in the eloquent opening periods of *The First Anniversary.* The rhythms of Walton's book— recurrent, seasonal, and cyclical—are leisured, loose, playful, and careless in the broadest sense of the term:

> A beggers life is for a King:
>   Eat, drink and play, sleep when we list,
>   Go where we will so stocks be mist.
>   Bright shines the Sun, play beggers, &c.
> . . . .
>   Thus beggers Lord it as they please,
>   And only beggers live at ease:
>   Bright shines the Sun, play beggers play,
>   here's scraps enough to serve to day.
>
> (113)

The "Beggars' Song" is a mildly ironic and socially particular version of the ethos of leisure, and that ethos is central to the broadly con-

templative mode that *The Compleat Angler* argues as the highest mode
of human behavior. Angling, with its submission to seasonal and cyclical rhythms, is an emblem of leisure echoed in the scenes of social
conviviality that recur throughout the book. Song, drink, play, and
hospitality form the elements of rural communion, and they are
poised against strife and contention:

> Oh the brave Fishers life,
> It is the best of any,
> 'Tis full of pleasure, void of strife,
> And 'tis belov'd of many:
> > Other joyes
> > are but toyes,
> > only this
> > lawful is,
> > for our skil
> > breeds no ill,
> but content and pleasure.
>
> (148)

Angling is the higher recreation, an art based on the proper uses of
leisure, surrounded by poetry and song, set in the innocence of nature,
free from ambition and strife, those "restless thoughts and contentions
which corrode the sweets of life" (150).

Formulated into a whole, the arguments of nature, of social relations, and of poetry and antiquity articulate a politics of society and
man. *The Compleat Angler* is not, of course, Aristotle's *Politics;* it eschews
method and is anything but systematic; but out of its diversity we
might assemble a coherent ethics, something more than the musings
of a sequestered royalist. Not only does the book argue the innocence,
indeed the virtue, of its social vision; it means to console and to con-
front, to suggest not simply a defeated alternative but something of
a celebration of social and political hierarchy and harmony, a coherent
vision of the art and the welfare of the properly constituted man and
community. Beyond private consolation the book is imagined as an
argument for the coherence, the virtue, the resourcefulness of a beleaguered community whose embrace of common values and virtues
will prevail in the long cycle of pastoral ways.

Like Marvell's angler at the close of *Upon Appleton House,* Walton's
Piscator is watchful, even perhaps wary; he lives in common with all

those "that hate contentions, and love quietnesse, and vertue, and Angling" (163). They await a better day, but Walton inspects pastoral retreat without any of the vivid ironies that qualify the scene of angling in *Upon Appleton House*. Walton's angler does not hover at the edge of apocalyptic transformation. There is no figure like Maria utterly to transform nature and suggest the power of man to reform the social community and redeem history. Marvell is poised between the dangers of retreat and reform. In one direction, a direction that he knew very well indeed, angling and idling lead to the lyric and the contemplative, to pastoral and amatory song, to eclogue and complaint. These are genres that Marvell practiced brilliantly, and they are worked through in the retrospective tour of the Fairfax history and estate. The mixed modes of the poem allowed Marvell the complete run of pastoralism in all its spectacular variety: the amatory pastoral, the piscatory eclogue, the pastoral of retreat and complaint, the sacred pastoral, pastoral drama and masque, and paradisal verse. Had Marvell wished to follow the social and political path to royalist poetics, he knew not only the way but how to perform its various modes.[33] *The Compleat Angler*, though not the text that Marvell would have composed, is a version of pastoral that we might have imagined for Marvell had he chosen to remain in the retirement so suggestively figured at the edge of the river Denton. Except for that astonishing and fleeting moment in *The Last Instructions* where Marvell frames the Dutch invasion of the Medway and Thames with a scene of pastoral delicacy and delight, pastoral was not again to be his mode. The world Marvell next embraced can be examined by following the figure of the poet from the angler and idler of *Upon Appleton House* to the shrill huntsman of *The First Anniversary*.

❧

Here I want to begin with some reflections on the literary mode of *The First Anniversary* since Marvell explicitly and not surprisingly addresses the issue of poetics, revealing what manners the polemicized muse might adopt in a godly republic. The passage to which I refer is something of a pressure point in *The First Anniversary*, suggestive of formal matters—poetics and rhetoric—and revealing about the difficulties encountered or anxieties released by the conjoining of poetry and polemic. It occurs at the point where Marvell turns from

Cromwell to the foreign princes, that chorus and foil for the brilliant anomaly of the Lord Protector:

> Unhappy Princes, ignorantly bred,
> By Malice some, by Errour more misled;
> If gracious Heaven to my Life give length,
> Leisure to Time, and to my Weakness Strength,
> Then shall I once with graver Accents shake
> Your Regal sloth, and your long Slumbers wake:
> Like the shrill Huntsman that prevents the East,
> Winding his Horn to Kings that chase the Beast.
> Till then my Muse shall hollow far behind
> Angelique Cromwell who outwings the wind;
> And in dark Nights, and in cold Dayes alone
> Pursues the Monster thorough every Throne:
> Which shrinking to her Roman Den impure,
> Gnashes her Goary teeth; nor there secure.
>
> (117–30)

First the passage twins poetry with reformation, that program of international Protestantism that included the defeat of Antichrist, the conversion of the Jews, and the hastening of the end of time.[34] The Lord Protector blazes an incandescent and lonely trail, and his laureate turns prophet of the apocalypse. The accents of such a prophet shake regal sloth and stir the slumbering princes; the language at this point becomes particularly interesting for its musical and metrical specificity. The analogy between the huntsman and the laureate has been prepared by the twinning of Amphion and Cromwell, and Amphion and the poet. Musician, architect, and statesman, Amphion creates the harmonious state through music; in turn, the lute becomes a personal allusion to Cromwell and a figure of the instrument of state as both political and panegyric device.[35] Tucked within this analogy is the reference to Amphion's "graver Notes" (63), a musical and political idiom that raises the columns of the temple and orchestrates the sanctity of the state. These are notes of public works, of polemic and panegyric, *gravitas* suggesting seriousness of subject and dignity and authority of manner.[36] In turn, the "graver Accents" of the next scene are those that announce reform and raise temples; they bespeak elevation of purpose and manner. Marvell's passage of poetic self-definition suggests both a role and a manner for the public muse. In the hands of Amphion, the muse creates the harmonious state; in the hands of Marvell, the muse transforms lyric measures into public notes that harmonize the state and galvanize the elect. But the poet as "shrill Huntsman" conjures as well a rather different figure from Amphion as lyric legislator or David as prophet and psalmist. In 1654 the pressing matters of state included not only the defeat of Antichrist but quelling dissent and foiling plots against the person of the protector and the protectorate.[37] To those ends lyric poetry, pastoral ironies, even the Davidic psalm were not sufficient, and the Cromwellian laureate took a moment out of the programmatic concerns of his poem to suggest his awareness of the demands such a program placed on poetry. The poem that he made is an experiment in civic style.

The rather stiff decasyllabic couplets of *The First Anniversary*, its learned and allusive manner, the ceremoniousness of its panegyric form and conventions—these are choices befitting the new role of poet as huntsman of the apocalypse. Deliberately setting aside lyric measures, the poet assumes *gravitas* in his anniversary piece. Part of his project is to define the politics and ethos of the protectorate; part is to assert its poetic mode, carefully to differentiate its manner from the lyric measures not only of his own career—I now lay aside those playful forms—but more generally of cavalier lyric, of those royalist lyric anthologies of the 1650s. Walton's Piscator hopes to convert the hunter into the angler; Marvell has made the opposite move. He has put aside angling measures and languishing numbers for "graver Accents"; in that phrase, with its suggestions of statecraft, reformation, and the *gravitas* of the republic, he rededicates his muse. As early as 1649 Marvell had contemplated the dialectic of lyric measure and *gravitas*. The die was cast in *The First Anniversary;* and though some have regretted the loss of lyric poet to civic prophet, there was nothing casual about the decision. These lines in *The First Anniversary* bespeak a high and suggestive awareness of the role and character of public poetry. Amphion and David are models; but the poet further understands that in 1655 the measures must be both grave and piercing; there must be both dignity and penetration to his numbers.

I want to allow one further meaning for the passage about poetry and poetics; once again the angling episode in *Upon Appleton House* and *The Compleat Angler* provide context and gloss. There is in Walton's book an insistent overlapping of leisure, song, and the art of angling: *The Compleat Angler* is a treatise on the mysteries and arts of recreation. No one need have tutored Marvell on the relations between poetry and play, a conjunction of which he is profoundly and strategically aware in *Upon Appleton House*. The angling episode, where the poet is narrator and idler, closes with Maria shaming a poet surprised in play:

> Oh what a Pleasure 'tis to hedge
> My Temples here with heavy sedge;
> Abandoning my lazy Side,
> Stretcht as a Bank unto the Tide;
> Or to suspend my sliding Foot
> On the Osiers undermined Root,
> And in its Branches tough to hang,
> While at my Lines the Fishes twang!
>
> But now away my Hooks, my Quills,
> And Angles, idle Utensils.
> The young Maria walks to night:
> Hide trifling Youth thy Pleasures slight.
> 'Twere shame that such judicious Eyes
> Should with such Toyes a Man surprize;
> She that already is the Law
> Of all her Sex, her Ages Aw.
>
> (641–56)

The direct reference is to the lines and rods of the fisherman, but the figure also suggests the measures of lyric poetry. Marvell had once before reflected on idleness and lyric measure (*An Horatian Ode*, 1–4); the confrontation in *Upon Appleton House* is both sharper and psychologically more complex when the poet and angler must be shamed into *gravitas*. For Marvell, putting aside lyric poetry was a literary act, but the social, psychological, and political pressures under which that choice was made allow us to see just how clearly and sharply implicated are literary choices in the political conditions of revolutionary moments. Marvell's awareness of the costs and seductions of lyric poetry lends a dazzling complexity of tone to the poet's handling of the conventional topos. Under the pressure of and deeply responsive to the imperatives of public life, this lyric poet had come to see that statecraft was wholly implicated in polemic, a mode that provides analogy with the hunt, that implies literary warfare, military engagement, and heroic endeavor. Polemic is a mode not for shepherds and anglers but for the huntsman of the apocalypse and the captain of the latter days.

To suggest that Marvell was not aware of the costs of such choices would be naïve. Both his tribute to apocalyptic poetics in *The First Anniversary* and the contest he stages at the close of the poem (349–402) bespeak a high awareness of literary mode and a certain anxiety about literary authority. The verse in which Marvell concedes a kind of rhetorical defeat not only allows the strategic rhetoric of weakness and distance but suggests a regretful understanding of diminution, the loss of literary authority this poet felt in his assumption of prophetic robes:

> Pardon, great Prince, if thus their Fear or Spight
> More then our Love and Duty do thee Right.
> I yield, nor further will the Prize contend;
> So that we both alike may miss our End:
> While thou thy venerable Head dost raise
> As far above their Malice as my Praise.
> And as the Angel of our Commonweal,
> Troubling the Waters, yearly mak'st them Heal.
>
> (395–402)

The confession of greatness from an adversary is a convention of panegyric that Marvell had already exploited in the *Horatian Ode* (73–80); and the contest of praise allows an international perspective: European awe for the achievements of the Lord Protector, his program of reform, and his democratic humility, themes spun out through the whole of the poem. But what the passage underscores in the context of poetics is the high degree to which contention is the aim not only of the formal contest of praise but of the poem as a whole, and, further, what kinds of anxiety such overt contestation must have raised in this poet.

The First Anniversary not only makes rather bold with the formal conventions of panegyric but is peculiarly combative and contestative. It reflects the polemicized atmosphere of literary culture in the 1650s, the sharpness of attack under which the protectorate found itself in its first year, but it also suggests a broader literary siege. *The First Anniversary* has been carefully glossed, its polemical encounter with radical dissent and royalist suspicion fully measured, but the poem's contention for literary authority has not been as exactly gauged, and it is this contestative aspect of *The First Anniversary* that I want further to address.

The Compleat Angler offers a guide to contestable territory in the politics and the social and literary culture of the early 1650s. Mixing ballad and lyric with piscatory and pastoral elements, Walton effects a marriage of art and leisure, a union of cavalier and royalist genres and modes with folk materials. And such colloquy between poetic mode—indeed, poetic meter—and political sympathy is embedded in a long literary tradition. By the early 1650s the association of the Caroline court and of cavalier poets such as Suckling, Lovelace, and Herrick with song would have been nearly complete.[38] Milton had written in lyric measure in the 1630s and reprinted those efforts in 1645,[39] but the heroic sonnets of the 1650s suggest the *gravitas* of *The First Anniversary* rather than the lyric measures of *L'Allegro* and *Il Penseroso*. It is not only cavalier verse that is under scrutiny here, however. Marvell's own deployment of lyric measure for philosophical reflection, for pastoral irony, for testing the costs and limits of engagement is just as clearly under inspection in this passage as are the broad associations between lyric and courtly modes. But lyric was not the only mode in contest in this poem. Like Walton, Marvell summons the whole of nature, though a nature carefully selected, to bear witness to the politics of reform in the early 1650s.

The Compleat Angler suggests, then, a politics of lyric verse and pastoral landscape.[40] The argument is not topical but cultural; the countryside is a source of social values, a locus of amity and innocence; it represents a world nostalgically associated, like much of Caroline pastoral, with purity and simplicity. To the sequestered royalist driven into the solacing green of the countryside, pastoral landscape might have seemed a repository of sentiment and sympathy. Of course, to embed the landscape with political and social values was not the exclusive prerogative of royalist sentiment. Nostalgia and polemic could allow quite diverse political ideals within the same patch of green. The conjuring had important differences, however, and I want to look at the discourse of nature in *The First Anniversary* to suggest some of the polemical values the millenarian might find in nature. Pastoral retreat was a subject over which few had exercised greater mastery than Marvell. But neither the pastoral estate nor the private garden anticipates the images of nature in *The First Anniversary*, images at once mysterious and marginal. The order of nature is thrust into such stark opposition with the realm of grace at the opening of the poem that it never recovers from that dialectical swerve. Now the poet associates decline and disappointment with nature, the realm of mortality and monarchy. It is not the river Denton into which the sinking weight of the opening lines disappears, but a far more mysterious stream.

The river landscape at which we left the poet in the summer of 1651 is Denton at Nun Appleton; the salmon fishers there suggest the possibility of amphibious man living within the realms of history and grace. By the late fall of 1654 Marvell was less sanguine over the prospect of amphibiousness. What he contrasts in *The First Anniversary* is declining man in the shallows of the river and the apocalyptic force of Oliver Cromwell:[41]

> Like the vain Curlings of the Watry maze,
> Which in smooth streams a sinking Weight does raise;
> So Man, declining alwayes, disappears
> In the weak Circles of increasing Years;
> And his short Tumults of themselves Compose,
> While flowing Time above his Head does close.
>   Cromwell alone with greater Vigour runs,
> (Sun-like) the Stages of succeeding Suns.
>
>   (1–8)

At the opening of the poem Marvell imagines the Lord Protector in relation to the elements, a vitrifying and redemptive force; at its close Cromwell returns as angel of the apocalypse, troubling the waters, healing and settling the nation. But here the realm of nature threatens disorder and dissolution. Rather than a source of solace or continuity, nature is mortality and sin, conspiracy and shipwreck. Landscape in *The First Anniversary* is quite marginal to redemption; here nature is reluctant and slothful. The oppositions in this poem are not between contemplation on the one hand and commerce, warfare, or litigation on the other, but rather between the long, slow cycles of mortality and the dynamism of Cromwell's new order. The rhythms of nature are circular and cyclical, but its force is also centrifugal, dissolutive, and disorderly. Nature is the realm of monarchy and mortality, of scattered effects and scattering time, of traffic and commerce, of conspiracy, rebellion, and sin, of justice obscured and reason fooled, of deceit, of adultery, of envy and false inspiration. The true prophetic mode is Cromwell's alone. All who oppose or resist the prophetic order participate in fallen nature; all who obstruct the dynamism and the Lord Protector's promise of reformation hinder the millennial hopes of the elect.

The dialectic between nature and redemption suggests how deeply Marvell has committed himself in this poem to a repudiation of the philosophical, disquisitional, and ironic past. To Walton's suggestion that the ancient debate between contemplation and action is resolved in the art of angling, Marvell answers with the restless energy of the Lord Protector:

> Cromwell alone with greater Vigour runs,
> (Sun-like) the Stages of succeeding Suns:
> And still the Day which he doth next restore,
> Is the just Wonder of the Day before.
> Cromwell alone doth with new Lustre spring,
> And shines the Jewel of the yearly Ring.
> 'Tis he the force of scatter'd Time contracts,
> And in one Year the work of Ages acts.
>
> (7–14)

Cromwell reverses nature and condenses time, and the verbs in this poem make that aggressive rush, that apocalyptic surge, push aside the older, cyclical order: Cromwell runs and contracts, he hies and cuts, tunes and orders, he hurls the world around him and outwings the wind; he is redeemer and huntsman of the apocalypse—judge, captain, and angel of the commonweal.[42] This is a language of scriptural prophecy and Protestant reform; the degree to which it is not simply distant from but in contention with the language of contemplation and meditation is striking.

Angling and hunting figure not simply the pace of retreat and reform, but suggest a mode for the whole of the society that they address. Walton's sweet fraternity—his convivial and sociable countryfolk, his society of versifiers, anglers, and antiquaries—composes a sociable ideal. It is a model for the whole of a peaceable nation now torn by disputation and dissension, and though Walton's assertion of the politics of that social ideal is dispersed through his text, it nonetheless gathers the force of argument. Walton lives not in foreshortened time, not in the realm of prophecy and revelation, but in time diffused, dilated, and lengthened, in the realm of projects forsworn. Against the hurrying and purposive reformation of nature and man that *The First Anniversary* promises—a vision glimpsed in Maria's symbolic vitrifying of nature in *Upon Appleton House*—Walton poses the pastoral certainties of natural wisdom. And here the function of a naturalist lore reaching back to Pliny is to insist on the slow, continuous wisdom of the natural world. What Pliny describes in his *Natural History* Walton recovers from the river Ware in 1653. The art of angling is the art of recapturing what was known in the past, what has been handed down from generation to generation by oral tradition and by pondering the wisdom of old books.

The idioms of *The First Anniversary* could hardly be more sharply differentiated. The wisdom of nature, the veneration of the past, the assurance of cycle: all are burst by Cromwell. He brings about not continuity with the past, but knowledge of the future. What he proposes is not to recapture ancient wisdom but to transform knowledge. He promises not connection to past communities, but an utter break with the chain of mortal time. Walton contrasts the arts of angling and hunting; his work is to praise contemplative virtue; Marvell's poem is a treatise on the pursuit of the beast. To Walton's question "Whether Contemplation or Action be the chiefest thing wherin the happiness of a man doth most consist in this world"(69), Marvell urges a constant readiness to act:

> And well he therefore does, and well has guest,
> Who in his Age has always forward prest:
> And knowing not where Heavens choice may light,
> Girds yet his Sword, and ready stands to fight.
>
> (145–48)

To Walton's inquiry, Marvell returns the answer of the prophet: be urgent and seasonable, bend to the protector's will, hasten the elect in their momentous work, transform self and society. In this poem we live on the edge of apocalyptic change, balanced between the abyss of mortal time and transformation into the prophetic order. Pastoral had long twinned complaint and prophecy,[43] but Walton's pastoral is antiapocalyptic; it is a critique of chiliasm and eschatology. It imagines, not the end of time, but the endless fluctuations of nature. The vision is steadily backward: to literary authority from the past, to ballads and lyrics of an earlier generation of writers, to the wisdom of ancient naturalists, to the tranquillity of a mythologized golden world. Like the progressive and apocalyptic idealizations of *The First Anniversary*, the slow pastoralism of *The Compleat Angler* is not only vision but also argument; it is a polemical text that counters militant puritanism at every point: on the nature of man, on the ideal of society, on the character of piety and wisdom. It is something of the genius of this book that its program should be so fully integrated with its lore, its naturalism; we ought not to underestimate the shrewdness of *The Compleat Angler*, the carefulness of its construction, the highly artful ways in which the political and social arguments are dispersed through the materials of the book. Although its initial and subsequent audiences may not have parsed the text in quite the manner that I have suggested, the force and coherence of its argument must have been apparent. Its quite artful twinning of idioms—the natural and the social, the naturalist and the political—allowed the work a remarkable longevity. It is the naturalist's manual that promises a coherent social and political vision. And yet that vision is so neatly accommodated to the lore of the book that it can remain idle and uncultivated; it is a book of naturalist lore with deep social resonance.

The First Anniversary, by contrast, conceals none of its political argument or polemical design. It urges the blessings of the protectorate and the blessedness of the protector; it contests and combats dissension and criticism of all kinds. It would, by the most energetic and argumentative of means, wield a whole out of what must have looked like disparate fragments of a society reluctant to be thrust toward the end of time under the stern rod of the captain of the latter days. We have considered the discourse of literature and nature in these works. I want finally to consider the discourse of society. The idioms of sociability provide one of the most striking features of *The Compleat Angler*. As dialogue, the book takes its form from social interaction; this is a society in casual, at points intimate, and always considerate discourse. The cups of ale, the meals carefully described and pleasurably consumed, the singing matches: all the actions of the book are accompanied by sociable interchange. Though angling suggests contemplative privacy, Walton's anglers are companionable, at points voluble. There is nothing contentious or contestative in a discursive world where talk "seems to be Musick" (73). The arcadian society of *The Compleat Angler* knows only a language of amity that excludes legal contention, religious controversy, and civil combat. And it is neatly emblematic of Walton's notion of discourse that the lines between conversation and song should be so fluid within the work. The mixed genres of *The Compleat*

Angler argue both its indeterminacy of mode and the proximity of talk, verse, and song; but Walton also suggests the harmoniousness of all language within a world where song and conversation are natural extensions of the same sociable impulses.

The anglers of Walton's arcadia do not have exclusive claims on harmony. Harmony, after all, is a figure of political coherence that Marvell carefully deploys in *The First Anniversary*, where the civilizing achievements of the Lord Protector are expressed by earthly and celestial music. But Walton's language of sociability becomes in *The First Anniversary* an idiom of single attainment. The figures of heroic endeavor are singular musicians and instruments of state: Amphion, David, Cromwell. But their music is not sociable discourse. Indeed, the figure of the single musician—the shrill huntsman, the psalmist, Amphion—is set against the discord of society. These are musicians of solitary genius, not of sociable harmony; political discourse is contentious and ill-tempered, and must be tuned by the mysterious figure, the single musician. The Lord Protector is distinguished from mortal monarchs; his laureate singly winds his horn. The Lord Protector is set apart not only from mortal monarchs but from tedious statesmen, stubborn minds, political dissent within, and envy without, the commonweal. He is a prince isolated from his peers and subjects, bent on a task isolate, lonely, and dark.

Perhaps the most striking separations and distinctions are suggested by Marvell's condemnation of the sectaries. These groups are figured as societies of dissent: they are locusts and liars, a frantic army, mobs of confusion; Cromwell, by contrast, is the single man, Adam in the first world. At the end of the poem the credulous ambassadors close rank to stand in envy and awe of the single man. Society in *The First Anniversary* is the world of plots, confusion, dissent, and error. Of course, the business of panegyric is to celebrate the single man, but the conventions of panegyric usually figure the hero in concert with a people, in fruitful matrimony with the state: a figure above, but contingent on and given form and potentiation by, his subjects. Sociability is implied by the idioms of his calling: domestic care, patriarchy, civil ardor. Indeed, the language of desire was crucial to Renaissance notions of the body politic, and especially to royalist idioms of the state; nowhere would the political argument of passion be more obvious than in the Restoration poems written for Charles II. But the language of domestic propriety, patriarchy, and civil ardor is strikingly absent from *The First Anniversary*. That is a language, if not held in contempt by the Cromwellian laureate, hardly useful to his work. The older idioms of patriarchy and political communality are not simply foreign to this republic; they are at cross-purposes to its visionary mode. Marvell understood what it meant to portray the Lord Protector as isolate hero; he is at once distancing Cromwell from the older idioms of the political imagination and creating a new heroic mold for his country gentleman and army general. He fashions, in this anniversary poem, a method of argument meant to break molds, to suggest distance and difference. *The First Anniversary* celebrates not the vulnerability of its forms but revolution. The poem has more conservative polemical work to conduct as well, and Marvell does so in the management of some of its other languages, in the poem's fierce contest with the political radicalism of Quakers and Anabaptists; but it is striking to see just how isolated and desocialized is the figure of the Lord Protector. Indeed, this poem conducts an argument with sociability itself; it is the man standing apart who is the instrument of change. Marvell's distinction is between the individual conscience and sociability. Walton sees virtue as social discourse; Marvell suggests virtue as the isolated hunter, the sole millenarian: he alone will chase the beast and bring society to the brink of its final reform.

One additional turn is given to the issue of sociability in *The First Anniversary*. Toward the end of the poem Marvell constructs a critique of democratic tyranny: " 'Tis not a Freedome, that where All command; / Nor Tyranny, where One does them withstand" (279–80). Cromwell is the one righteous man who withstands the many; but Marvell also suggests the possibility of Cromwell as patriarch, a language surprisingly close to that widely espoused convention of patriarchy in which the king is so frequently figured and which is carefully put aside at the opening of *The First Anniversary* with its decisive rejection of lineal descent. And yet the analogue for Cromwell suggested here is Noah: "Thou, and thine House, like Noah's Eight did rest" (283). Some students of the poem have suggested that Marvell seems here to allow for a "house of Cromwell," a rule of patrimonial descent.[44] But the poet quickly deflects that possibility with an episode that extends and undercuts patriarchy:

> That sober Liberty which men may have,
> That they enjoy, but more they vainly crave:

And such as to their Parents Tents do press,
May shew their own, not see his Nakedness.
(289–92)

In this reworking of Genesis (6–9), Marvell attacks dissent as drunken license. Not only does the passage subvert republican patriarchy, but the idioms central to Walton's sociability, to the higher leisure, are denied together with patriarchy. In a sweeping argument that collapses the whole of the radical opposition to Cromwell's rule into Noah's drunken descendants, Marvell suggests not only the singularity of Cromwell's rule, but the isolation and distance of the great captain from all societies: sociable, libertarian, radical, or patriarchal and monarchical. It is central to the method of *The First Anniversary* to celebrate Cromwell as heroic isolate, a figure distinguished from, as much as analogized with, other models.[45] In the powerful dialectic of this poem, Cromwell is finally unlike any other figure, distinguished in the form of his governance not only from foreign princes but from his nation as well.

One of the deepest puzzles of this anniversary poem is the kind of society that might be imagined for Cromwell to protect and reform. It seems at best a society willful and fragmentary; the people are at one point stubborn and unyielding, at another giddy and drunken; they are swayed by malice and error; they offer conspiracy and resistance. The Lord Protector is shielded from the wicked and the commonplace by his singular virtue; but he must steadily do battle not only with Antichrist but with the stubborn minds and tedious statesmen of his own nation. Like Amphion, Cromwell wrings harmony from discord, but Marvell must harmonize the disparate episodes, the distractions and fragmentations, of a poem that suffers a powerful centrifugal drag. The work of Cromwell's laureate is to give not simply coherence but redemptive meaning to a social and political experience that threatens dissolution and disarray. In such work *The First Anniversary* is cast into vivid relief by *The Compleat Angler,* a text that lacks the complex formal machinery of Marvell's poem but yields an argument of ineffable coherence. The piscatory idyll is not only a sustained meditation on natural bounty and ease; it is an encomium to social coherence. Amphion fixing the contentious stones of a temple whose cohesion relies on tension is answered by Walton's angler, meditative and idle. For Marvell, poetry in *The First Anniversary* is the constructive force of grave accents and shrill notes; it supports the urgent structure of statecraft. In *The Compleat Angler* song is play. The visions could hardly suggest greater distance on the nature of poetry, on vocation, on civil society. The Lord Protector and his laureate are heroic isolates; Walton as Piscator is in steady dialogue, one within a community of rustics, poets, antiquaries, and gentlemen. Poetry in *The Compleat Angler* has something about it of the corporate enterprise; the book as anthology is an argument for the social community of letters. The shrill huntsman and angelic Cromwell are singular in the landscape of *The First Anniversary;* they are invested with powerful social and political meaning, but they are not imagined within a community.

It is one of the sharpest ironies and incongruities of *The First Anniversary* that the poet announces renewal and return, that Marvell allows within the image of the sinking weight at the poem's opening a figure of repetition, an echo to be placed at its close; and yet that so much of the poem is fixed in the imagination of the apocalypse. Uniqueness, foreclosure, the mysteries of time, the latter days: these are the tags not of renewal but of the end of time. A poem that calls itself "the first anniversary" suggests repetition, and yet there is little here to allow iteration; its argument is political and social uniqueness. The poem struggles with the burden of putting into pattern what is singular, of suggesting the coherence of time imagined as prophetic and redemptive. *The First Anniversary* was, I suspect, an impossible act to follow in 1656. *The Compleat Angler* also closes with a recollection of its opening. The book is not utterly an argument for stasis; after all, conversion has taken place, for by the work's close the hunter has "turned Angler" (163). And Walton's book ends not only with this conversion, but with the promise of returning celebration; the two men part at the point where they met and fix a time exactly one year hence, the anniversary of this trip, to meet again, to renew acquaintance and that recreative idyll passed in conversation and leisure. Like *The First Anniversary, The Compleat Angler* ends with scriptural citation: the "blessing of Saint Peters Master be with mine" (163), the evocation of quietness, virtue, and angling. Marvell's poem closes with Cromwell as the angel of St. John's gospel, stirring the waters to heal the troubled commonweal. The poet undoubtedly imagined an audience in the Lord Protector; how much broader an audience his materials and arguments might have yielded is difficult to know. *The First Anniversary* is a brilliant, embattled, and finally incoherent work, both as form and as an act of social imagination. The poem is set within time and within society, but its energies are devoted to escaping those structures. And while Marvell's redemptive message has meaning only within the social construct of an elect nation, the poet finally abandons the possibility of redemption for an act of commemoration.

It is not difficult, by contrast, to see why *The Compleat Angler* found an audience. Its argument is consoling and restorative. Set in its initial moment of creation and reception, the early 1650s, the work offers an image of the nation before the wars, prior to the destruction of the church, the extirpation of monarchy, and the symbolic dismemberment of hierarchy. Of course, the interregnum did not efface all privilege, ceremony, and pleasure; but *The Compleat Angler* not only creates an idealized moment, a world that stands apart from the apocalyptic rush of the 1650s; it assures us of the timeless, cyclical return of its own terms. The acts of obeisance toward an earlier age, the quotations of authority and poetry, all the small gestures of piety toward the past—these are arguments of continuity and promises of return. The book is anything but a call to arms; it must, however, have had both consolatory and polemical powers. Walton's book is capacious, with curious disproportions—indeed, nearly without structure; perhaps that too was part of its appeal, for the work contains nothing that is compulsory or unequivocal. It was a book for "profit or pleasure" (59), a project to which Walton returned four times in his own life. If there is something patchwork about *The Compleat Angler,* it also suggests a world that has not accounted for loose ends; there is nothing here monolithic, no general field theory of politics or society. Unlike the prophetic imagination that would organize all experience and all detail into coherent, redemptive meaning, *The Compleat Angler* allowed revision, expansion, and collaboration.

In its very success, *The Compleat Angler* created something of the sociability it took as the burden of its argument; in that project, it succeeded beyond Walton's dreams. Although *The Compleat Angler* does not exactly deny the Second Coming, it certainly does not argue preparations against that day. Marvell's poem is under pressure of and suffused by the apocalypse. The two works stand at the poles of experience and imagination at midcentury; *The Compleat Angler* and *The First Anniversary* may seem improbable interlocutors, but their very antinomy provides its own steady illumination.

4 The Politics of Pleasure:
Annus Mirabilis, The Last Instructions, Paradise Lost

It would be an exaggeration to say that the restoration of Charles II produced unparalleled and unalloyed celebration, and yet such an impression is not difficult to gather from the sheer abundance of verse and song, thanksgiving sermon and broadside, letter and diary entry that recorded and represented the event.[1] We cannot gauge the extent to which the written record covered over the anxieties and regrets that must also have accompanied the return of Stuart monarchy, but the records we do have suggest something like a moment of unanimous jubilation.[2] In London the king's return was marked "with a Triumph of above 20000 horse & foote, brandishing their swords and shouting with unexpressable joye: The wayes straw'd with flowers, the bells ringing, the streetes hung with Tapissry, fountaines running with wine ... such a Restauration was never seene in the mention of any history, antient or modern, since the returne of the Babylonian Captivity, nor so joyfull a day, & so bright, ever seene in this nation."[3] In Edinburgh the celebrations included the raising of a cross "covered with artificiall Vines loaden with Grapes, both white and good Claret Wines springing out from all it's Pipes or Channels; on it's Head a Bacchus bestriding a Hogshead with two or three Satyrs, did with their mimick Gestures entertain the beholders. A little below the Crosse ... divers exotick Trees were raised loaden with their leavs and fruits. ... The Musick and breaking of glasses were seconded by three general Vollies of the Horse and Foot ... and all were ecchoed by joyfull acclamations of the people."[4]

The revolution was wrought whole and bloodlessly from the confusions of Richard Cromwell's protectorate; it came without apparent effort or resistance; and a mood of national exultation, though not quite so univocal or undisturbed,[5] extended over the next two years to embrace the coronation in April 1661 and the king's nuptials in May 1662.[6] The public themes of those first months argued the Restoration not only as a return of the person of the king and the office of kingship but as a broader renewal: a restoration of arms and arts, a reinvigoration of science and letters, a revival of wit and eloquence, an elevation of style and manners, and for our purposes, most especially a restoration of abundance and pleasure.[7] At the center of these hopes and idealizations stood a king whose words announcing return, and spoken frequently thereafter, promised indulgence and liberality, themes that would, in ways both expected and unexpected, become the signature of his reign.

National renewal centered on the person of the king, but it extended to aristocrats and courtiers, dependents and hopefuls, a network of privilege, power, and aspiration. Those celebrating and being celebrated in the Restoration had every reason to cultivate its association with privilege, ceremony, and pleasure. Indeed, the revival of court culture proved a self-fulfilling prophecy: those who had most to gain from its elaboration also had most reason to promote its values, to provide occasion, protection, and example. Images and ideals arguing the return of privilege, pleasure, and art were embraced together with a broader program, a mythic English past of caroling and delight as well as the more immediate pleasures of the theater and the alehouse. The arts and gratifications of Charles's court would prove rather more complex, strategic, and finally more subversive than could have been reckoned in the months following the king's restoration, but who would have gainsaid forgiveness and liberality?

In charting the public mood of the early 1660s we must recognize that the themes of pleasure and indulgence, while celebrating the present, also allowed a sharp engagement with the immediate past. Public pronouncements of the Restoration urged forgiveness and liberality, but this same literature deplored the past, at times blackening and repudiating the figures, politics, and social theories of the republic. What seem to our eyes innocent and bucolic gestures—indeed, the entire culture of pleasure—formed an important polemical position in the 1660s. Delight and abundance played their own role in denying a once much-trumpeted piety and saintliness.[8] That the 1650s were a good deal more complex hardly needs assertion;[9] but what does need stressing is that while the themes of this Restoration projected ideals for the future and idealized images of the present, they also allowed in quite conscious and perhaps not quite so conscious ways a powerful engagement with puritan moral regulation and reformation.[10] In that project, abundance, liberality, and pleasure played a significant role.

It may have been chance that the person of Charles II allowed so much of this work to be done, that his history of exile and restoration so neatly offered a parallel with David in godly election as in sexual history, and that the king's personal inclinations so fully accommodated the themes of abundance and liberality that were claimed for the Restoration as a whole, king and subject alike.[11] The generosity of spirit announced at Breda would come to characterize much about his reign;[12] and though some who felt themselves ignored or scorned would contest and decry the objects of his generosity,[13] none denied the easy impulses, what must have been something like a true liberality of spirit in which the king came back to England. Nor can the king's wit and playful sense of irony be doubted; it is not difficult to believe that the restored court provided a model for repartee in the comedy of manners, that the satires of Rochester, scurrilous and brilliant, found a forgiving audience in the king, or that he would have grasped immediately the ironies and pleasures of the opening lines of *Absalom and Achitophel*. Abundance and generosity took their cue from the person of the king, but they had a broader life in the literature promoting, celebrating, and defending his kingship. On the abundance of the king turned the patronage system in its entirety: both the literal and the figurative system of rewards and generosity of personal attention, protection, place, and pension.[14] It was not only in the defensive and partisan gestures of *Absalom and Achitophel* that the paternalism of the king was urged as an aspect of patronage, stability, and national abundance; those combined hopes were expressed at Charles's return and frequently thereafter.[15] Sexual abundance, the nation assumed, would be harnessed by marriage and progeny,[16] but the twinning of personal and national fertility is found in the first poems written to greet the Restoration.[17]

Indeed, the king's procreative promise formed the very center of a politics of abundance.[18] Charles's return was repeatedly celebrated in a language of passion and pleasure. Nor does the explicitness of the language derive simply from what was known or rumored of the king's private pleasures; it derived from conventional assumptions about the role of those pleasures in the state.[19] The royal capacity for abundance promised stability and continuity, qualities much prized after two decades of political turbulence. As the king observed in announcing his marital intentions to Parliament in May of 1661:

> I have been often put in minde by My friends, that it was high time to marry; and I have thought so My Self ever since I came into England: But there appeared difficulties enough in the Choice, though many overtures have been made to Me; and if I should never marry till I could make such a Choice, against which there could be no foresight of any inconvenience that may insue, you would live to see Me an Old Batchelor, which I think you do not desire to do. I can now tell you, not onely that I am resolved to marry, but whom I resolve to marry, if God please; And towards my resolution, I have used that deliberation, and taken that advice as I ought to do in an Affair of that importance; and trust Me, with a full consideration of the good of My Subjects in general, as of My Self; it is with the Daughter of Portugal.[20]

We have come to associate Charles II's court with bawdry and heartless license, but there is nothing in the slightest licentious in the high-minded verse that celebrates this sexual restoration. At its center was fixed the ideal of patriarchal continuity; from the promise of royal abundance followed a series of topics that bound sexual fertility to those very qualities that the king had pronounced on his return home: liberality, generosity, and forgiveness.

If the domestic politics of the early 1660s are best unfolded by allowing pleasure and sexual abundance their full political meaning— their celebratory and contestative edge—the mid-1660s can only be understood by considering how much darker and more complex, and how much more varied, the polemical charge of these themes had become for a public disappointed by the barrenness of the royal marriage and the license of the court. When the king returned, pleasure and fertility meant both a repudiation of the immediate past and hopes for the sexual and commercial abundance and political stability of the future; by the mid-1660s such hopes had not altogether vanished, but the king and nation were no longer united in a bacchic embrace. The disappointment of returning cavaliers has been amply documented,[21] but it was not only those trying to get their own back who were not wholly gratified by this Restoration. Dissenters were harried and threatened, and though some had turned to quietism under the new regime, they had not disappeared.[22] The Clarendon

Code was harshly restrictive, and while the king attempted Indulgence in 1662, his Cavalier Parliament was not in a mood to grant such an indulgence to dissenters.[23] The king and many in Parliament had spoken against division and recrimination,[24] but sharp words were not long in coming. The first real crises of the Restoration arrived, however, with a force beyond anyone's reckoning.[25] The middle years of this decade brought unparalleled military, fiscal, natural, and political disaster: the Dutch invasion of the Medway and Thames and destruction of a good part of the English fleet; the plague that decimated London's population; the Great Fire, which leveled huge tracts of the city and left rumors of conspiracy in its wake; and the hounding from office of the lord chancellor in a parliamentary mood that reminded some of the destruction of Strafford.[26] The combination of fire, plague, and military defeat left the impression that the four horsemen of the apocalypse had descended on London in rapid order; cries of divine judgment were not long in coming, nor was the apocalyptic significance of the year 1666 lost on millenarian sensibilities.[27]

By now the failure of the king's legitimate sexual abundance was only too obvious, and the morals of the royal family were searched for explanations of that failure. License and fornication had come to have an urgent political significance. Who could have missed the application implied by the publication in 1667 of a sermon on Hebrews 13:4 entitled *Fornication Condemned*,[28] or the significance of sermons preached before the king at Whitehall in 1667 on sensuality, lust, and passion?[29] In the midst of disaster, these were subjects as dangerously charged as ministerial incompetence and greed, naval mismanagement and cowardice, fire and plague. The royal extravagance came under parliamentary scrutiny and displeasure in 1667;[30] but it was not only in Parliament that the appetites and luxuries as well as the valor and integrity of the court were contemplated.

Political resentments and blame had not yet hardened into a system of opposition politics as they would in Exclusion, but the disasters of the mid-1660s produced a flood of polemical activity, much of it addressed to the politics of pleasure. At the base of such activity were squibs and lampoons, materials that often did not reach print;[31] but above the satiric, at times pornographic, ephemera rose a socially and aesthetically more complex literary structure that included old and new satiric forms, experiments in panegyric, drama, verse history, and epic. All the literary forms, both popular and elite, were responsive to and helped shape and interpret the crises of the mid-1660s.

They often shared tropes and idioms and deployed similar figures of politics and speech. Their full representational force comes clear as we watch their contestative work, here shoring, there reinterpreting, and more than occasionally exploding the conventions of Restoration politics and culture. It is in that context and along such a spectrum of literary and political concerns that I want to locate *Annus Mirabilis*, *The Last Instructions*, and *Paradise Lost*, poems of that year of literary wonders and political disasters, 1667.

I want to begin, however, at a slightly more optimistic moment: June 3, 1665. Shortly after the Battle of Lowestoft, the first English victory of the Anglo-Dutch wars, Edmund Waller wrote a new style of court panegyric, a poem of ostensible *Instructions to a Painter*.[32] The fiction allowed Waller vividly to illustrate the colors and imagery of combat and conquest; his celebration of the victory at Lowestoft may not have been the first effort to politicize pleasure and honor in the mid-1660s, but the poem's visible and vulnerable moves were taken up both by satirists and by those defending the court's honor. In its optimistic elevation of tone the poem gave an opening to those skeptical of the court and of panegyric efforts to claim on its behalf the laurels of military honor, the pleasures of gallant display, or the authority of literary culture. Waller's poem was quickly answered, and not only by military defeat, but by a group of satires that engaged the premise, topics, tropes, and style of his verse.[33] In the satiric reversals of Waller's piece, the conduct of the war, the character of the admiralty, the quality of the court, and finally the negligence and indulgence of the king himself were put under harsh scrutiny; indeed, the breadth and density of satiric attack were such that the polemical literature itself became part of the crisis. The court was put on the defensive against defeat and disaster, against scurrilous charges leveled at its conduct and character, and ultimately against accusations that such conduct was itself responsible for the divine judgment now so clearly visited on the nation. Poems of praise and blame addressed the prosecution of the war, its heroes and heroics, and the conduct of the ministry and admiralty; but they also undertook to manage images of the court, to represent its principals, and, rather more specifically and daringly, to address the king's sexual conduct.

Waller begins his work with ships and battle gallantry; but a third of the way through the poem, in a portrait of the duchess of York at Harwich, he expands his poem to suggest the role of love and beauty in a proper courtly economy. Not only is the navy victualed and supplied at Harwich; valor itself is renewed, heroic resolve affirmed by the "beauties of the British court" (80). The episode is brief, but Waller's portrait of the duchess proved of surprising literary importance: variations on the portrait, spun together with attendant themes of love and valor, were played out in *The Second Advice,* in Dryden's dedicatory verse to *Annus Mirabilis,* and most damagingly and brilliantly in Marvell's *Last Instructions.* First, Waller's complimentary and classicizing "instructions":

> But who can always on the billows lie?
> The wat'ry wilderness yields no supply:
> Spreading our sails, to Harwich we resort,
> And meet the beauties of the British court.
> Th' illustrious Duchess and her glorious train
> (Like Thetis with her nymphs) adorn the main.
> The gazing sea-gods, since the Paphian queen
> Sprung from among them, no such sight had seen.
> Charm'd with the graces of a troop so fair,
> Those deathless powers for us themselves declare,
> Resolv'd the aid of Neptune's court to bring
> And help the nation where such beauties spring.
> The soldier here his wasted store supplies
> And takes new valor from the ladies' eyes.
>
> (77–90)

For the moment, Waller would have us contemplate the duchess of York as a goddess of the sea, the divinity of love and fertility, supplier of arms to Achilles, the very source of heroic resolve. Conventional and innocent enough, one might have thought, but in *The Second Advice* (1666) both Waller's subject and his literary manner come under scornful attack.[34] Here is no Aphrodite with her train of nymphs, but a caricature of Waller's portrait that rewrites the idiom of love in the language of appetite:

> But, Painter, now prepare, t' enrich thy piece,
> Pencil of ermines, oil of ambergris:
> See where the Duchess, with triumphant tail
> Of num'rous coaches, Harwich does assail!
> So the land crabs, at Nature's kindly call,
> Down to engender at the sea do crawl.
> See then the Admiral, with navy whole,

To Harwich through the ocean caracole.
So swallows, buri'd in the sea, at spring
Return to land with summer on their wing.
One thrifty ferry-boat of mother-pearl
Suffic'd of old the Cytherean girl;
Yet navies are but properties, when here
(A small sea-masque and built to court you, dear)
Three goddesses in one: Pallas for art,
Venus for sport, and Juno in your heart.
O Duchess! if thy nuptial pomp were mean,
'Tis paid with int'rest in this naval scene.

(53–70)

The "glorious train" has become a "triumphant tail," and in that translation we can anticipate much of the satiric contest over love and honor. Waller's elevated tone is ridiculed, his mythology exploded, his extravagance regretted. And *The Last Instructions* provides a much harsher and nastier explicitness. Throughout the satires—in *The Second Advice, The Third Advice,* and *The Last Instructions*—the elevated language of love and honor, so conspicuous in Waller's poem and more largely in the literature of court compliment, is inverted vividly and exactly. The satirist traditionally exposes vice, extravagance, and folly, but in the middle of this decade he fixes on enormity and appetite. It was clear by the mid-1660s that a deep vulnerability in the court's armory lay in the king's morals: his appetites, his personal indulgences, and his sexual follies. The satirist is keen to lower the tone, to debunk epic gestures, to debase and embarrass, but his steady aim is to connect sexual greed and political corruption. What he angles after throughout is the matter of governance.

Given the king's crucial role not only in governance but in the literature of governance, it may seem puzzling that the attacks on appetite and license should have been repeatedly directed at the duchess of York and, by implication, at the duke of York, rather than against the king himself. But the vivid accounting of the king's sexual appetites that we have from the 1670s and after should not obscure the fact that direct, published attacks on the person of Charles II were quite new in the polemic of the mid-1660s.[35] As it had long been customary to address failures in the king's policies by denouncing his "evil ministers," so was it now easier to attack Charles's morals through his relatives and mistresses; moreover, such targets underscore how the king's corruption permeates the family and the state. Further, the duchess of York was particularly vulnerable to such attack; she had been the subject of scandalous rumor at the time of her marriage to the duke, and she was the daughter of the reviled and (by the middle of 1667) discredited lord chancellor. One of the charges against Clarendon was his aim to load the king with a barren wife so that the lord chancellor might ascend, through his grandchildren, to the throne, an accusation frequently coupled with charges against his appetite, grandeur, and arrogance.[36] By the time of *The Second Advice* and Dryden's *Annus Mirabilis*, the duchess of York's vulnerability to attack and defamation must have been resplendently clear, although the virulence of *The Last Instructions* seems unusual and daring. Not all, however, was accusation and vindictiveness.

The verses addressed to the duchess of York in the essay that prefaces *Annus Mirabilis*, like the poem itself, must have been intended to combat the scurrility of *The Second Advice* and to defuse, in a more general way, such a concentrated attention on the lewdness of the duke and the vulnerability of the duchess. The preface and the poem aimed to rescue a poetic mode and to recall the more hopeful days when royal paternity might tangle together sexual vigor and national abundance. By 1667 that was a project to strain the resources of even the most ambitious of court poets. Dryden's first essay in sexual politics is not as fluent and daring as the case he would make during Exclusion, but it is obvious that he grasps the fundamentals of the polemical problem and that *Annus Mirabilis* is in its own way a deeply resourceful poem.

It is quite typical of Dryden first to address rudeness and scurrility by altogether denying them. The complimentary verses tucked into the prefatory essay to *Annus Mirabilis* begin with the poet's wonted high-mindedness, an altitude and a mild obliqueness quite of a piece with his praise of the city of London for its "true Loyalty, invincible Courage and unshaken Constancy."[37] London's role in the parliamentary effort during the civil wars was well known, as were its tradition of radicalism and current ambivalence toward the royal family.[38] And in the face of both past and present, Dryden exalts the duchess' spiritual fortitude and piety, her beauty and honor, the faithfulness of the duke, and the chastity of their union.

> Then with the Duke your Highness rul'd the day:
> While all the brave did his command obey,

The fair and pious under you did pray.
How pow'rful are chast vows! the wind and tyde
You brib'd to combat on the English side.
Thus to your much lov'd Lord you did convey
An unknown succour, sent the nearest way.
New vigour to his wearied arms you brought;
(So Moses was upheld while Israel fought.)

. . . .

Thus Beauty ravish'd the rewards of Fame,
And the Fair triumph'd when the Brave o'rcame.
Then, as you meant to spread another way
By Land your Conquests far as his by Sea,
Leaving our Southern Clime, you march'd along
The stubborn North, ten thousand Cupid's strong.
Like Commons the Nobility resort
In crowding heaps, to fill your moving Court:
To welcome your approach the Vulgar run,
Like some new Envoy from the distant Sun.
And Country Beauties by their Lovers go,
Blessing themselves, and wondring at the show.

                          (21–51)

Rumor and innuendo told a rather different story of Anne Hyde and James Stuart; the duchess of York was famed neither for chastity nor for beauty, and the duke's lechery, perhaps not as well publicized as the king's, was hardly private. But the point of Dryden's verses to the duchess was not really to argue the case for her beauty and chastity but rather to assume it, high-mindedly to refuse polemical engagement on this topic by including the verses as stylistic exemplar, as a model for "softness of expression, and the smoothness of measure, rather then the height of thought" (207–8). By citing these verses as a point of literary rather than political contest, Dryden moves the problem of style to the center of attention and rather blithely assumes that the claims of the verse as representation can stand uncontested. Such a maneuver is of a piece with the essay's elaborate argument, which aims generally to cover the quite contestable and highly idealized images of the war, the king, and the royal family with the loftiness and blandness of generic argument, stylistic contest, and literary precedence. Literary debate might indeed have been an interest of this preface, and literary authority is certainly one of the claims that the poet is busy making in his essay, but the materials of the essay and the poem itself also include quite combustible and contentious representations of the war, of the conduct of its principals, of the court and its agents, and most especially of the duke of York and his yet more visible brother.

Deep within the web of conceits, images, analogies, and rhetorical colors so self-consciously displayed by this poem, Dryden chose to address what he must have been aware of as an explosive issue, but one that needed to be addressed, or rather handled, managed, and dispersed. While satire and lampoon had by the mid-1660s begun to take up the open lewdness and license of the court, such behavior did not long remain only a matter of low defamation. Nothing brought home their significance more sharply than interpretations of the plague and fire as God's judgments on and displeasure with the court. Milton had prophesied the Restoration as the choosing of "a captain back for Egypt";[39] more such reflections were now ready to hand. Nor was it simply the voice of suppressed dissent decrying lust and sexual profligacy; at the center of the court there was also disapproval. Clarendon's displeasure was well known—his part in the frustration of the king's sexual pleasures cost him Charles's loyalty in the impeachment proceedings.[40] Just as telling, the king's own chaplain preached before the king on the anniversary of Elizabeth's accession, November 17, 1667, a sermon on James 4:7: "Resist the Devil, and he will flee from you."[41] The sermon is a generalized warning against the "carnal prejudice of infidelity"; of course, preaching such a sermon to the king demanded generalized and high-minded morality, but who hearing this powerful denunciation of lust and infidelity could have doubted the fitness of such an audience for such sermonizing?

Whether or not Dryden knew of a particular innuendo, satire, or lampoon, the barrenness of the royal couple and the sexual profligacy of the king were very well known indeed by the mid-1660s, and Dryden must have felt compelled to address these problems. He could not alter what most obviously could not be altered, but he might through a quite masterful deployment of images of paternal solicitude transform the king from an unfaithful husband in a barren marriage to a pious and tender father of his people. The issue of patriarchalism is quite sharply deployed in this poem, which seeks at once to portray the king and his court in the most advantageous light and to suggest that paternity has more than one form when the father in question is the king and his family is the state. But the patriarchal argument is not made in so simple a fashion, and the poem does not begin with the solicitude of the king as its subject. It begins rather with a coupling of commerce and pleasure. The Anglo-Dutch war, *Annus Mirabilis* urges, has harnessed valor to commerce, and commercial empire is celebrated at both the poem's opening and its close as the source of ripeness and luxury. This is a war for spice and perfume, for commercial splendor and luxury; in such terms the king's interests are aligned closely but not exactly with his nation's:

> In thriving Arts long time had Holland grown,
>> Crouching at home, and cruel when abroad:
> Scarce leaving us the means to claim our own.
>> Our King they courted, and our Merchants aw'd.
>
> Trade, which like bloud should circularly flow,
>> Stop'd in their Channels, found its freedom lost
> Thither the wealth of all the world did go,
>> And seem'd but shipwrack'd on so base a Coast.
>
> For them alone the Heav'ns had kindly heat,
>> In Eastern Quarries ripening precious Dew:
> For them the Idumaean Balm did sweat,
>> And in hot Ceilon Spicy Forrests grew.
>
> . . . .
>
> What peace can be where both to one pretend?
>> (But they more diligent, and we more strong)
> Or if a peace, it soon must have an end
>> For they would grow too pow'rful were it long.
>
> . . . .
>
> This saw our King; and long within his breast
>> His pensive counsels ballanc'd too and fro;
> He griev'd the Land he freed should be oppress'd,
>> And he less for it then Usurpers do.
>
> His gen'rous mind the fair Idea's drew
>> Of Fame and Honour which in dangers lay;
> Where wealth, like fruit on precipices, grew,
>> Not to be gather'd but by Birds of prey.

> The loss and gain each fatally were great;
>> And still his Subjects call'd aloud for war:
> But peaceful Kings o'r martial people set,
>> Each others poize and counter-ballance are.
>>>> (1–48)

Luxury and abundance can be obtained by sacrifice, but the nature of that expense, carefully weighed by the king, is slighted by a nation that clamors for war. While the poem seeks to identify the king with abundance, it is an abundance of the mind and temper, a valor of the spirit, a sense of honor. The poem also aligns him with prudence and solicitude—this prince would gladly forgo luxury for peace—but public clamor tips the carefully balanced scales. A nation's appetite and a king's daring finally determine for war. Dryden's stanzas associate empire, abundance, and solicitude with the king; they heighten valor as a princely motive and argue commercial gain as the national will. The distinction between abundance as a motive to valor and abundance as appetite is delicately assayed, for while Dryden is happy to allow delight, abundance, and pleasure as general concerns of the commonwealth, generosity and solicitude are reserved for the king alone.

That dialectic governs the opening, indeed the entire first half, of the poem: on one side we find abundance and valor; on the other, appetite and violence. The primary work of this dialectic is to discriminate English from Dutch motives and character, but it also allows an elevation of the king above his people and of old social hierarchies over newer challengers. Both sets of oppositions are spun around images of fertility and sensual delight: laboring suns, waxing and waning tides, balms, scents, spices, as well as eunuch guardians, frantic passions, and jealous husbands. The dialectic allows Dryden to associate the king with empire, valor, and solicitude, to separate his motives and abundance from those of his people, and to distinguish the entire nation from the Dutch. Within this complex of associations and discriminations Dryden fixes the business of the first half of the poem: the elaborate, at times fantastic, descriptions of naval battles. Such descriptive passages allow for the wonted, indeed absolutely generic, celebrations of honor and valor, and Dryden turns both victory and defeat into occasions for praising the valor of the English nation and its royal family: the dukes of Albemarle and York and, of course, the king himself. By contrast, the Dutch are cowardly and weak, driven solely by commerce, devoid of valor and splendor.

A rather more interesting set of arguments is folded within the obvious dialectic, for along with commerce and appetite, celebrations of valor, and denunciations of cowardice, we find a second set of images and arguments that figures war and commerce as sexual violence, passion, and domestic and paternal solicitude and care. Warfare absorbs sexual violence in martial valor; like marriage it regulates and bridles passion, transmuting sexual appetite into honor, the conventional program of epic and romance. But Dryden finds a pointed use for this program at a time when appetite and sexual indulgence have become such important polemical subjects. What the court displayed and what the king exemplified was an abundance of appetite and a disappointing capacity either for legitimate paternity or valor. The Dutch wars, the poem rather subterraneously suggests, absorb and channel the sexual aggression of a king and his people; through such sublimation are valor and commercial empire achieved. For the nation, pleasure and luxury are the rewards of valorous battle; for the king, sexual potency is translated into military authority and paternal solicitude. This war, in fact, allows a scope for sexual energy that domestic life does not offer. Dryden does not, of course, suggest that the king's domestic sexual performance is indifferent, or inconstant, or inappropriate, but it is the war and national calamity that allow the appropriate scope and meaning for his sexual authority and paternal solicitude. The battles with the Dutch are figured with a variety of hunting, chasing, and sexual images, but it is the restoration of the fleet that binds sexual with military power:

> Our careful Monarch stands in Person by,
> His new-cast Canons firmness to explore:
> The strength of big-corn'd powder loves to try,
> And Ball and Cartrage sorts for every bore.
> (593–96)

The puns allow a kind of explicitness to what is otherwise most often implicit in scenes of the chase and assault (cf. lines 521–28); and the restoration of the fleet with its twinned images of sexual and military potency is resolved into a scene bright with gallant trim and sanguine streamers. In return for the city's martial gift, the king offers his vigor and paternal solicitude. The deflection of sexual force into military authority is the poem's argument for the "civilizing" arts of warfare, an argument that acknowledges the energy and aggression of sexuality and lends to it epic dignity and civic care. Paternity in the form of martial authority and leadership is crucial to the presentation of the duke of York and of Charles II. Moreover, Dryden provides another set of images to lend dignity and domestic affect to the king's paternalism. Accompanying the scenes of sexual aggression, images of domestic sentiment are scattered in both the first and second halves of the poem. In the midst of fire and plague, those images have an obvious polemical force.

They argue, of course, a caring monarch, pious and solicitous, the sacrificial servant of his people; and that figure is anticipated in the earlier scenes of domestic solicitude:

> The Son, who, twice three month's on th' Ocean tost,
>   Prepar'd to tell what he had pass'd before,
> Now sees, in English Ships the Holland Coast,
>   And Parents arms in vain stretch'd from the shore.
>
> This carefull Husband had been long away,
>   Whom his chast wife and little children mourn;
> Who on their fingers learn'd to tell the day
>   On which their Father promis'd to return.
>   (129–36)

Such scenes illustrate the inscrutability of providence, Dryden's ostensible and politically useful theme; where providence is inscrutable, blame is difficult to fix. But rather more interestingly, these scenes offer images of fathers and husbands, of chaste unions and pious familial relations and restorations. They depict appetite domesticated, providing a countermeasure to and conjuring a world quite distant from the one with which the king's sexual pleasures were more and more frequently and more and more polemically associated. Dryden's full argument about such royal domesticity and sentiment is realized in the long passages where Charles acts out the role of solicitous patriarch, but these scenes of domestic sentiment have an important polemical design. That they display not so much sentiment as sentimentality, that they are hopelessly generalized and abstracted, suggests the difficulty of Dryden's job in discovering appropriate domestic

counters for the king's private life. What they also make clear is the
need for associating the court with solicitude and domesticity in a
context that stressed martial vigor.

At a time when fire, plague, and sexual indulgence might have
discovered a more appropriate analogue for the king in Nero than
in Christ, such images of domesticity and propriety took on vivid
polemical life. Fire and plague might not seem to offer ripe occasion
for domesticity and civic care, and yet Dryden uses exactly these materials to argue the king as Christic redeemer—"On me alone thy just
displeasure lay, / But take thy judgments from this mourning Land"
(1059–60). Yet more crucially, he retraces the sexual thematic, using
the fire as a foil against which to display the chastity and piety of the
king. In the depiction of the origins and progress of the fire, the
dominant language is sexual impropriety. At first, the fire is associated
with the republican past; but as Dryden develops the imagery, he
presses the analogy with sexual passion:

> The winds, like crafty Courtezans, with-held
> > His flames from burning, but to blow them more:
> And, every fresh attempt, he is repell'd
> > With faint denials, weaker then before.
>
> And now, no longer letted of his prey,
> > He leaps up at it with inrag'd desire:
> O'r-looks the neighbours with a wide survey,
> > And nods at every house his threatening fire.
>
> The Ghosts of Traitors, from the Bridge descend,
> > With bold Fanatick Spectres to rejoyce:
> About the fire into a Dance they bend,
> > And sing their Sabbath Notes with feeble voice.
> > > (881–92)

This scene, rather daringly I think, takes up that central courtly
subject—sexual license, illicit and uncontrolled passion—and instead
of denying its existence, associates it with political and social tumult,
with regicide and republican anarchy, with social leveling and religious
fanaticism. Against those images, Dryden poses an innocent citizenry
and a pensive king. The domesticity and tranquillity of the present
are contrasted with the unbridled passion and fanaticism of the recent

past. Perhaps in the mid-1660s the translation of sexual passion into a figure for leveling and fanaticism would not have been argumentatively convincing, but Dryden was not alone in such work, nor was the activity of the poem so much rational debate as the orchestration of a complex set of negotiations between past and present. The fire blazes through the night; men are bewildered, mothers are distressed, children weep, all are dependent on the comfort and reassurance that the paternal care of the monarch provides:

> Now day appears, and with the day the King,
> > Whose early care had robb'd him of his rest:
> Far off the cracks of falling houses ring,
> > And shrieks of subjects pierce his tender breast.
> . . . .
> More then his Guards his sorrows made him known,
> > And pious tears which down his cheeks did show'r:
> The wretched in his grief forgot their own:
> > (So much the pity of a King has pow'r.)
>
> He wept the flames of what he lov'd so well,
> > And what so well had merited his love.
> For never Prince in grace did more excel,
> > Or Royal City more in duty strove.
>
> Nor with an idle care did he behold:
> > (Subjects may grieve, but Monarchs must redress.)
> He chears the fearful, and commends the bold,
> > And makes despairers hope for good success.
> > > (949–68)

To underpin the suggestion of a nation fitted out for thanksgiving and gratitude for monarchical government and for the person of Charles II, Dryden provides a public prayer replete with memories of the civil wars and the republican past, and God casts a pitying eye, mercy touches his melting breast. God relenting of his punishment echoes the king asking forgiveness for his people; and this celebration of the king as patriarch and suffering servant returns us explicitly to the argument of plenitude with which the poem begins:

> The Father of the people open'd wide
> > His stores, and all the poor with plenty fed:

Thus God's Annointed God's own place suppli'd,
  And fill'd the empty with his daily bread.

This Royal bounty brought its own reward,
  And, in their minds, so deep did print the sense:
That if their ruines sadly they regard,
  'Tis but with fear the sight might drive him thence.
                                        (1141–48)

The poem then closes with the restoration of commerce rendered in both mercantile and pastoral terms, a vision of London as the new Eden where abundance is legitimized by the suffering, commercial energy, and appetites of the nation, and by the charity of the king. Given the poem's argument about commerce, abundance, and luxury, it seems particularly significant that royal plenitude should be associated with charity and that the appetite for luxury should be again associated with the commercial nation. It is a program not simply distinct from but intended to contest the conventional and now damaging association between the consumption of luxury and the expenditures of vast sums of the national wealth at court. The structure, argument, and language of *Annus Mirabilis* are designed to combat the polemical drive against the court, to disperse accusations of indulgence and extravagance, to translate sexual aggression into civic paternalism. In that dispersal the poem is well occupied indeed.

❧

Of course, *Annus Mirabilis* was not the last word in the depiction of the court's principals, in the display of love and honor at Whitehall, in the conjuring of passions, or inquiries over desire. These subjects are addressed repeatedly and with a sharp satiric insistence throughout the mid-1660s. Nowhere, however, is the inquiry conducted more brilliantly and savagely, or the address to the political meaning of the sexual appetite and indulgence more exact, or the general scrutiny more corrosive than in *The Last Instructions to a Painter*.[42] Marvell's attention is absorbed by luxury and vice, by physical appetite in all its unedifying variety, and most important, by the relations between sexual indulgence and political ruin. So the poem begins in its depiction of court politics, and so the poem ends in its daring portrait of Charles II in his bedchamber. Between lies a world of appetite, vice, and folly.

The attribution of corrupt politics and sexual profligacy to a single court appetite begins in *The Last Instructions* with a portrait of Henry Jermyn, earl of St. Albans, at the French court:

> Paint then St. Albans full of soup and gold,
> The new Courts pattern, Stallion of the old.
> Him neither Wit nor Courage did exalt,
> But Fortune chose him for her pleasure salt.
> Paint him with Drayman's Shoulders, butchers Mien,
> Member'd like Mules, with Elephantine chine.
>
> (29–34)

Succeeding portraits are more daring and violent, but this sketch has its own lovely economy. The conjoining of soup and gold explicates the embedded pun on bullion, linking not excrement and treasure but appetite and greed; and that argument is coupled through a pun on his office of Master of the Queen's Horse to the crucial third term in the suggestion of Jermyn's sexual service to Henrietta Maria, "The new Courts pattern, Stallion of the old" (30). At the Restoration, Jermyn was created earl of St. Albans and posted ambassador to the French court; by the time Marvell wrote *The Last Instructions* the Queen Mother was an aged widow,[43] and the suggestion that Jermyn, debauched in appetite, besotted with food and drink, was stallion to Henrietta Maria is both lurid and comic. Pepys records the rumor that St. Albans was married to the Queen Mother,[44] but Marvell's image does not conjure nuptial propriety; Jermyn is "pleasure salt," language that conjoins sexual and physical appetite. Here ingestion and copulation are one; "pleasure salt" recalls the initial figure of Jermyn, bloated with soup and gold, and its implications are extended in images of physical force and lechery: "Paint him with Drayman's Shoulders, butchers Mien" (33). And the physical image is but a prelude to the argument of political treachery: "He needs no Seal, but to St. James's lease, / Whose Breeches were the Instrument of Peace" (41–42).[45] By fixing the political in explicitly sexual terms, the portrait of Henry Jermyn anticipates the coupling of sexual defilement and political corruption throughout the poem and most damagingly in the portrait of Charles II in his bedchamber.

More immediately, the portrait of Jermyn prepares the terms for the figure of the duchess of York drawn in the succeeding lines:

> Paint then again Her Highness to the life,
> Philosopher beyond Newcastle's Wife.
> She, nak'd, can Archimedes self put down,
> For an Experiment upon the Crown.
> She perfected that Engine, oft assay'd,
> How after Childbirth to renew a Maid.
> And found how Royal Heirs might be matur'd,
> In fewer months than Mothers once indur'd.
>
> . . . .
>
> Express her studying now, if China-clay,
> Can without breaking venom'd juice convey.
> Or how a mortal Poyson she may draw,
> Out of the cordial meal of the Cacao.
> Witness ye stars of Night, and thou the pale
> Moon, that o'rcome with the sick steam did'st fail;
> Ye neighb'ring Elms, that your green leaves did shed,
> And Fawns, that from the womb abortive fled.
> Not unprovok'd she trys forbidden Arts,
> But in her soft Breast Loves hid Cancer smarts.
> While she revolves, at once, Sidney's disgrace,
> And her self scorn'd for emulous Denham's Face;
> And nightly hears the hated Guards away
> Galloping with the Duke to other Prey.
>
> (49–78)

The portrait is an anthology of gossip circulated about and accusations laid against the duchess of York from the time before her marriage, through her childbearing years, the deaths of her own sons, and the poisoning of her husband's mistress. The lines mingle lechery and grossness with accusations of infidelity, rapacity, and greed, and the whole is swathed in anger and disappointment. The portrait is at once astonishing and brilliant in its complication of detail, its degrading mixture of intimate domestic story with criminal accusation, its twinning of appetite with disgust and coupling of desire with conspiracy and murder. Here and throughout the satire, Marvell argues enormity, appetite, and luxury while insisting on sterility and death. The concentration on physical detail allows him to conjure in this court a chaos of waste and passions, an unmatched violence and degradation of taste; and always, Marvell carefully and steadily argues the dissonance, in this world, between pleasure and production.

The portrait of Henry Jermyn glances slanderously at the Queen Mother; the address to Henrietta Maria's daughter-in-law is frontal and direct. Jermyn may be the Queen Mother's stallion, but the duchess of York is a whore. The accusations were familiar enough by the time Marvell drew up his indictment: her sexual career preceding marriage to the duke of York (rumored to include the earl of St. Albans's nephew and namesake, Henry Jermyn), her political ambition, her supposed murder of Lady Denham, the enormity of her appetite and body, and her sexual servicing by Henry Sidney, Groom to the Bedchamber of the duke and duchess and her Master of the Horse.[46] The insults echo the attacks on Lord Chancellor Hyde and taint the royal family, but in their violence they go quite beyond smearing accusation. Appetite and debauchery are satiric commonplaces, but the particular insults of *The Last Instructions* are quite this poet's own:

> Paint her with Oyster Lip, and breath of Fame,
> Wide Mouth that Sparagus may well proclaim:
> With Chanc'lor's Belly, and so large a Rump.
> There, not behind the Coach, her Pages jump.
>   (61–64)

The image may have begun in Waller's "glorious train," but who would have recognized in that phrase the potential for degradation in this portrait? The particulars are not only degrading, gross in every sense; they also position the rule of appetites at the center of a realm in which governance is out of control. Slandering the duchess of York may have been good sport in the satires of the 1660s, but in the structure of this satire, the escalating attacks bring the denunciations of raging appetite ever nearer to the body of the king. Whoring and misgovernance are the central charges laid against the king at the close of the poem, and they are prepared from its beginning.

Pierre Legouis has assured us that "the more revolting charges [against Anne Hyde] may be safely rejected";[47] he means, of course, that they were false. But they may not be rejected if we are correctly to read their most important claim. For *The Last Instructions* attacks not simply the physical excesses of individuals but the political deformity of the body politic, and the one is insistently a metaphor of the other. Marvell's "revolting" charges against Jermyn, the duchess of York, and the countess of Castlemaine are intended with the utmost seriousness. They aim to disgust in their violence and particularity, and they intend our sense of disgust to be brought finally to bear against the inmost center of the body politic. The high-mindedness of this satire has been praised, its avoidance of debasement and its careful exemption of the king from personal abuse; but it is the low-mindedness of this poem that carries its most urgent argument. For *The Last Instructions* insists on, and makes central to its political argument, the deformity, the appetites, the personal vulgarity of the Stuart court. It may be difficult to reconcile the salacious and vulgar materials of *The Last Instructions* with the delicacy of Marvell's lyric muse, but to stress only the high-mindedness of his satire is to gloss over the vigor and particularity of Marvell's opposition poetics and politics, their connection to and incorporation of cruder forms of popular print culture, and finally to slight the matter of sexual misconduct so important to the depiction of the court and Charles II's pride of place in its articulation.

The portrait of the duchess of York juxtaposes sexual indulgence and appetite with images of sterility, corruption, and death. Here is no twinning of pleasure and ease, sexual fecundity and national abundance, but an image of desire and indulgence that is poisonous and sterile, an inversion of the promise of pleasure and abundance that had proclaimed the sexual restoration of the court. The final portrait in the opening trilogy comes yet closer to the center of the body politic; it is a portrait of the king's then most notorious whore, the countess of Castlemaine:

> Paint Castlemaine in Colours that will hold,
> Her, not her Picture, for she now grows old.
> She through her Lacquies Drawers as he ran,
> Discern'd Love's Cause, and a new Flame began.
> Her wonted joys thenceforth and Court she shuns,
> And still within her mind the Footman runs:
> His brazen Calves, his brawny Thighs, (the Face
> She slights) his Feet shapt for a smoother race.
>
> (79–86)

The portrait is exclusively sexual in content; the burden of Marvell's argument is that the servicing of Castlemaine by her lackey is a humiliation of the king's mistress and of the king himself. Love's cause in this scene is anatomy; but while Castlemaine discerns love's cause in her lackey's drawers, it is not in copulation that Marvell portrays the king's whore, but in a lurid rubdown of her groom:

> Great Love, how dost thou triumph, and how reign,
> That to a Groom couldst humble her disdain!
> Stript to her Skin, see how she stooping stands,
> Nor scorns to rub him down with those fair Hands;
> And washing (lest the scent her Crime disclose)
> His sweaty Hooves, tickles him 'twixt the Toes.
>
> (91–96)

In a blasphemous mockery of Luke 7:37–38, this woman of sin washes and anoints not the feet of her lord, but the "Hooves" of her groom. The figure cuts against Lady Castlemaine and the quality of the entire court; it offers a momentary and shocking juxtaposition of high and low. The scene is aligned with and inverts the Gospel, a fitting culmination to the initial argument of court corruption, for the actors in the scene are unaware of the travesty, but the reader is not allowed their brazen naïveté. The opening portraits fix the terms of the *The Last Instructions,* and they are nothing so simple as slander and outrage. Uncontrolled appetite, lust, and debauchery confounded with greed and corruption: these are the terms important not only to the poem's satiric portraiture but as well to its discursive passages on governance and war and to the figure of the king that closes the poem. They are also the terms brilliantly rewritten in the portraits of Admiral de Ruyter and Archibald Douglas that illumine the center of the poem.

At line 523 Marvell takes up his description of the Dutch invasion of the Thames and destruction of the English fleet. What is shocking about the poet's handling of the narrative is not the violence of the scene but its elevation, the pastoral setting given to military plunder and destruction. As de Ruyter sails from ocean to river, the poem turns from heroic to pastoral scenery; the invasion is rendered as a scene perhaps from an illustrated Ovid:[48]

> Ruyter the while, that had our Ocean curb'd,
> Sail'd now among our Rivers undisturb'd:
> Survey'd their Crystal Streams, and Banks so green,

And Beauties e're this never naked seen.
Through the vain sedge the bashful Nymphs he ey'd;
Bosomes, and all which from themselves they hide.
The Sun much brighter, and the Skies more clear,
He finds the Air, and all things, sweeter here.
The sudden change, and such a tempting sight,
Swells his old Veins with fresh Blood, fresh Delight.
Like am'rous Victors he begins to shave,
And his new Face looks in the English Wave.
His sporting Navy all about him swim,
And witness their complaisence in their trim.
Their streaming Silks play through the weather fair,
And with inveigling Colours Court the Air.
While the red Flags breath on their Top-masts high
Terrour and War, but want an Enemy.
Among the Shrowds the Seamen sit and sing,
And wanton Boys on every Rope do cling.
Old Neptune springs the Tydes, and Water lent:
(The Gods themselves do help the provident.)
And, where the deep Keel on the shallow cleaves,
With Trident's Leaver, and great Shoulder heaves.
Æolus their Sails inspires with Eastern Wind,
Puffs them along, and breathes upon them kind.
With Pearly Shell the Tritons all the while
Sound the Sea-march, and guide to Sheppy Isle.

(523–50)

The pastoral is finally shattered by the bombardment of Sheerness (560), but the long portrait of de Ruyter's invasion is rendered in a most self-conscious and heightened style. What might properly be figured as violence and plunder, rape and violation, is magically transformed into a pastoral of gallant love.

What is especially curious in its opposition to the portraits that open and close the poem is Marvell's invitation to imagine the scene as a field of modest sexual delight. The violation of English territory by the invading Dutch is softened, rendered amorous and nearly comic. De Ruyter is transformed from an aging admiral to a gallant lover; the streams are crystal, the skies are clear, and the air is sweet. Here amorous passion is all delicacy and courtliness; rather than coarse bodily function, love in this passage is filtered through a diaphanous pastoral. Not that the matter of desire is entirely dispersed, but it is heightened, rarefied, mythologized. The banks boast shy nymphs hidden in verdant green; the Dutch sailors look longingly from ships that fly streaming silks: all is rendered innocent through song and myth. The distance from the harsh verisimilitude and coarse imagery of the opening portraits could hardly be greater. Satire, now the only literary kind fit to render the Stuart court, is transformed when the identities of the characters change. The mixed modes of *The Last Instructions* are determined not by the poet's will but by his subject matter. Like the commemoration of Archibald Douglas that follows, the Dutch pastoral is strikingly literary in texture and detail. The juxtaposition of pastoral and satire not only allows Marvell to play foreign and republican virtue against native and monarchical vice; it also allows the poet to remind us of the idioms and images of Stuart panegyric, of that language of abundance and pleasure so insistently invoked for those halcyon days in 1660.

The portrait of Douglas (649–96) extends both the literary and political terms of the passage on de Ruyter and makes one further point. The nymphs and lovers of the Dutch pastoral are at once shy and gallant, an inversion of love at the English court; but the elegy for Douglas carries a more complex argument. In this scene the gallant is no aging admiral but an androgynous beauty, a nymph among nymphs, a vestal virgin, yet the hero of the English fleet. The portrait of Douglas answers the figure of de Ruyter but further complicates its terms. For while de Ruyter prepares for amorous play, Douglas is a denial of sexual desire: he is innocence in a world of corruption, beauty among the deformed. It is bravery and honor that Marvell celebrates in Douglas, fortitude and constancy, virtue in all its complex senses:[49]

> Not so brave Douglas; on whose lovely chin
> The early Down but newly did begin;
> And modest Beauty yet his Sex did Veil,
> While envious Virgins hope he is a Male.
> His yellow Locks curl back themselves to seek,
> Nor other Courtship knew but to his Cheek.
> Oft has he in chill Eske or Seine, by night,
> Harden'd and cool'd his Limbs, so soft, so white,
> Among the Reeds, to be espy'd by him,
> The Nymphs would rustle; he would forward swim.

> They sigh'd and said, Fond Boy, why so untame,
> That fly'st Love Fires, reserv'd for other Flame?
> (649–60)

In part the initial terms anticipate Douglas's immolation aboard the *Royal Oak,* but the portrait offers other displacements and claims. Heroic and steadfast, Douglas is yet hardly of age; the valiant Scot not only shames the English youth; he also rebukes the aging pimps and whores of the English court. More than that, he is the very denial of sexual passion. Douglas rejects the river nymphs and embraces only the flames in which the *Royal Oak* is consumed:

> Like a glad Lover, the fierce Flames he meets,
> And tries his first embraces in their Sheets.
> His shape exact, which the bright flames infold,
> Like the Sun's Statue stands of burnish'd Gold.
> (677–80)

Although Douglas was married at the time of his death, in the economy of *The Last Instructions* his virginity denies not chaste marriage but the outrageous sexual appetites and deformities of the poem's opening scenes. More important, it anticipates the closing portrait of the king, itself prefaced by an anecdote of lust and infidelity. In death, Douglas is the "glad Lover"; here passion is explicitly a civic duty, love is the embrace of honor, the defense of king and country. The sexual ambiguity of the figure allows Douglas to be hero and victim: the true embodiment of loyalty and honor, the innocent sacrificed to the flames created from the court's lust and dishonor.

In an effort to rescue the seriousness of *The Last Instructions,* to differentiate it from more libelous and libidinous satires, some students of the poem suggest that the closing portrait of Charles II (885–906) is neither harsh nor critical.[50] They assume that Marvell's envoy to the king (949–90) alters the terms of the portrait, that the poet seriously intends the device of the king's evil ministers to paper over his harsh criticism of the monarch. Such a reading would have Marvell close *The Last Instructions* by blaming others for the havoc wreaked by the king's passions and follies. But read in terms of the other figures in Marvell's gallery, the portrait of the king dreaming in his bedchamber is the most serious and most daring satire, and quite properly the culminating argument of *The Last Instructions.*

The portrait is immediately prefaced by a group of nasty lines on Sir Edward Turnor, Speaker of the House of Commons; lust and infidelity anticipate the king's vision. What the painter next sees, disclosed by candlelight, is the king in his bedchamber, startled from sleep by the apparition of a bound virgin:

> Paint last the King, and a dead shade of Night,
> Only dispers'd by a weak Tapers light;
> And those bright gleams that dart along and glare
> From his clear Eyes, yet these too dark with Care.
> There, as in the calm horrour all alone,
> He wakes and Muses of th' uneasie Throne:
> Raise up a sudden Shape with Virgins Face,
> Though ill agree her Posture, Hour, or Place:
> Naked as born, and her round Arms behind,
> With her own Tresses interwove and twin'd:
> Her mouth lockt up, a blind before her Eyes,
> Yet from beneath the Veil her blushes rise;
> And silent tears her secret anguish speak,
> Her heart throbs, and with very shame would break.
> The Object strange in him no Terrour mov'd:
> He wonder'd first, then pity'd, then he lov'd:
> And with kind hand does the coy Vision press,
> Whose Beauty greater seem'd by her distress;
> But soon shrunk back, chill'd with her touch so cold,
> And th' airy Picture vanisht from his hold.
> In his deep thoughts the wonder did increase,
> And he Divin'd 'twas England or the Peace.
>
> (885–906)

The portrait is a daring and subtle gesture, an image prepared by the opening portraits and by the elegy for Archibald Douglas. Douglas as "the Sun's Statue ... of burnish'd Gold" is the counterpart of the bound virgin illumined by candlelight. And now the argumentative force of Douglas's virginity is brought home, for he is both an analogue for the virgin England and a reminder of the civic uses of passion. The slumbering monarch reaches for the captive virgin; excited by her distress, he would satisfy his appetites on this hapless figure, and in his lust he misreads the emblem. This king cannot distinguish between matters of state and erotic fantasy, exactly the charge that

Rochester would lay against him in one of the most famous, indeed infamous, satires of the age.

Luxury and sensuality at the center of the court are fundamentally political in character: pleasure rather than honor or abundance is the aim of this monarch; private passion rather than public trust is the principle of this court. Though not in detail as vile as the images of the courtiers earlier offered in the poem, the implications of the king's undifferentiating appetites are, if anything, more damaging. What the scene finally urges is the recognition that England herself has become matter simply for sexual consumption, the nation a body used mainly to excite and relieve the king's desires. Perhaps because the indictment is read so directly against the king, Marvell casts it as a dream vision, a device that allows him to soften the scene. But it also permits him to historicize the scene, to anchor it in an episode of the king's erotic history that works, with a wonderful economy, against the scene's elevation. For the allegory is a redaction of Charles's pursuit of Frances Stuart, the most protracted and least successful of the king's sexual ventures.[51] The combination of allegory and historical narrative conjoins, as does the poem throughout, politics and whoring; and rather than disperse the criticism, the covering of the narrative by allegory concentrates the indictment and sharpens the explicitness of the case.

The shape raised up of virgin's face had appeared at court in 1662. Painted by Lely as Diana, twice by Huysmans, and by Cooper, Frances Stuart was widely admired for her beauty, and by no one more than the king.[52] Her sexual history was the focus of interest and gossip throughout the early 1660s, an interest heightened in 1667 when in February she sat, at the king's direction, for the figure of Britannia that appeared on the Peace of Breda Medal created by Roettier (hence her certain identity in line 906 as "England" or the "Peace").[53] At the end of March she secretly eloped from Whitehall to marry the duke of Richmond.[54] In so eluding the king's sexual demands, she was rumored to have been assisted by the lord chancellor, who (the king believed and others suggested) had arranged the secret marriage to frustrate the king's passions and correct his morals. Charles's anger and frustration help to explain his otherwise unaccountably vindictive attitude toward Clarendon.

The brief scene records several details of Charles's pursuit of Frances Stuart: her resistance, her virtue, her fondness for games, including, suggestively, blindman's buff—a detail that renders both poignant and ridiculous the blindfolded figure in the vision—and, of course, her escape from the king's hold and his surprise and frustration over her disappearance into the night. The most telling juncture of detail is provided by the puns of the portrait's final line, where the language tangles together coins, whores, medals, and politics. "England" and the "Peace" (906) allow the medal struck to celebrate naval victories in the Dutch wars to be collapsed with the meaning of piece as "whore" and piece as "money," meanings already conjured with reference to Frances Stuart at lines 761–62, where Marvell alludes to her appearance as Britannia on the farthing. The puns underscore, as does the whole scene, the compounding of lust with policy and so serve as structural and argumentative cruxes, linking the king's dream to the dismissal of Clarendon in the next scene. The fall of Clarendon is determined, the structure of the poem argues, by the lord chancellor's role in the frustration of the king's appetites and by the chief architects of the king's new policy, Bennet and Castlemaine (927–42), who had been linked in their efforts to use Frances Stuart to influence the king. In this poem, so drenched in topicality and so insistent on its author's high-mindedness, the king's dream occupies a special position, conducting its argument simultaneously as allegory and gossip.

The coldness of the virgin shocks the king into an awareness of the allegory, educates him in poetics; but the king's heroic resolve proves nothing more than fixing on a device to disperse criticism. Rather than reform his own appetites and understanding, the king indulges the fiction of "evil ministers," a fiction deployed at the close of the summer of 1667 to appease the hunger of the House of Commons and savagely ridiculed in *The Last Instructions* in the parliamentary chorus that would blame all naval disasters on Commissioner Pett (765–90). The sacrifice of Clarendon befits the wise designs of Castlemaine, Bennet, and Coventry, those emblems of lechery and mistrust. While Marvell hardly means to allow sympathy for Clarendon, the valor of the king's resolve is itself a disgrace.

The envoy (949–90) doubtless softens the closing representation: Marvell's address to the king invokes familiar literary and political sentiments and conventions—the poet's own modesty, the purity of his aims, the conservative constitutionalism of his politics—but its very reliance on the trope of the king's evil ministers damages the credibility of the envoy.[55] It is difficult indeed to reconcile the formal pieties of the envoy with the scathing tone Marvell achieves at the close of the king's portrait or to assume that the device of Hyde's disgrace would effect the restoration so affectingly glimpsed in the pastoral couplet lodged between images of scratching courtiers: "But Ceres Corn, and Flora is the Spring, / Bacchus is Wine, the Country is the King" (973–74). Given the structure of the *The Last Instructions*, its steady accretion of images, its length, the poem's satiric density and particularity, it is hard to imagine how courtly panegyric could have been successfully wrought from satire. The pastoral figures tucked into the envoy bear an inordinate weight if they are truly to counterpoise the violence and corruption cataloged in the body of the poem.

I suspect that Marvell was aware not only of the failure of resolution in the envoy, but also of the aesthetic and political difficulties of resolving this satire. Though the poem wanders toward a conclusion with images of the good subject, of "gen'rous Conscience and . . . Courage high" (985), the line that finally brings the poem to an end is anxious and dissonant: "Give us this Court, and rule without a Guard" (990). The line recalls the closing of the portrait of the duchess of York, her humiliation and longing, her anger at sexual betrayal, and the suggestive coupling of appetite and violence, as nightly she hears "the hated Guards away / Galloping with the Duke to other Prey" (77–78). For the king, the warning conjures the bleeding ghosts of Henry IV and Charles I (918), a mood of anxiety and equivocation closer to those spirits of the shady night in *An Horatian Ode* than to the harmonies and abundance of the pastoral state.

The restoration of Charles II in 1660 had twinned hopes of pleasure and abundance with the person of the king: "Our water laughs it self now into Wine, / Bacchus extends beyond his wonted line."[56] That this king's private pleasures and civic care should have proved so fruitless and so negligent was a conclusion to which Marvell and a number of his contemporaries had come by the close of 1667; as Pepys noted that summer, "the King and Court were never in the world so bad as they are now for gaming, swearing, whoring, and drinking, and the most abominable vices that ever were in the world—so that all must come to naught."[57]

❧

It is possible that the fleeting pastoralism of Marvell's lines projected an ideal to which the poet was still willing to cling. In a different mood he had once celebrated the redemptive promise of gardens and meadows at the Fairfax estate; and however harsh the satire of *The Last Instructions* or deep the poet's misgivings in 1667, Marvell might still have allowed the premise of royal and national fertility as a true coupling of pleasure and abundance, an ideal widely embraced in 1660. In the midst of the disappointments and disasters of the mid-1660s such a gesture would not have been difficult to make, nor should we dismiss the polemical advantage of launching a scurrilous attack on the court, on the quality and most intimate conduct of its principals, and proclaiming oneself an ally of the true marriage of pleasure and abundance. Few would have opposed its reality, although one among those who had warned against a return to the "detested thraldom of Kingship" now stood quite firm.[58] Milton had his own uses for Ceres and Bacchus and his own vision of the marriage of pleasure and abundance, but had the author of book 4 of *Paradise Lost*—that supreme essay on the union of chastity and fecundity—been made an audience to Marvell's *Last Instructions,* he would have been deeply sympathetic with his compatriot's project. Who better than Milton understood the personal and civic import, the polemic force in charges of sexual corruption?[59]

Formal verse satire was not the mode of *Paradise Lost,* nor topical argument Milton's immediate concern, perhaps least so in book 4; and yet I want to suggest that Milton shared not only in Marvell's politics but also in his rhetorical aims and ambitions. The meditation on pleasure, sexuality, and corruption in book 4 of *Paradise Lost*—subsumed though it may be within the vast structure and economy of the epic, responsive to a myriad of themes and arguments beyond those that drove the political satire of *The Last Instructions*—was shaped in part by similar contestative ambitions. Milton was not about to concede pleasure or abundance or sensual delight and fecundity to a Stuart court any more than he would have abandoned Ovid or Virgil to the embrace of Stuart publicists. Indeed, one of the deepest aims and most moving achievements of Milton's pastoral vision is the reclaiming of the aesthetics and the politics of chaste union. To that end and with such contestative aims book 4 of *Paradise Lost* was imagined and composed.

It can hardly surprise us at this point in our appreciation of Milton's achievement as a controversialist,[60] or in our reading of his adventurous song, with its steady (if only occasionally declared, and at times quite baffled and occluded) literary ambitions, to discover, even in the inmost reaches of his poem, Milton's engagement with the aesthetics, morals, and politics of his contemporaries. Yet it is one sort of argument to declare that a particular style has polemical resonance or that Milton's address to a subject like kingship is invariably complicated by a polemical urgency that thrusts myth into historical allegory; it is quite another to contemplate Milton's garden state as an essay on the politics of pleasure.

And here I want to begin, not with the protean character of contestation, but with a set of images that returns us to the pastoral moment of *The Last Instructions*, even perhaps to the exotica of *Annus Mirabilis* with its vision of Eastern treasure swelling London's tide, of commercial energy and sexual prowess transforming the shepherdess Augusta through the "Arts of Modern pride."[61] In Dryden's progress piece, history perfects myth; the fall into commerce and sexual knowledge transforms rude Augusta into modern London, that famed emporium. Milton too aims to inform the mythic with the historical—indeed, to argue a kind of perfection of myth in history—but *Paradise Lost* is a progress piece of a very different kind. While he insists that the mythic gathers fullest meaning only through history, the meaning of history in Milton's pastoral is violence and desecration. The poet's method is to imagine our approach to paradise from history. That perspective allows Milton to moralize geography, to cover the vision of plenitude with regret and despair, to heighten our appreciation of what was with the knowledge of what cannot be, and to insist that we discover the unspoiled wonder of Eden—that we contemplate its sensuality and its untainted capacity for sexual delight—from within personal and historical knowledge of passion and corruption. Personal knowledge allows us to spiritualize the poem, to apply it in a timeless and intimate way to our experience of good and evil; historical knowledge makes other, and more guarded, rhetorical and political claims. In Milton's poetic the spiritual and the political are ultimately one, though the unfolding of these layers of implication and argument is not necessarily simultaneous.

Of course, such devices and perspectives are not peculiar to book 4, though Milton puts them to an especially complex use here as he excites and darkens the literal and literary and mythological memory of the garden state.[62] As with all the urtexts of *Paradise Lost,* the primary image is steadily rewritten, enlarged, and complicated, as the materials are extended into history, a method used to brilliant and poignant effect with "Paradise, so late their happy seat."[63] This is particularly so when Milton begins to compromise the images of pastoral abundance with narratives of violation; and it is in the play between the vision of innocent delight and those narratives where the most excited contest over the uses of delight takes place. Listen, for example, as Milton presents the "happy rural seat of various view":

> Groves whose rich trees wept odorous gums and balm,
> Others whose fruit burnished with golden rind
> Hung amiable, Hesperian fables true,
> If true, here only, and of delicious taste:
> Betwixt them lawns, or level downs, and flocks
> Grazing the tender herb, were interposed,
> Or palmy hillock, or the flowery lap
> Of some irriguous valley spread her store,
> Flowers of all hue, and without thorn the rose:
> . . . .
> The birds their choir apply; airs, vernal airs,
> Breathing the smell of field and grove, attune
> The trembling leaves, while universal Pan
> Knit with the Graces and the Hours in dance
> Led on the eternal spring. Not that fair field
> Of Enna, where Proserpine gathering flowers
> Her self a fairer flower by gloomy Dis
> Was gathered, which cost Ceres all that pain
> To seek her through the world; nor that sweet grove
> Of Daphne by Orontes, and the inspired
> Castalian spring, might with this Paradise
> Of Eden strive; nor that Nyseian isle
> Girt with the river Triton, where old Cham,
> Whom Gentiles Ammon call and Lybian Jove,
> His Amalthea and her florid son
> Young Bacchus from his stepdame Rhea's eye;
> Nor where Abassin kings their issue guard,
> Mount Amara, though this by some supposed
> True Paradise under the Ethiop line
> By Nilus' head, enclosed with shining rock,
> A whole day's journey high, but wide remote
> From this Assyrian garden, where the fiend
> Saw undelighted all delight, all kind
> Of living creatures new to sight and strange.
>
> (4.247–87)

Milton aims first to flood our senses with vernal delight; beyond such proliferation, he seems interested in contest, the "striving" of pagan with sacred garden.[64] Yet who could have doubted victory here? The fabled groves offered something more than an opportunity for Eden to triumph over Enna: they allowed Milton to point the sacred garden into myth and history, to make fable true both in the primary sense his words at first imply and in a darker way as the fables of violation discover their truth in history. Eden is the overarching model; Enna, the grove of Daphne, and Mt. Amara, an afterlife that recaptures the original but points the meaning of change.[65] These are groves of delight and loss, nor is the nostalgia sentimental and generalized but sensual and specific. The juxtaposition contrasts sensual wonder with lust and violation.

It is Milton's thesis, announced early in book 4, that Eden is the geography of undreamt sensual delight, and the poet unstintingly catalogs the ways in which all the senses are given play within this "delicious Paradise" (4.132), a garden of bliss and abundance, of Eastern balms and native perfumes, of spicy shores and ambrosial fruit.[66] But this is no garden of recumbent pleasure;[67] here the principle of steady profusion reigns, abundance is the mainspring of Eden, and profusion embraces the union of pleasure with grace. Here universal Pan orchestrates the dance of the Graces, assuring eternal spring.

What, then, of Ceres and Bacchus? In Marvell's hands, they might just allow the conjunction of abundance and pleasure as the union of country and king. In a world where the interests of the king are truly united with those of the country—rather than yoked by violence or lust or luxury—abundance is the product of pleasure. So the king's panegyrists had argued, and so perhaps the virtuous country politician might be persuaded still to allow, though the tone of Marvell's pastoral in *The Last Instructions* can at best be thought wishful and nostalgic. What Milton does with these stories is quite different, for through the Ovidian materials he exposes not nostalgia but death, the inevitable consequence of carnal appetite and illicit desire.[68] Ceres stands not for the marriage of bounty and pleasure (cf. 4.980–83) but for the consequences of sexual plunder; Daphne is translated into a tree not to evince eternal spring but to escape violation; and the florid Bacchus is here neither god of wine nor emblem of spiritual frenzy but the child of illicit desire. These stories are positioned in Milton's catalog as if they might fulfill the dance of the Graces, for in the structure of book 4 they follow directly on the invocation of Pan; but they altogether deny pastoral innocence. The fragments of Ovidian narrative extend Eden into myth and history: the images are born in classical texts, but they have pointed and timely application in a world where sexual abundance had been celebrated as the true source of national wealth and was now bitterly denounced when pleasure at the Stuart court promised little by way of either stability or abundance. Book 4 complements Marvell's allegory of the "sudden Shape with Virgins Face"; Marvell's condemnation works by driving the topical into the allegorical, raising the literary stakes, complicating the texture of pastoral with gossip and slander. Milton's evocation runs in the opposite direction, suggesting that at the far reaches of the mythic we might discover innuendo and application. Contemporary politics had transformed appetite and abundance into history, though it is Milton's delicate assay of sensual abundance and erotic violence that allows the shadow of polemic to cross over the descriptive and narrative materials of book 4.

The marriage of pastoral abundance with sexual delight is an aspect of Milton's Eden that has been much noted in appreciations of the fullness of the poet's psychological and moral vision; I want to suggest that Milton's presentation of marital bliss is also an aspect of the polemic of pastoral in book 4. For if the myths of sexual violence are partly explicated by the ways in which they include the present, Milton also means to reclaim sexual experience, to redeem the most debased contemporary images of the body by restoring sexual delight to its proper position within the hierarchy of innocent pleasure. Milton's presentation of Eden, it has long been noted, combines sensual with more explicitly sexual materials. Indeed, the first glimpse of paradise is an astonishing synthesis of the broadly sensual and the specifically sexual:

> So on he fares, and to the border comes,
> Of Eden, where delicious Paradise,
> Now nearer, crowns with her enclosure green,
> As with a rural mound the champaign head
> Of a steep wilderness, whose hairy sides
> With thicket overgrown, grotesque and wild,
> Access denied; and over head up grew
> Insuperable highth of loftiest shade,
> Cedar, and pine, and fir, and branching palm,
> A sylvan scene, and as the ranks ascend
> Shade above shade, a woody theatre
> Of stateliest view.
>
> (4.131–42)

The editors of the Longmans Milton cite C. S. Lewis's slightly defensive and scolding recovery of the sexual content of this scene: "The

Freudian idea that the happy garden is an image of the human body would not have frightened Milton in the least."[69] Far from frightening Milton, the synthesis of the broadly sensual with the explicitly sexual is the very program of book 4; little wonder that the discovery of Eden as sexual allegory should be preceded by that epithet "delicious Paradise." For Milton's argument, it is crucial that Satan appreciate the explicitly sexual character of paradise;[70] this, Milton suggests, is the cruelest knowledge of all for him. Adam and Eve in conjugal embrace is a hateful, tormenting sight: "these two / Imparadised in one another's arms / The happier Eden" (4.505–7). Perfect intimacy is part of the meaning here, but sexual delight, and most especially human fecundity, are the glory of this generative paradise, the very center of Milton's insistent coupling of pleasure and production. As book 9 insists, shame and lust, not sexual pleasure, are the product of the Fall. On this subject Milton is explicit, almost pedantic; he turns away neither from nudity nor sexual pleasure in his portrait of Eden. In staging nuptial bliss, Milton carefully and repeatedly argues the spiritualized character of carnal union: the nuptial bower is "a place / Chosen by the sovereign planter ... sacred and sequestered" (4.690–91, 706); copulation is the "crown" (4.728) of Edenic bliss, an emblem of divine love, a promise of fecundity, a religious mystery.

The language could hardly be more exalting; indeed, so insistent, perhaps aggressive, is Milton's spiritualized dwelling on the subject of sexual bliss that we cannot be wholly surprised by the historical turn that he takes after the hymn to wedded love.[71] To that hymn I return shortly, but listen as Milton bends the hymn in the direction of a more timely engagement:

> Here Love his golden shafts employs, here lights
> His constant lamp, and waves his purple wings,
> Reigns here and revels; not in the bought smile
> Of harlots, loveless, joyless, unendeared,
> Casual fruition, nor in court amours
> Mixed dance, or wanton mask, or midnight ball,
> Or serenade, which the starved lover sings
> To his proud fair, best quitted with disdain.
>
> (4.763–70)

Whatever else Milton means to do in this excursus,[72] it is clear that he intends an explicit, perhaps taunting application. Who could have doubted the implications of this language? And yet this is a more delicate assay of court pleasures than Marvell had provided in *The Last Instructions,* and there is a mildly antiquated, even euphemistic quality both to Milton's topics and his diction. Who in the mid-1660s would have been worried about mixed dancing or shocked by "court amours"? Even the reference to wanton masques seems either delicate or dated. Rochester would not compose *Sodom* until the early 1670s,[73] but "wanton mask" seems demure given the polemical fury with which Milton had denounced Charles I's court and prophesied its corrupt return in Charles II. And yet the savage exposition of sexual license is not the most urgent work of Milton's hymn. Milton wants to indicate this topic, to juxtapose the casual and loveless pleasures of the court with the exalted mysteries of sexual delight in Eden, to argue the capacity of right love to reclaim revelry. But the theme of Milton's hymn points a yet more important contemporary argument. For the pleasures of wedded bliss are only in part physical and psychological. One additional term is indicated, and while it is bound to the other mysteries of his theme, Milton gives pride of place to the generative promise of chaste union:

> Hail wedded love, mysterious law, true source
> Of human offspring, sole propriety
> In Paradise of all things common else.
> By thee adulterous lust was driven from men
> Among the bestial herds to range, by thee
> Founded in reason, loyal, just, and pure,
> Relations dear, and all the charities
> Of father, son, and brother first were known.
>
> (4.750–57)

If there is a topical urgency to Milton's exposition of wedded love, to his counterpointing of chastity and court amours, its center is to be found at the beginning of the hymn. The juxtaposition of wedded love and adulterous lust turns specifically on the production of offspring; it is chaste union alone that guarantees familial affection and secures propriety, both of which, as the republication of Filmer's *Patriarcha* and the fury of Exclusion would demonstrate, are crucial legal and political states. The most urgent and the most polemical point of Milton's invocation of the mysteries of wedded bliss turns out to be that "mystery" of patriarchalism. The explicitly political implications of wedded love are repeatedly underscored as Milton documents the privileges of such production: "Relations dear . . . all the charities / Of father, son, and brother." Why, we might wonder, does he identify these charities exclusively with the male line? This oddly gendered account of charity underscores the relations among the sanctity of wedded love, governance, propriety, property, and the purity of the bloodline. Milton's juxtaposition of wedded love and adulterous lust could hardly be more conventional, but the additional terms he provides suggest more than spiritual union. Wedded love in his account is not only the source of affective relations but the origin of propriety at a point in mythic history when real and movable property had not yet fallen under the regulations of the market economy. Having argued the intimacy of marriage and property rights, Milton underscores their political implications by insisting that patriarchal relations are founded in the sanctity of the marriage bed. First and foremost, then, adultery is a crime against the state.

I have spun out the politics of this passage in ways that have not been the primary terms for reading the hymn to wedded love; and yet in 1667, and for an audience that may have had in hand such other verse of that year of wonders as *Annus Mirabilis* or *The Last Instructions*, was there a more urgent frame than politics within which to contemplate the mysteries and sanctities of wedded bliss? Adam and Eve are the great and undefiled example of contractual love in Eden, but another example of contractual love was prominent to view in England, one that had begun, like the union of Adam and Eve, with the rich promise of, if not nuptial bliss, then surely the blessings of "human offspring." Such a juxtaposition may be surprising, perhaps alarming, and yet if we were to meditate on the politics of marital bliss, we might ask if there were a marriage more crucial to those politics in the 1660s than that of Charles II and Catherine of Braganza, or a union headed toward a more profound generative disappointment than that of the royal couple.

Paradise Lost was, of course, a project long meditated; we do not know with certainty when it was written, how much of its composition reaches back to the tragedy that Milton had outlined in the early 1640s, what was composed after the collapse of the protectorate and what after the Restoration. There is no question of Milton's long polemical engagement with kingship; his campaign against the brutality, luxury, and sexual defilement of monarchy must be read against the courts of both Charles I and Charles II. We need only recall the language of abuse in *The Tenure of Kings and Magistrates* and *Eikonoklastes*, or the allegory of political slavery and sensual indulgence that informs the whole of *The Readie and Easie Way,* to appreciate the dynamic of Milton's campaign against courtly corruption. The imagery of chaste union in Eden surely reclaimed the court symbolism of Charles I and Henrietta Maria; but in his great essay on chastity and fecundity, Milton counterpoints the long perspective of antiquity not only with secular histories but with a sharp and local topicality. The energy of Milton's Eden derives in part from the play between sacred and secular myth. But the figure of paradise is also charged by the encounter that sensuality and pleasure allowed with a world that in 1667 must have seemed very close to hand, a world easily conjured through the harsh indictments and powerful images hovering over the corruption and generative disappointment of the Stuart court. We cannot with any certainty argue that the pastoral moment of *Paradise Lost* was composed after such themes as sensuality and luxury had become matters of rumor, innuendo, and public pronouncement; and surely we need not assume that Milton was responsive to a specific text or particular rumor. But the poet's engagement with the entire set of themes, and the crucial political turn that he gives those themes as he drives wedded love into the domain of propriety, argues the contextual importance for Milton's Eden of the polemical work, both panegyric and satiric, that had been done with pleasure and sensuality from the moment of this king's return.

The responsiveness of Milton's pastoralism to the culture and politics of pleasure need not reside wholly within intention. It was surely Milton's aim to recover from the stews and brothels of a king's court not only sensual pleasure but sexuality, to reclaim Christian abundance and delight from those dominions where pleasure and abundance had pitched their tent. And yet we might loosen the model of contestative engagement, for while a good deal of the drama that we have examined derives from models of direct and self-conscious encounter, it is also the case that words, images, and ideas have a contestative life quite independent of the recoverable or hypothesized intentions of their authors.

I want to conclude by meditating for a moment on the resonance of Milton's images and by proposing mediation between intentional and contextual models of contest, for surely both are at play. Without suggesting a system of cross-reference, or even for the moment contending that *Paradise Lost, The Last Instructions, Annus Mirabilis,* or a number of other works were either intentionally or unintentionally interrogating one another, I want to consider them as works situated within, perhaps occupying, particular cultural and political moments, and to propose that the crucial sites of occupation in 1667 included pleasure and sexual abundance. Dryden and Marvell were skirmishing, firing salvos, claiming and denying direct and damaging hits, and all the while Milton was hovering not in the wings but sublimely— and at times not so sublimely—above the battlefield, which in this case proved to be nothing less than the bower of bliss. "Here Love his golden shafts employs"; so Milton began the brief satiric engagement with court amours, but myths and histories, Dis and Asmodeus, also had the power to move and to inform his contemporaries. Who among this poem's audience, either in league with or outraged by the politics and the pieties of Milton's poem, could in 1667 have altogether denied the sting or the pathos of Satan's plea and promise:

> league with you I seek,
> And mutual amity so strait, so close,
> That I with you must dwell, or you with me
> Henceforth; my dwelling haply may not please
> Like this fair Paradise, your sense, yet such
> Accept your maker's work; he gave it me,
> Which I as freely give; hell shall unfold,
> To entertain you two, her widest gates,
> And send forth all her kings.
>
> (4.375–83)

5 Paternity, Patriarchy, and the "Noise of Divine Right": *Absalom and Achitophel* and *Two Treatises of Government*

John Dryden and John Locke were close contemporaries, the poet born in August 1631 and the philosopher in August 1632. In the 1640s they were students of Dr. Busby at Westminster; in the 1650s they wrote panegyric verse on Oliver Cromwell;[1] in the 1660s they celebrated the return of Charles II with published verse;[2] in the 1670s they were attached to two of the most powerful political actors in the nation, the duke of York and the earl of Shaftesbury; and by the fall of 1681 they had composed their masterpieces on the Exclusion Crisis.[3] *Absalom and Achitophel* aroused immediate attention and indignation and became a touchstone of Tory rhetoric; Locke's *Two Treatises* took a more cautious and circuitous path to the world, but its importance to the shape and the rhetoric of modern political discourse is so broad and so well established that it need not detain us here.[4] Rather, what interests me is the notion of these texts as contemporary rhetorical and political events, as competing interpretations of the origins of government, the nature of royal authority, and the political meaning of paternity and patriarchy. Historians of politics and students of literature have given us accounts of the lineage and afterlife of these texts as literary and political classics, but they have described each work so as almost wholly to exclude the other.[5]

On occasion Locke appears in notes to *Absalom and Achitophel* as a contemporary theorist of the origins of government, but Dryden is rarely mentioned in work on *Two Treatises*.[6] We do not know if Locke and Dryden had personal contact in the early 1680s, though clearly they knew each other as schoolboys, and in the fall of 1681 Locke must have learned of the laureate's brilliant and damaging portrait of his patron.[7] Did their paths cross when Locke was living at Thanet House and Dryden in Longacre? The parallels in their careers, their common experience, and even their physical contiguity are intriguing, but what is especially striking is the common space of ideas and idioms that the work of the two men occupied. They shared a broad set of concerns; they wrote meditations on a set of common themes; and they composed in genres that were intended to argue elevation and authority and, just as important, to make a contribution to party polemic in the midst of the most serious political crisis since the collapse of the protectorate.

A list of key words in the opening lines of *Absalom and Achitophel* identifies the most important topics in the opening chapters of book 1 of *Two Treatises:* patriarchy, paternity, succession, law, slavery, the state of nature, liberty, and freedom. Though it might appear from such an index that Locke and Dryden were in intimate colloquy during the Exclusion Crisis, Dryden had no knowledge of *Two Treatises,* and Locke's tract takes as its rhetorical target not *Absalom and Achitophel* but the *Patriarcha* of Sir Robert Filmer.[8] This common vocabulary might alternatively suggest that Dryden had also engaged with *Patriarcha,* a work written before the civil wars but first published in 1680 when it became important to the Tory program in Exclusion.[9] But the relation of the poem to *Patriarcha* is not simple; although Dryden is alert to the general force of Filmer's treatise and its particular cogency in Exclusion, his poem is not an orchestration of *Patriarcha,* nor were Locke and Dryden the only players in the crisis to respond to Filmer. There may in fact be something of a triangulation of texts in relation to *Patriarcha:* Filmer's work is situated at the apex, the responses of Locke, Tyrrell, and Sidney forming one angle, those of Dryden, Mackenzie, and other Tory apologists running at a quite different angle.[10] While Filmer's treatise is important to the idioms of the crisis, its arguments were not adopted wholesale by Tory ideologues, and Dryden's use of patriarchalism is at once cautious and daring. The laureate could see both the advantages and authority of the patriarchal argument and the vulnerability in Filmer's handling of absolutism, its excess baggage, the burden of a rhetoric run to extremes. And, of course, neither Locke nor Dryden was constrained by *Patriarcha.* Locke's careful refutation of Filmer occupies a good deal of space and energy in *Two Treatises,* but he was absorbed in a much grander scheme. He had his own foundations to cast and a rhetorical and theoretical construct of his own to erect; with those fundamental constructions *Patriarcha* had only casual connection. Moreover, Dryden had satiric and panegyric aims and clients quite different from those of Filmer. Yet patriarchy, paternity, and royal authority are the originary points, and much more, for both Locke and Dryden. In those two, Filmer had found his shrewdest exegetes.

❦

Students of *Absalom and Achitophel* have observed the convenient indeterminacy of its opening lines, the pleasant haze of scriptural sanctity that Dryden casts over sexual abundance and indiscretion. England as elect nation allowed Dryden to remark the Davidic identity of the king—long a valued idiom for celebrating Charles II—in terms that denominate appetite as divinity. But the lines are not only convenient and clever. The complex polemical life of pleasure and abundance in the first two decades of the king's rule endowed the idioms with which Dryden chose to open the poem with a rich set of associations. Now in the middle of a crisis brought on by the royal failure to beget a legitimate heir, a crisis heightened for some by the very promiscuity celebrated in those lines, Dryden daringly proffers the king's sexual conduct as a sign of the sanctity and fecundity of his reign. Further, by tracing Charles's power to patriarchal origins, he urges a no less efficient and significant argument, for bound together with paternity and patriarchy as sexual signs are political issues. The publication of Filmer's *Patriarcha* in 1680 set one of the crucial terms of polemical debate for the Exclusion Crisis, and Locke's opening remarks on Filmer's book make clear the persuasive force of founding the origins of government in Genesis, for Locke cannot proceed without first, and at length, discrediting the patriarchal model as a political argument. In *Patriarcha* the absolute and complete sovereignty of Adam over creation, and hence the absoluteness of all sovereignty, can be traced to two sources: the original donation to Adam and Adam's sovereignty over his family. The strenuous and detailed responses of Locke, Tyrrell, and Sidney to this case suggest that Filmer had struck a sound chord in situating the origins of absolute and divine-right rule simultaneously in the donation to Adam and in the model of the original family.[11] That God endowed Adam with domestic and universal if not absolute sovereignty is an obvious reading of Scripture; what Filmer erects on that donation—a structure of

political absolutism Dryden carefully deflects from his poem—occupies
Locke for the whole of the first book of *Two Treatises.*

"Slavery is so vile and miserable an Estate of Man, and so directly
opposite to the generous Temper and Courage of our Nation; that
'tis hardly to be conceived, that an Englishman, much less a Gentleman, should plead for't" (I.1). Locke could hardly have chosen better
than to open with *slavery;* it was a key term in the assault on the duke
of York and a Catholic succession. A long train of abuses was called
into prospect by the linking of popery with slavery: their intimate and
polemical association with French politics and religion—an association
Locke directly makes by suggesting that the fashion for French at
court runs concurrent with Filmer's "short System of Politics, viz. Men
are not born free" (I.5); the threat of Louis XIV's "invasion" of English
rights and liberties; and the final reduction of English property and
property owners to chattel and slaves. All these associations were
unloosed by the prospect of the accession to the throne of a professing
Catholic. The aim of Locke's sentence is not only to reject slavery as
a miserable estate consequent on the absolutist doctrine of *Patriarcha,*
but more practically and polemically to warn against James's accession.
He argues the antiquity of liberty, its social elevation, its indigenous
English character. He intends to blacken patriarchalism as a foreign
and slavish invention not fit for a gentleman, to ring the term with
suggestions of oppression, associations of popery, and the contami-
nation of France and Rome. Dryden does valiant work on the question
of English "character" in *Absalom and Achitophel* ("Those very Jewes,
who, at their very best, / Their Humour more than Loyalty exprest"),[12]
its giddy disloyalty, its savage atomism; but first he must attempt to
define what patriarchy and patriarchalism might have meant.

It did not take Locke's opening exposition of Filmer to suggest the
vulnerability of patriarchalism, although the economy of Locke's sentence provides a suggestive counterpart to the compactness and brilliance of Dryden's first sentence:

> In pious times, e'r Priest-craft did begin,
> Before Polygamy was made a sin;
> When man, on many, multiply'd his kind,
> E'r one to one was, cursedly, confind:
> When Nature prompted, and no law deny'd
> Promiscuous use of Concubine and Bride;
> Then, Israel's Monarch, after Heaven's own heart,

> His vigorous warmth did, variously, impart
> To Wives and Slaves: And, wide as his Command,
> Scatter'd his Maker's Image through the Land.
>
> (1–10)

Here Dryden carefully addresses the very points of theoretical and polemical vulnerability that Locke exposes. Although Dryden later toys with the French identity of Catholic ritual (118–21), in the opening lines patriarchy is firmly situated in a jointly English and Old Testament past and present. The resonance and implication of patriarchalism are familial first and political at a distant second.[13] David's appetite is sensual rather than political; his sentiments are paternal rather than civic. Patriarchy as a political model has honorific associations for any kingship, and Dryden does not aim wholly to disperse these, but Filmer's *Patriarcha* had burdened the political as opposed to the domestic meaning of patriarchy with the heavy weight of absolutism. Locke's reading of patriarchy attacks not the propriety of the domestic model, but only the outlandish civic implications of "This Fatherhood which is to design the Person, and Establish the Throne of Monarchs" (I.72). For Locke, men live not as mere children to the father/king of the nation but as citizens of a state. Dryden carefully avoids this issue, linking the patriarchy of *Absalom and Achitophel* with the abundance and generosity of paternity; but he is wary of its role in political argument. It fell neatly to Dryden's hand that such generosity, warmth, and abundance had long marked Charles's rule; it was such generosity and warmth that the king had brought to England in 1660 and that he had, in a number of ways, made his own over the next two decades. Dryden had first explored these themes in his Restoration poems and had carefully calculated their civic force in *Annus Mirabilis;* now the theme was sounded in a number of "royal and loyal" Exclusion pieces.[14] That there was an underside to this argument, that it had vulnerability as well as appeal, does not deny the long and plausible string of associations among this monarch, his Davidic counterpart, and the life of sensual vigor, appetite, and paternal indulgence.[15]

The opening of *Absalom and Achitophel* promptly takes up the thematics of patriarchy and casts them in such a way that the trope excites associations rather different from those Locke infers and unfolds from *Patriarcha*. Dryden was happy to bathe the king in the warm glow of patriarchal indeterminacy; he sought the authority of that argument; he toyed with its plausibility. He was also aware, however, of the less happy associations that might be excited from the patriarchal model of governance, and those are buffered at every point in these lines. Here is so little suggestion of tyranny or absolutism or negligence of the law that Charles's kingship is presented as a study in acquiescence to the unnatural laws of monogamy.[16] What patriarchs might once have done in their expansive and legitimate pleasure, this king, in his strict observance of the legal force of monogamy and its implications for inheritance, refuses. Although the king is blessed with a graceful son, he cannot inherit the throne since he is not by law a legal heir. The opening juxtaposition of law and polygamy underscores the king's scrupling legalism and suggests that those who would lay aside such laws to prefer the illegitimate heir provoke a state of nature that even this forgiving patriarch would resist. In a set of complex and ironic moves, Charles II becomes champion of the laws and monogamy, and those who argue Exclusion advocate a state of nature, appetite, and indulgence that may not wholly contradict the king's personality but denies monogamy and legal scruple.

Students of the poem have often contrasted the indulgent father of its opening lines with the severity of its closing image, the king as reluctant but vigorous lawgiver. Some have seen in this transformation Dryden's attempt to reform Charles by dialectic. In fact, the indulgence and leniency, the art and generosity of this paternal beginning are a response not to the king's present, lamentable behavior, but rather to the powerful if ambiguously useful suggestion of patriarchy as a political model that publication of Filmer's tract had deposited in 1680. The penumbra of sexuality and indulgence that covers these lines is created not to combat or deplore the king's character, but to rearticulate patriarchalism in terms that carried none of the damaging associations of tyranny and absolutism so quickly detected in *Patriarcha*. As the laureate well knew and as the king would soon again demonstrate, harsh and repressive political measures might be acted out under rubrics far different from absolutism and tyranny. Insofar as the patriarchal model had dignity and authority, Dryden was quite happy to manipulate its associations, nor was he really free to disregard it; but he was also aware of patriarchalism as a figure of political and rhetorical speech to be handled with some care. His solution is a calculated dispersal of one set of associations and the invocation of quite another. That the paternal and the generative argument rather neatly devolved from the personal as well as official instance of this king and kingship it did not take Dryden long to recognize. The lines at the beginning of the poem are so rich and complex in their handling of the twin subjects of paternity and patriarchy that we must imagine less a careful exegesis than a brilliant and intuitive grasp of the problems and potentials of the trope. Nor have I fully unveiled the politics and poetics of these lines.

In its opening lines the poem, like *Patriarcha* and like Locke's *First Treatise,* is intent not only on patriarchy and paternity but on slavery, tyranny, and that useful and ambiguous state called "nature." Dryden's elaboration of the paternal aspect of patriarchy, his emphasis on appetite, pleasure, and indulgence, was one address to the charges of slavery and tyranny not only leveled at *Patriarcha,* but repeatedly brought against the French court of Louis XIV and rampant in the Exclusionist tracts of 1679–81. So far from a tyrant, the figure of "Godlike David" in these lines, as well as in the extensions and variations of the character played throughout the poem, reiterates indulgence, patience, and mercy. As the narrator indignantly and naïvely, if ingenuously, avers:

> Nor is the Peoples Judgment always true:
> The most may err as grosly as the few.
> And faultless Kings run down, by Common Cry,
> For Vice, Oppression, and for Tyranny.
>
> (781–84)

The charge of tyranny is carefully and cautiously inspected and dismissed as the "Standard" of the "fickle rout" (785);[17] so far is it from the character of this king that tyranny might be dismissed as the language of public lunacy. And when David at last emerges to speak in his own words, he begins by reiterating a careful selection of the topics with which the poem began: he has "dissembl'd" wrongs (940); he has delayed revenge; he has been moved and swayed not by the impulse of a tyrant but by "native mercy" (939). It is exactly the integrity of "character" in our sense of the word that Dryden aims to achieve in the opening lines of David's speech as he reviews his "tenderness of Blood" (947), his paternal indulgence, and his general clemency before unveiling the language of "Lawfull Pow'r" (1024), and with it the glittering sword of justice. Even here, where Dryden is clearly intent on menace, he shadows the sword with the language of the law.[18] The careful iteration and reiteration of the language of law are intended to encounter and combat exactly those charges of tyranny and oppression that had not only been raised by Whig pamphleteers but indeed had been allowed by that very cornerstone of Tory propaganda in the Exclusion Crisis, *Patriarcha*.

What, then, of that other instrument of Whig rhetoric that Dryden seems to acknowledge in so peculiar a fashion at the opening of the poem? Twice in the first fifteen lines Dryden plays on a word that Locke boldly announces in his opening sentence: "Slavery is so vile and miserable an Estate of Man...." The word *slavery* runs dangerously vivid through Exclusionist pamphlets and will make a notable appearance in the apologetics for the Glorious Revolution. Instead of ignoring this dangerous word, Dryden toys with it. He is cautious and practiced in such play, and rather than deny slavery, as he openly denies tyranny and oppression late in *Absalom and Achitophel*, he chooses a different tactic; he introduces the word in an explicitly sexual context:

> His vigorous warmth did, variously, impart
> To Wives and Slaves: And, wide as his Command,
> Scatter'd his Maker's Image through the Land.
>
> . . . .
>
> But since like slaves his bed they did ascend,
> No True Succession could their seed attend.
>
> (8–16)

What the lines seem to propose is that some subjects and this sovereign do indeed have a relation that might be denominated slavery. Why, one wonders, since there is a kind of political explosiveness attendant on the word, does Dryden admit the language of slavery into the opening precincts of his poem and then defend it by irony and innuendo? Locke's "Slavery is so vile and miserable an Estate of Man" suggests the force of the term in contemporary political rhetoric; its power and authority are such, it seems surprising that Dryden is willing to allow the word any entry into the intricate network of his opening lines. Of course, we might argue that Dryden so wholly redefines the term, so narrows and excludes its political associations, that he can risk its appearance in order to cast it utterly into a sexual context. The first appearance of the term is in fact technical in a way, for it names one of the two categories of sexual partners that legally belonged to patriarchs: concubines. And the second use of the term echoes but makes slightly more vivid that category: "But since like slaves his bed they did ascend." The line first reiterates the distinction between wife and slave: from the wife comes one line; from the concubine, another. But there is further argument here, for the line suggests not just a technical category but sexual slavery or slavishness. The image of a succession of female slaves "ascending" the king's bed engages with the politics of absolutism and slavery, not through denial or even through irony and defusion, but rather by making a crude joke out of the word. A dispersal of seriousness is here achieved through a bluntness that has the aim not to offend but to disable the word, to obliterate its capacity to carry serious political meaning.

Dryden achieves the same kind of verbal and argumentative coarseness in the joke made about Catherine of Braganza, who is given a humiliating couplet that isolates her simply as an instrument of infertility and ingratitude: "A Soyl ungratefull to the Tiller's care" (12). The joke is broad enough to run rather crudely over the issue of infertility as judgment on the king's excesses. There is something about the boldness of the joke that has the effect not so much of dissipating the issue as obliterating it. Of course, a calculation is involved, that the boldness and crudeness of the wit will not endanger its force as mask—and we have no certain way of knowing how different parties within the poem's immediate audience received the jokes. Among Dryden's antagonists were those who professed offense at his scandalous treatment of the monarch; they were claiming scandal not on behalf of the maligned monarch, who had borne and enjoyed much lewder celebration at Rochester's hands, but in hope of embarrassing or discrediting his laureate.[19] I suspect, however, that these topics—the nature of slavery in a body politic, the failure of the queen's fertility with all its political consequences—were so important that the laureate was willing to risk offense to defuse them.

Dryden's approach to Roman Catholic ceremony a bit later in the poem is determined by similar motives. In order to disable tyranny, popery, and slavery—three of the most important terms in Exclusionist propaganda—he was willing to run substantial risks. In his final engagement with the term *slave,* at the conclusion of a short generalizing portrait of the nation—"The Jews, a Headstrong, Moody, Murmuring race" (45)—he directly confronts its Whig applications. One of Locke's crucial projects in *Two Treatises* is to combat Filmer on the topic of those natural rights that guarantee a subject some "freedom" from the monarch's "Absolute, Arbitrary, Unlimited

...Power...his unbounded Will" (I.9).[20] Locke uses natural-rights theory to argue the fundamental nature of self-preservation (I.56–86, 88) and to assert the superiority of natural man to custom, civility, and fashion (I.58). Thus Locke attacks precedence as an undignified creation of fashion and custom:

> And when Fashion hath once Established, what Folly or craft began, Custom makes it Sacred, and 'twill be thought impudence or madness, to contradict or question it. He that will impartially survey the Nations of the World, will find so much of their Governments, Religions, and Manners brought in and continued amongst them by these means, that he will have but little Reverence for the Practices which are in use and credit amongst Men, and will have Reason to think, that the Woods and Forests, where the irrational untaught Inhabitants keep right by following Nature, are fitter to give us Rules, than Cities and Palaces, where those that call themselves Civil and Rational, go out of their way, by the Authority of Example. (I.58)

The coincidence of language in Locke's evaluation of natural man and Dryden's condemnation of natural man's liberty or perhaps "libertinism" is so striking that it looks as if one passage might have been intended as a gloss on the other:

> These Adam-wits, too fortunately free,
> Began to dream they wanted libertie;
> And when no rule, no president was found
> Of men, by Laws less circumscrib'd and bound,
> They led their wild desires to Woods and Caves,
> And thought that all but Savages were Slaves.
>
> (51–56)

Locke's "Woods and Forests" are the source of greater natural dignity than those "Cities and Palaces" that breed slavishness toward the authority of example. Dryden's couplets contest exactly this point. His twinning of savagery with slavery, his reduction of the natural-rights argument to antithetical extremes, his linking of limitless political desire with savagery itself, his conjoining of rule and precedent in the bounding of "wild desires": all the suggestion and innuendo of these lines is used to caricature the argument for natural rights and to ridicule the use of the word *slave* as a way of denominating the loss of natural rights and political liberty. The ridicule is effected by conjuring savages roaming, unlimited, in the full extent of wild desires, over a lawless terrain. Savagery is a matter of landscape and behavior; Locke's debunking remarks on cities and palaces form the counterpart. Both argue by innuendo and opposition; and it is in the full run of this argument about natural man that Dryden deposits, one final time, and then rather gingerly linking savagery and slavery, his comment on slaves. It is only those very Jews, those "Adam-wits," who would contest their freedom with accusations of slavery. Dryden's argument polemicizes *freedom* by linking it with savagery and limitless desire. The play with this term proceeds cautiously from the opening lines with the obvious difference that in the second encounter Dryden allows the term *slave* contact with politics and philosophy in order to debunk slavery as an adequate account of rights and liberties bounded by the law. What is especially interesting about the polemical reappropriation of the word is Dryden's suggestion that liberty is not simply license but savagery and wild desire. Locke aligns slavery with cities and palaces, freedom with forests; Dryden's argument here is not exactly an inversion of Locke's, but something like a conjoining of liberty with libertinism. "Wild desires" might be thought to approach "diviner Lust" (19), but Dryden's opening lines suggest desire as warmth and paternity. It is lawless political ambition that is best denominated wild desire, and it is on such a combination of license and appetite that Dryden later impales Shaftesbury. But the poet is wary of the term *slave*, and while he is intent on introducing the language of tyranny and slavery, he does so in contexts where he may rigorously control its exposition.

❦

The noble savage raises a central topic in both *Two Treatises* and *Absalom and Achitophel*.[21] Locke sets out a theory of nature as that presocial condition from which men may remove themselves into the convenience of politic society and to which they may return through the dissolution of political union. Unlike Hobbes's state of nature, whose brutality compels men to abandon all rights—except the right to life—in an irreversible political compact, Locke's nature allows men to enjoy liberty, equality, and the use of reason. Though he recognizes "partiality and violence" in human nature (II.13), Locke describes the move from natural to civil society as voluntary and convenient, a remedy for the "defects and imperfections" of man (II.15). To place Locke's discussion of this theme in colloquy and contest with Dryden's is to bring together disproportionate expositions, for what is in Locke a cornerstone on which to erect the state is, in *Absalom and Achitophel*, a shadow in one corner of the poem. Locke's discussion of property is premised on nature as abundance governed by reason (II.6); for Dryden, the politics of nature in a fallen world can best, perhaps only, be examined through civil society. The very disproportion in Locke's and Dryden's exposition of nature is itself evidence of their disparate notions about the foundations of political society. The colloquy is illuminating by its very asymmetry.

"When Nature prompted, and no law deny'd": Dryden could hardly have been unaware of the vast territories of speculation—political and philosophical—that he brings into play with the first half of the line and denies in the second. Indeed, I think one of his aims in the line is to excite as large a territory of politics and philosophy as he could manage. A more self-consciously delineated address to theories of governance comes late in the poem; but the intriguing opposition of nature and law in the poem's fifth line has a fair amount of work to do, and surely one of its rhetorical aims is to suggest that the poem will address major questions of political theory. As theorist of the state, Dryden posits a topic here that, like patriarchy, was not only of conventional interest but of a vivid currency and import. The opening lines of the poem quickly identify a large number of crucial topical issues—patriarchy, priestcraft, nature, law, legitimacy, succession. It is hard to think how these lines might have contained more of contemporary political and theoretical interest than they do; they form something of a register of the significant topics of political theory in 1681, and not the least of these is the state of nature.

What, then, are we to make of the poem's argument about this condition, if anything at all can be educed from half a line? The alignment of piety and nature and polygamy is striking, as is the opposition of nature to the law, and of piety to priestcraft. The oppositions have something of the air of paradoxes and puzzles, and we ought to recognize paradox as one desired effect. But the "state of nature" with all its philosophical import suggests, even in this abbreviation, something more than paradox. For while the alignment of polygamy and abundance recalls something of Locke's own exposition of nature, Dryden has the further and rather different aim of associating pleasure, polygamy, and abundance with the king himself. This much we can readily glean from the collocation. Where the combination of effects begins to puzzle is in the opposition of abundance and the law; for just as surely as Dryden means to identify the king with abundance, he also means to associate him with scrupulous legality in matters of succession, property, and patrimony. Why else should he so suddenly and sharply reverse the fifth line: "When Nature prompted, and no law deny'd"? The opposition of nature and the law distinguishes the patriarchal past (blurring at some point with the state of nature) from the monogamous and juridical present. The paradox allows Dryden, and this chiefly by sleight of hand, first to associate the king with the state of nature, that is, with abundance and fertility—indeed, even with the acquisition of property through labor, in this instance the labor of tillage—and then to insist that while abundance and fertility may be all to the good, the present tense of this poem is being imagined neither in the state of nature nor in the patriarchal past, but in civil society where laws govern marriage, succession, and inheritance as well as determine and delimit authority and the relations between monarch and subject.

In the context of Exclusion, certainly the context that put the most insistent pressure on this text and its original readers, the juxtaposition of nature and the law must have excited association with the much-debated and currently inspected state of nature. It took advantage of that discussion to situate the king as a high-minded and principled exponent of the law even in defiance of his own "natural" propensities. Dryden's opposition further discovers in the "naturalism" of the Exclusionists the libertarian and polygamous implications of Whiggery, nor was he now alone in that argument. Associating political radicalism with sexual libertinism had been standard in the civil war years.[22] Here, although the case might appear incredible at a time when the king's libertinism was so notorious, in a way the very crux of the problem, the lines rather triumphantly associate the king with monogamous legalism and the true descent of property, and his critics with a libertine neglect of the law.

It is hard to imagine that Dryden's audience parsed the lines with the studious care we might now be tempted to expend on them, or that they could possibly have been swayed by such arguments and associations. And yet the case was not exactly being "argued" in the poem; the lines seem to work not by exposition and distinction; the effects are at once faster and more puzzling. Seriously to argue that Charles II was an advocate of monogamous legalism and that Exclusionists were proposing a return to the polygamous, libertine primordial age was so preposterous that none could have seriously entertained the suggestion. But to conjure such a case obliquely and paradoxically, by sleight of hand and through suggestion, gives the proposals unusual spirit and wit. If there was a case to be made for the king as both polygamous progenitor and scrupling husband, Dryden was clearly the one to make it, and it is that case that we find in the opening lines of *Absalom and Achitophel* with its invocation of nature and the law.

So delineating the state of nature is one of the effects of Dryden's opening lines; but he has more to say on this subject, much of it reminiscent rather of Hobbes than of Locke.[23] Dissolution to the state of nature is clearly one of the threats to which the laureate is alert in 1681, and his address to the state of nature in a political context is harsh: where governance is concerned, the state of nature is ferocious, arbitrary, and lethal. Politic society is the only bulwark against the savagery of man in the natural state. "Self-defence," which Dryden ironically allows as "Natures Eldest Law" (458), is a specious device to resist legitimate authority, a cover for ambition and greed. The attack on self-defense is an attack on resistance theory in general and on those who had sworn oaths of nonresistance and passive obedience and would now contemplate the abrogation of such oaths. Natural law as a cover for resistance was much debated in the literature on resistance theory, whose expositor, in this poem, is the earl of Shaftesbury:

> Resolve on Death, or Conquest by the Sword,
> Which for no less a Stake than Life, you Draw;
> And Self-defence is Natures Eldest Law.
>
> (456–58)

What Shaftesbury is made to counsel in this poem is defiance of loyalty, affection, and gratitude: the violation, that is, of all the conventions of politic society.[24] To urge exclusion of the rightful heir is to counsel not only rebellion against the king but the dissolution of government, a condition figured in this poem as nature's state, "where all have Right to all" (794). This is the state brilliantly etched in *Leviathan,* a state of continual warfare in which man is subject to perpetual threat against life and property. Locke addresses this very issue in the last chapter of the *Second Treatise:* "He that will with any clearness speak of the Dissolution of Government, ought, in the first place to distinguish between the Dissolution of the Society, and the Dissolution of the Government" (II.211). But Dryden had no interest in that distinction or its implications, and even less in Locke's definition of clear speaking. In Locke's scheme the dissolution of society is consequent only on conquest from without; the dissolution of government is internal and follows on any of several acts: altering the legislative, hindering its assembling, altering elections, delivery of the people into foreign subjection, the prince's neglect or abandonment of the government (II.212–19). As Laslett and others have pointed out, Locke's remarks in this chapter were most likely added after 1688: they pointedly address James's "abdication" of the government in the fall of that year. When the government has been dissolved, Locke goes on to argue, "the People are at liberty to provide for themselves, by erecting a new Legislative, differing from the other, by the change of Persons, or Form, or both as they shall find it most for their safety and good" (II.220). Self-preservation is not only the right of the individual; it is a fundamental of civil society, which "can never, by the fault of another, lose the Native and Original Right it has to preserve it self" (II.220). Locke's politic society is conceived and enjoined for the protection of life and property; when the legislative forms devised for their preservation no longer function to that end, then resistance to aggression and defense of that property are not only rights but, by the force of Locke's rhetoric, obligations.

Dryden's orchestration of these themes is rather different; he decries resistance as rebellion driven by greed and ingratitude, and he regrets the state of nature as perpetual war. It is hardly surprising that an apology for Exclusion would handle the dissolution of government in the coolest and most reasonable tones. And Dryden, of course, is just as alert to the inflammatory potential of "Civil Wars," a theme he announces early in the poem when he praises the bulk of the nation for political passivity and sobriety:

> The sober part of Israel, free from stain,
> Well knew the value of a peacefull raign:
> And, looking backward with a wise afright,
> Saw Seames of wounds, dishonest to the sight;
> In contemplation of whose ugly Scars,
> They Curst the memory of Civil Wars.
>
> (69–74)

What is additionally interesting in Dryden's handling of rebellion is the steady emphasis he places on the bonds of society, that is, on the piety—paternal, familial, social, and civic—that counsels against Exclusion at every point. By presenting this network of bonds, the obligations of son to father, protégé to patron, subject to sovereign, Dryden is able to insist, in a language none would have contested, that certain threads in the fabric of civil society are sacred and inviolable. Locke's rhetoric is designed to handle in a temperate idiom— indeed, in as impersonal, almost mechanical, a language as he can manage—what others insisted on arguing in the most vivid and personal of terms.

Nor had the "Curst" memory of civil war become wholly historical memory; for some players in Exclusion, not least the king and his brother as well as the earl of Shaftesbury, civil war was a matter of the most profound and powerful kind of personal memory. Just as the point of Locke's rhetoric—the rhetoric of philosophical inquiry and first principles—is to cast the discourse of *Two Treatises* as cautious and rational, so Dryden's language of bonds and gratitude is meant to excite personal praise and blame, to provoke deep and partisan response to persons and principles. Where Locke's language wraps polemic within the folds of philosophy and moves his audience toward the realm of theory even while trailing hints of persuasion, Dryden's language embroils his audience in the personal. On this point Locke and Dryden occupy opposite ends of the rhetorical spectrum; nor is it accidental that so much of Dryden's poem should be absorbed in the eccentricities of personality or that Locke's essay, by contrast, should be so deeply impersonal. It hardly needs observing that Locke's work is that of a political philosopher; but as Richard Ashcraft has recently emphasized, to write in the midst of a political crisis and to advocate resistance to authority and the raising of arms is to be guilty of inciting to treason and provoking civil war.[25] If only out of self-defense and self-preservation, the author of such proposals might well find the genre of political theory usefully deliberative in the handling of incendiary topics.

❧

The state of nature is one of the crucial idioms in Locke's political arsenal; a second is property. Locke's development of a theory of property is not only central to *Two Treatises;* it becomes one of the most significant themes in the eighteenth-century development of "possessive individualism."[26] And certainly the rhetorical fervor surrounding the language of property was vivid in the Exclusion Crisis and yet more heated in 1688 when this language was exalted to a "revolutionary principle." The argument that a Catholic succession posed a threat to property, conceived in the most material as well as in the broadest theoretical sense, was a powerful engine in the rhetorical campaign against the duke of York, and its prominence in *Two Treatises* provides a certain kind of testimony to this status. Locke meant to combat absolutist theories of the state that argued the prince's original and patriarchal possession of all property, to urge property as a "natural" and inalienable right, and to dignify property as one of the principles of resistance to tyranny. In *Absalom and Achitophel* Dryden glances at the political uses of property in the rhetoric of revolution:

> By these the Springs of Property were bent,
> And wound so high, they Crack'd the Government.
> The next for Interest sought t' embroil the State,
> To sell their Duty at a dearer rate;
> And make their Jewish Markets of the Throne,
> Pretending publick Good, to serve their own.
> . . . .
> These, out of meer instinct, they knew not why,
> Ador'd their fathers God, and Property.
>
> (499–536)

What Locke capaciously defines as life, land, material, and labor, Dryden narrows into a commodity. Locke aims to dignify property into a principle of politics; Dryden aims to degrade the term as a rhetorical ploy, a fuel to rebellion, and a justification of greed.[27] He surrounds the term with the language of interest, seduction, and avarice; in this setting, *property* is a device to market political rebellion and mask self-interest. The steady degrading of the term suggests that Dryden was well aware of its currency and its force. He will return to the assault on property in a more concerted and vivid engagement after the Glorious Revolution, but here he manages the issue in a few dismissive couplets and in one rather more serious address within the passage on theories of governance:

> Add, that the Pow'r for Property allowd,
> Is mischeivously seated in the Crowd:

> For who can be secure of private Right,
> If Sovereign sway may be dissolv'd by might?
>
> (777–80)

This passage closes with the Hobbesian invocation of that state of nature "where all have Right to all" (794); it signals Dryden's awareness, beyond the earlier couplets, of the cogency of the language of property. For in this passage he recognizes the abstract and theoretical sense Locke assigns to the term in *Two Treatises*. But while Dryden allows that property includes "propriety"—the capacity of ownership, the "Pow'r for Property"—he suggests that endowing men with a right to property, as distinguished from its donation by the monarch, is the most fundamental threat to its security. Once we acknowledge through such an act as Exclusion the capacity to elect the destination of a man's property—in this instance, sovereignty (in the abstract) and the crown (in the concrete)—then all rights and property are subject to popular whim. Consequent on a theory of property as inalienable right is Dryden's threat of imminent reversion to that state of nature "where all have Right to all." It is exactly such a consequence that Locke means to combat through a theory of property based on the inalienable character of labor. Dryden counters the rather startling implications of such a theory of property not on philosophical grounds and not on Filmer's grounds—that is, not on the grounds of absolute ownership of all property by the divine prince—but on grounds of prudence, dignity, and antiquity. Such is obviously the answer not of a theoretician of politics but of a man of shrewd rhetorical skills. One has the feeling that Dryden may have been aware that he had by the tail a rather powerful and fundamental set of arguments; he chose to combat the rhetoric and principles of what came to be known as Lockean property not with direct refutation but by derision and innuendo, with the shadows of civil war and the conjuring of fear.

Two Treatises as guide to the political poem suggests, among other things, how broadly Dryden casts his poem into the network of political themes of the Exclusion Crisis: property, paternity, patriarchy, the state of nature, self-defense, rebellion, resistance, succession, and sovereignty—all are handled in *Absalom and Achitophel*. At times Dryden is simply deflecting the Whig use of a particular theme; at other points he softens or disperses or conceals problems exposed by such royalist political theory as Filmer's *Patriarcha*. Two passages in the poem, however, are rather more directly concerned with political theory. The first is an account of the principles of succession and election; the second is as close to a full-scale rehearsal of the theory of sovereignty as Dryden comes in this poem. The address to succession is planted on Shaftesbury, where it is aimed as a persuasion to Monmouth to seize the crown; it is also more broadly suggestive of sovereignty through election:

> If you as Champion of the publique Good,
> Add to their Arms a Chief of Royal Blood;
> What may not Israel hope, and what Applause
> Might such a General gain by such a Cause?
> Not barren Praise alone, that Gaudy Flower,
> Fair only to the sight, but solid Power:
> And Nobler is a limited Command,
> Giv'n by the Love of all your Native Land,
> Than a Successive Title, Long, and Dark,
> Drawn from the Mouldy Rolls of Noah's Ark.
>
> (293–302)

The notion of election as expression of the popular will and the nice if paradoxical doubling of solid power with limited command suggest the sleight of hand with which this seduction takes place. The passage becomes especially interesting when Dryden has Shaftesbury handle the topic of succession. The aim of contrasting election and succession, from his point of view, is to argue that popular sovereignty guarantees Monmouth more power than a successive title. The contrast is premised on the false assumption that Monmouth has equally in his grasp the authority of popular sovereignty and successive title. The only title that Monmouth has in his grasp is offered by a Bill of Exclusion. Monmouth's choice is between a "Legacy of Barren Land" (438) and the limited command endowed by election, "the Love of all your Native Land." Dryden closes the passage by having Shaftesbury deride "Successive Title, Long, and Dark, / Drawn from the Mouldy Rolls of Noah's Ark" (301–2), in order to register Filmer's argument about the source of sovereignty and succession from Adam through Noah to Charles II and to recall the covenant, the injunction to fruitfulness, and the sanctity of a line of patriarchal succession back to Noah and through him to Adam. But the poet wants to admit these topics into his text in such a way as not to take full responsibility for the flaws and burdens of the system they imply. He therefore gives an ironic and debased version of patriarchal succession to Achitophel, allowing the sanctity and privilege of lineal succession to be cast aside through the aspersions of the chief architect of Exclusion. Without burdening himself with the full run of the patriarchal argument, he places it within the poem and by implication and innuendo endorses its language and principles. This handling of succession through patriarchy is similar to the brilliant and sketchy invocation of patriarchy as generative principle, as leisure and abundance, in the poem's opening lines. Dryden allows himself to touch on the themes of royalist absolutism, hinting at their arguments and their sanctity, while hedging against what was vulnerable and debilitating in their full-dress presentation. With loyalty, gratitude, and obedience he had no need for the shield of these brilliant ironies, and they are rather more straightforwardly engaged than are such themes as lineal descent and the patriarchal origins of government.

The fullest rehearsal of political theory in the poem is the narrator's soliloquy beginning, "O foolish Israel! never warn'd by ill" (753). Here and for the next sixty lines Dryden entertains, in his most unguarded manner, a variety of political theories and accounts of sovereignty.[28] It is a little difficult to specify the rhetorical, structural, or even political aim of this passage since in it Dryden tries on a variety of accounts of sovereignty and then draws the passage to a conclusion in which no general theory of sovereignty is allowed dominance. Indeed, at its close the narrator meekly withdraws into a kind of minimalist position endorsing antiquity and decrying innovation. It is in fact a position of least exposure and slightest venture; in the company of Locke and Hobbes, for example, it seems alarmingly thin. Since the soliloquy is placed between the lengthy account of the plot and plotters and the briefer file of the righteous whom David musters in his defense, it has, I suspect, the aim of leavening personality with theory. It provides materials for political reflection that gather up in an abstract and dignified manner the theoretical implications of the actions so fully laid out as personality in the preceding several hundred lines. The accounts of sovereignty also preface the presentation of the king, who speaks in his own voice at the poem's close and articulates his own account of divine sovereignty with an emphasis on justice, mercy, and the necessary effects of the law. But the king's speech is less a theory of sovereignty than a series of remarks on the character of power in the hands of a just and merciful lord. Where the poem most directly articulates theories of sovereignty is in the narrator's own address.

What is immediately striking about this exposition of theory is that it takes place in the form of a series of questions. Granted, they are cast as rhetorical questions, which imply their own response and contain it in such a way as to give the appearance of something like declamation, or disbelief, or even indignation. Nevertheless, the interrogative form of the review of sovereignty indicates a kind of obliqueness about the whole inquiry. Its presentation is in fact studiously rhetorical, an inventory of other men's arguments and positions. The passage allows the narrator to review and dismiss theories of sovereignty contemporary with Exclusion, particularly theories of limited sovereignty, election, and property, without committing himself to any single and vulnerable position. Dryden confronts the powerful propaganda of Exclusion by returning accusations of tyranny and arbitrary government in kind; he invokes the familiar and threatening shadows of civil war to argue popular resistance as regicide. Finally, and at length, he identifies the attempts to divert succession or limit the sovereignty of the king as a wholesale assault on the very essence of the commonweal, which, under such attack, must suffer dissolution to a state of nature where there is no safety of person or property. Though the Hobbesian threat is delivered in the bluntest of terms, Dryden's own remedy is not based on any theory at all. It is neither Hobbesian nor Filmerian, neither absolutist nor contractual; it is based on neither the divinity nor the necessity of monarchy. Dryden's remedy takes cover, and with a great raising of dust, behind a different issue altogether:

> What Prudent men a setled Throne woud shake?
> For whatsoe'r their Sufferings were before,
> That Change they Covet makes them suffer more.
> All other Errors but disturb a State;
> But Innovation is the Blow of Fate.
> If ancient Fabricks nod, and threat to fall,
> To Patch the Flaws, and Buttress up the Wall,
> Thus far 'tis Duty; but here fix the Mark:
> For all beyond it is to touch our Ark.
> To change Foundations, cast the Frame anew,
> Is work for Rebels who base Ends pursue:
> At once Divine and Humane Laws controul;
> And mend the Parts by ruine of the Whole.

The Tampering World is subject to this Curse,
To Physick their Disease into a worse.

(796–810)

What is immediately striking about the passage is its flight toward figurative language. After forty lines of theoretical, densely political idioms, suddenly, at line 799, the language turns metaphoric. Now the state is fabric, ark, frame, and foundation; politics is the business not of covenants, trust, and power but of patching, buttressing, mending, and tampering. Dryden seeks shelter and closure in what is at once the most familiar and for him one of the most frequently handled of idioms: the state as body politic, statecraft as physic. It is, of course, the metaphor with which the preface ends—"If the Body Politique have any Analogy to the Natural" (61–62)—and it yields the kind of verbal authority, determinacy, and sense of closure that is not very noticeable in the rest of this review of models of governance.

How, then, are we to evaluate the position that Dryden occupies in these lines? And how are we to judge the weight and authority of that position? These are different matters, but I think that they might be taken up together. Much of the effort at analyzing Dryden's politics in *Absalom and Achitophel* has been devoted to attributing to the poet the most palatable motives and passions that a modern reader might discover for a man whose job it was to celebrate what we have come to think of as the forces of reaction.[29] In such accounts, moderation and disinterest are triumphantly produced as the genuine politics of a man who, against his better judgment, but with an obvious dependency, had to betray his conscience to vindicate his patron. Nor is the conduct of this passage of alternative political theories much of a help in isolating the politics of the poet as private man. Although Dryden was extremely careful of his own opinions, he is obviously calling public attention to himself in these lines by speaking "in proper person," though we should add that this tactic is given an unusual turn by the poem's teasing anonymity, an anonymity immediately unmasked by the poem's first readers in 1681.

Yet the passage most clearly reveals neither the poet's admirable moderation nor his forgivable servility but his distinct uneasiness with the conduct of arguments of political theory. Nothing could be more striking in the colloquy between *Two Treatises* and *Absalom and Achitophel* than the poet's deep ambivalence toward political theory and his very real discomfort with that analytical idiom. That Dryden was aware of the necessity of playing within this arena is evidenced by his careful and repeated and at points quite brilliant display of its subjects and signs. He had read Plato and Aristotle on the state; he was familiar with Hobbes, Bodin, and Pufendorf; his reading in politics as in theology was sound and wide; and he understood that to be a serious player in the literature of political contest he must know its idioms and manipulate its languages. But how different and divergent are the energies of this text from those of *Two Treatises;* where the articulation of theory in *Absalom and Achitophel* is most exposed, there we find the least authority in the poem's conduct. Rather than first principles and full implications, what this passage offers is rhetorical questions and formulaic answers and, finally, collapse into a thicket of figurative activity that serves as camouflage for the poet's refusal to engage in theorizing. What are the implications of the metaphors at the close of this passage? What does it mean to patch flaws and buttress walls? Is this legislative reform? Is this control of monarchical power through parliamentary intervention? What is the relation between "Innovation" and "All other Errors"? What position does the narrator occupy on the source of monarchical authority, the foundations of government, the relation between privilege and prerogative? What, finally, does the narrator advocate as a resolution to the Exclusion Crisis?

It is difficult to answer these questions from the passage that seems most willing to address them, because that passage is hardly willing to address them at all. It is one thing to conjure a topic; it is another to supply an analysis of its character and implications. The passage on government offers very little guidance on the poem's central political themes. H. T. Swedenberg indulgently remarks, "In this passage Dryden glances at various theories then in the air and dismisses them all, for the most part on pragmatic rather than philosophical grounds. . . . [Dryden] appeals to the common sense of his countrymen."[30] But Dryden's is a rather peculiar appeal to common sense since it is made under the wraps of metaphor, and the commonsense effect is hard to discover when the practical consequences of the metaphors cannot be discerned. This is not to suggest that Dryden has no opinion on the practical and theoretical matters raised in the passage, but that he is reluctant or unable to address them in the passage designated "political theory." On the value, motives, and character of the Exclusionist effort, he is very opinionated indeed: Exclusion is an instrument cobbled together by ruthless, self-seeking politicians intent on profit and power. The principals of Exclusion ought to be dealt with through extreme, indeed savage, means. The figure of the sword hinted at in the preface—"the Chyrurgeon's work of an Ense rescindendum" (60)—and glittering in the king's speech gives fair warning of what was to come. We know that such revenge became official policy; the judicial murders of Russell and Sidney indicate the ruthless policy that the king would follow.[31] *Absalom and Achitophel* endorses that position, and it does so keenly aware of its implications. The poem advocates a hard and relentless line toward state innovation; but it does so only under cover of other, less direct expressions of politics and theory. Part of that expression takes place in the passage on government that, though the most obvious, is also the poem's murkiest example of political argument, a passage that at its close altogether abandons first principles and theory for homemade quietism, a politics of sewing, patching, and careful mending—needlework rather than governance.

Of course, Dryden did not call his poem "an essay of civil government," nor have I meant to suggest that the colloquy between Locke and Dryden ought to be conducted in order to expose weakness or deficit. Rather, I am interested in the ways in which both works responded to political crisis and responded in writing that bears the stamp of polemic and argument. I have not in this colloquy touched on the real center of energy in *Absalom and Achitophel:* the quite astonishing personalization of politics through portraits and caricature. For the authority of this poem dwells in the particular, the contingent, and the personal. It is part of the rhetorical principle on which this poem operates that personality and domesticity, the household and its contents, are as political and politicized as the most abstract theories of state. Quite clearly, Dryden knew his way around the management of character; moreover, everything in the poem moves in its own relentless way toward the immediate and the topical. The poem is an elaborate system of analogies that seems designed, at every point, to excite the contemporary reference; the pressure of the poem is almost exclusively on one half of the analogical system.[32] There is nothing in *Absalom and Achitophel* that would argue the propriety of the contemporary as commentary on Scripture: the illumination, the shading, and the argument all press toward 1681. The system is designed to bring the past to bear on the present in all its polemical particularity, particularity heightened by the poem's ability to hold the details at a very slight distance. Surely part of the pleasure and force of the insistent topicality of *Absalom and Achitophel* lay in the poem's historical reach, Dryden's ability to lift his work elegantly above lampoon while suggesting the damaging capacity of libel and slander. He later wrote of his masterpiece, "There is still a vast difference betwixt the slovenly Butchering of a Man, and the fineness of a stroak that separates the Head from the Body, and leaves it standing in its place."[33]

Locke's system of argument is tilted in exactly the opposite direction. The *Second Treatise* is designed to suppress topical application, to pull away from the contemporary into the timeless realm of first principles.[34] Locke investigates quite inflammatory topics in the most deliberative of manners, and he uses the mode of his work to guide its reception as discourse engaged in contemplative study rather than in problem solving. Yet both *Absalom and Achitophel* and *Two Treatises* deploy theory and polemic; both engage the abstract and the particular. Dryden self-consciously brings a full range of registers into play: the theoretical and the personal, but also the eternity, sanctity, and universal truth of Scripture. Locke dabbles in contemporary reference, touching, at a few points, and with great deftness, on such particulars as Monmouth, Judge Jeffreys, and the sloganeering of Exclusion; but the thrust of *Two Treatises* is in the opposite direction. The point of most telling contact between poem and political treatise is in the realm of the explicitly polemical.

Before addressing that encounter, I want to turn from Exclusion Crisis poem to Exclusion Crisis political theory. Here my interest is not in the content of Locke's argument but in its rhetoric and its rhetorical self-awareness. The latter point is the one least discussed by students of philosophy and political thought. Even those who have examined *Two Treatises* as a text within the history of political thought, even within the history of political conduct, have had considerably less to say about its self-awareness as a rhetorical event than about its rhetoric or its form, neither of which has attracted much attention.[35] I begin with the text's self-awareness as rhetoric because that self-awareness suggests ways of conceiving other formal and verbal problems that the tract poses. Peter Laslett contends that the *First* and *Second Treatise* were written together and not necessarily in successive order. He has found traces of each treatise so embedded in the other as to deny the neat sequence suggested by their joint publication as, first, polemical attack and, second, first principles and high theory. The rhetorical form they came to occupy is something like praxis and theory, polemic and abstraction, a clearing of the ground of absolutist patriarchal argument in order to allow a reconstruction from first principles. That the two should have been published jointly and that there should be a number of cross references gives *Two Treatises* a bibliographical and argumentative logic, coherence, and intelligibility. The most serious structural puzzle that remains, and it is a puzzle created by Locke himself, is the relation of the "beginning and end" to the reported middle.

Locke wrote a Preface to *Two Treatises* in anticipation of its publication in 1689 (Laslett speculates in August), "after the preparation of the text for the press."[36] The Preface is a rhetorical event to be situated in the months following the installation of William and Mary, and not, like the bulk of Locke's text, in Exclusion. "Reader, Thou hast here the Beginning and End of a Discourse concerning Government; what Fate has otherwise disposed of the Papers that should have filled up the middle, and were more than all the rest, 'tis not worth while to tell thee." So Locke began the Preface, announcing the work's incompleteness, yet justifying its current form as adequate to the task of establishing the throne of "our Great Restorer, Our present King William" (155). Locke then returns, with a show of anxiety, to the subject of the missing middle and insists that "there will be no great miss of those [papers] which are lost, and my Reader may be satisfied without them" (155). Having reminded us of the missing middle and justified the current form of the "Discourse," Locke circles back again to self-justification: "For I imagine I shall have neither the time, nor inclination to repeat my Pains, and fill up the wanting part of my Answer, by tracing Sir Robert again, through all the Windings and Obscurities which are to be met with in the several Branches of his wonderful System" (155). Once again, two sentences later, Locke reverts to the missing middle, encouraging his reader to strip bare those parts of Filmer's discourse "here untouched" (155).

The Preface is an altogether peculiar performance, most obviously because so much of it is taken up with prefacing the missing part of the *Treatise*, a part, Locke claims, that is longer than the *First Treatise* and the *Second Treatise* put together. The book that Locke published in 1689 was 467 pages; what he is describing is a middle section of perhaps 500 pages, a section that would have considerably altered the relation between the parts and the whole and substantially increased its heft. The *First Treatise* would have been something like a preface, and the *Second* a coda to the missing middle; and while Locke is at pains to suggest the importance of the missing middle, he also argues its inconsequence to the whole. The content of the *First Treatise* is a careful refutation of *Patriarcha;* the *Second Treatise* lays out the fundamentals of civil government. The relation of these parts to each other and their formation of a whole is clear and cogent. Moreover, the logic of refuting *Patriarcha*—a book published during the Exclusion Crisis to buttress Tory politics—before arguing the contractual and consensual nature of government and the causes of its dissolution is obvious. The missing middle, however, concerns neither *Patriarcha* nor first principles, but rather "the Windings and Obscurities which are to be met with in the several Branches of his wonderful System." Had Locke written a refutation of the whole body of Filmer's considerable writings on politics, it could well have run to his suggested five hundred pages; he would have had to address *The Free-Holders Grand Inquest* (1648), *The Anarchy of a Limited or Mixed Monarchy* (1648), *The Necessity of the Absolute Power of All Kings* (1648), *Observations Upon Aristotles Politiques* (1652), and *Observations Concerning the Originall . . . of Government* (1652). Locke and Shaftesbury had in their possession all Filmer's works except *The Free-Holders Grand Inquest* and *The Necessity of the Absolute Power of All Kings*.[37] There is reason to believe that Locke had not only mastered his opponent's work but could have effectively engaged Filmer on Aristotle—as had other Whig controversialists[38]—and contended with Filmer's other versions of monarchical absolutism.

But what would have been the cogency of doing so during the Exclusion Crisis? It was *Patriarcha* that had been published as the foundation of royalist political theory in 1680, and that text Locke refutes in detail. Few overt references to Filmer's other writings appear in *Two Treatises* (cf. I.14, 15). If the refutation of *Patriarcha* had served in Locke's "original" work as the first step in his handling of "the several Branches of his wonderful System," and the two together had preceded the *Second Treatise*, it is difficult to believe that not a trace of the "several Branches" of Filmer's other writings would have survived in the *Second Treatise*, especially given the cross-referencing between the *First Treatise* and the *Second*. Nor is there any reason to suspect that references to the middle section had been suppressed. Had Locke been interested in enhancing the formal integrity of *Two Treatises* as published in 1689/90 by suppressing references to Filmer's other writing, then the frequent references to the "missing middle" in the Preface make no sense. Why, then, does Locke refer repeatedly to this section of his work?

Locke invented the "missing middle," I suggest, as a rhetorical ploy in 1689 to enlarge the prospectus of *Two Treatises* and to disperse its origins in the arguments and circumstance of the Exclusion Crisis. The Preface unequivocally argues *Two Treatises* as justification of the Glorious Revolution: a restoration of natural rights and the preservation of a people "on the very brink of Slavery and Ruine" (155). Locke caught the idiom of the Glorious Revolution very nicely here. Though there is other language in the Preface that was neither common nor much courted in the apologies and justifications of the Glorious Revolution, *restoration* and *salvation* are words that appear in nearly every panegyric on William III.[39] Ashcraft has argued that Locke was a member of the circle of radical Whigs active during the Exclusion Crisis and that some ideas in *Two Treatises* conform to those proposed by the radicals during the crisis;[40] and yet Locke was so successful in suppressing the occasion of its composition that it took nearly three hundred years for Locke scholars to demonstrate it.[41] What I suggest Locke achieves with his reference to the "Papers that should have filled up the middle" is enlargement and elevation; for the missing middle implies that *Two Treatises* not only was intended to address the cornerstone of Tory polemic published during the Exclusion Crisis, but had the grander design of refuting the whole system of Filmer's politics. Such a system was hardly tied to Exclusion; it was situated further back in public memory, in the period just after the conclusion of the civil wars. By enlarging the polemic, Locke removes, as far as he can without actually producing the missing middle, the impression that the work was intended as a refutation of one book and as a response to a particular crisis.

The obvious advantage of Locke's rhetorical ploy was to dissociate the work from its radical origins and, further, to suggest a rhetorical character of rather grander authority than *Two Treatises* itself displays. As timeless political philosophy, a work fit to keep company with the writings of Grotius and Pufendorf, *Two Treatises of Government* seems peculiarly tied to *Patriarcha*. That the refutation of Filmer made more sense in 1681 than in 1689 Locke was quite aware. His response is a Preface that encourages its audience to consider *Two Treatises* as justification of the Glorious Revolution and as refutation of an entire system of political philosophy for which *Patriarcha* serves as a mere emblem. The allusions to the missing middle of his book allow Locke to portray the whole as a systematic inquiry into fundamentals rather than a caviling animadversion.

The character of the *First Treatise* as a confutation is so clear that it seems more or less taken for granted; but the *Second Treatise* has traditionally been read and received as "philosophy" with obvious stress on the value of its propositions rather than on their strategic, polemical, and political character. If my suggestion about the Preface and the missing middle is correct, then Locke's attitude toward the whole of his book as rhetorical performance needs more attention. He was shrewdly aware of reception, of rhetorical maneuver, of polemic, as well as of first principles. To argue natural rights, the state of nature, the dissolution of government, and to publish such an argument—even anonymously—on the coattails of a bloodless and successful revolution, is to perform the most self-conscious of rhetorical acts. Further, to suppress the origins of that argument in an unsuccessful effort to divert the "legitimate" rights of property and succession, an effort that resulted in the crown's accusations of high treason against some of the principals of Exclusion, including Locke's patron, is not only to move one's work strategically away from treason and failure; it is also to underscore the universal and timeless truths propounded in the "philosophical" half of the work.

In addition to suggesting Locke's concern for the reception of his work, the Preface lays the ground for his attack on *Patriarcha* as a rhetorical performance. That attack further underscores Locke's awareness of the rhetorical character of his own political writing. Laslett notes in a comment on Locke's and Tyrrell's references to Filmer's stylistic elegance that modern readers are puzzled by these compliments, that "as a writer of continuous, controversial prose Filmer is no more attractive than any of his contemporaries."[42] But the point of Locke's commendation is not aesthetics. The references to Filmer's flourishes of expression, to his glibness, to his well-sounding English, to the gravity of his title and epistle, to his simpering courtliness—these represent more than puzzling evidence of seventeenth-century rhetorical taste. For Locke means to contend with Filmer not only as purveyor of ideas but as purveyor of language. To do so Locke must refute and deny Filmer's principles and fundamentals, but he must also engage with *Patriarcha* as a piece of writing and with the powerful effects it has had on a public easily fooled by glibness and flourishes of expression. Locke's engagement with Filmer as stylist acknowledges the great noise that *Patriarcha* has made and the book's distribution by the "Drum Ecclesiastick" (156). The dismemberment of *Patriarcha* must take into account not only the substance of the work but also its reception. And here we might be reminded, if in a lower register, of that other champion of liberty, John Milton, confuting the stylistics of absolutism as he aimed to dismantle its logic and deny the authority of the great noise the *Eikon Basilike* had made coming into the world.

The attack on Filmer's "gentile stile"[43] addresses the vulnerability of the political audience and the nature of political language as persuasive instrument. By cautioning against caviling and railing in response to his own writing, Locke shows his awareness that political writing can be dismembered and discredited; rhetorical damage can be inflicted by the discovery and disclosure of the gaps between language and action. The rather backhanded compliments that Locke pays Filmer announce a point of vulnerability that Locke intends to exploit both as evidence of Filmer's incompetence and as a foil to his own style. Although the seeming neutrality of manner and abstractness of proposition in the *Second Treatise* have been widely noted, they have been remarked as if they were facts of nature rather than calculated effects. While a certain consistency of style runs through Locke's writing on a variety of subjects—the neutrality of manner, the ironic distance, the elevation to epithet and principle—the prose of *Two Treatises* is the expression neither of stylistic habit nor of conventional philosophical manners. Locke had a keen appreciation for the middle style, the gait of reason and self-evident truths; *Two Treatises* is composed in what Dryden calls the "Legislative style," the terrain that would rather reason men into truth than cheat them into passion.[44] Staking out this territory is a claim on the province of reason, that most important of polemical and stylistic geographies.

Moreover, the attack on Filmer's style is compounded with an attack on the ethics of an English gentleman who would plead for slavery on behalf of a nation of "generous Temper and Courage" (I.1). Like Milton and Marvell, Locke is alert to the polemical weight of court and country styles; he aligns *Patriarcha* with the corruption and exaggeration of a court that bows steadily in the direction of French manners and morals. Dryden was aware of the vulnerability of the court to these charges, and his efforts in *Absalom and Achitophel* to distance the court and indeed his own style from courtliness are a response to this vulnerability. Locke plays on such associations repeatedly in the *First Treatise:* in the rhetoric of the opening paragraph; in the reference to *Patriarcha* as the "Pattern in the Mount" (I.2) for tyranny (language that reminds us of Milton's address to the *Eikon Basilike*); in the association of absolutism as a system of politics with the vogue for French fashion at the court of Charles I (I.5); and in the ironic reference to Filmer's obeisance to the *arcana imperii* (I.6).

In attacking the politics of *Patriarcha,* Locke aims as well at the cringing morals of its author and at his intellectual manners, his "hudling several Suppositions together," his "medly and confusion" of terms, his "words of undetermined and dubious meaning," his "Incoherencies in Matter, and Suppositions without Proofs" (I.20). The careful exegesis that Locke must perform is demanded because Filmer's argument lies diffused over the whole of his *Patriarcha,* hidden behind rhetorical flourishes, masked by a lofty style, adorned by "well turned Periods" (155). Locke, as exegete, and here again he reminds us of Milton in *Eikonoklastes,* would hunt through the whole of his opponent's treatise, search out and expose every shred of its improbability, obliterate its arguments, explode its logic, ridicule its propositions. In part, of course, such exposition is conventional in seventeenth-century religious and political debate. Like his contemporaries, Locke was expertly trained in exegesis and animadversion; but we ought also to be aware of his particular rhetorical savvy in the *First Treatise,* of his sensitivity to *Patriarcha* as a public document, to the distribution of its ideas by the "Drum Ecclesiastick."

Locke is deeply responsive to the persuasive force of *Patriarcha,* to the appeal of its scripturalism, its dogmatism, its pretensions of title and manner, its eager reception by an audience sensitized to political debate. In the opening chapter and through the whole of the *First Treatise* Locke registers his awareness of the public space the *Patriarcha* occupies. The *First Treatise* begins with a reluctant and surprised admission of the great "noise" that *Patriarcha* made "at its coming abroad," and Locke is careful to deflate and to corrode with a rather delicate and pointed irony the public significance of this "Rope of Sand," this tract that dazzles and blinds the unsuspecting (I.1). While deflating its manner and deriding its proposals, Locke suggests his own public virtue: the point of the *First Treatise* is to unveil *Patriarcha,* to clear the eyes of those blinded by Filmer's dust, to point out that "Chains are but an ill wearing, how much Care soever hath been taken to file and polish them" (I.1).

Like the opening of *Absalom and Achitophel,* the first paragraph of the *First Treatise* is a complex and seductive piece of writing. Locke's management of tone, if not so dazzling as Dryden's, is varied and finely graded. The opening sentence is standard Lockean epithet combined with disingenuous and ironic surprise. The rest of the paragraph indulges an elegant mockery of Filmer's project. With coolness and affected naïveté, Locke registers surprise after surprise: he is astounded that a book of grave title and epistle, a book with a frontispiece, apparatus, and popular acclaim, should reveal itself to be so argumentatively thin, so intellectually shallow. A book "which was to provide Chains for all Mankind" turns out to be "nothing but a Rope of Sand, useful perhaps to such, whose Skill and Business it is to raise a Dust, and would blind the People, the better to mislead them, but in truth not of any force to draw those into Bondage, who have their Eyes open" (I.1). The metaphors argue the slightness of Filmer's treatise—from chains and bondage to sand and dust—and suggest that the very fabric of *Patriarcha* disintegrates under Locke's touch. The passage also demonstrates Locke's skill as ironist and confuter. He aims to identify himself as a logician, a man of plain words and clear exposition; but the elegance of the first paragraph tells an additional story: that *Patriarcha* will be subject to destructive scrutiny and that such scrutiny will at points be masked by irony, and throughout performed by an extremely agile intelligence. Locke's mastery of tone, this coolness in ridicule and deflation, is a crucial part of the verbal armory and authority of his work.

So too is his steady awareness of the issues of reception, of the public nature of political philosophy, and of its force as instrument of persuasion. This much Locke suggests in his reference to the "noise at its coming abroad" (I.1), the effective machinery engaged in the distribution of *Patriarcha,* and Filmer's wary concealment of errors of logic among a medley and confusion of terms. The rhetorical presence and power of Filmer's tract are repeatedly acknowledged in the *First Treatise,* justifying the lengthy and detailed response but also underscoring the role of language in political action.

The *First Treatise* offers, then, an example of an exact and detailed engagement with a text that, though not written during Exclusion, was made into an object of important contemporaneity by its publication in 1680. The cogency of *Patriarcha* for the crisis of confidence excited by the Whig Exclusionists must have been considerable, given the amount of serious attention expended on the tract. If the *First Treatise* alone had survived, or if it had been Locke's only Exclusion

Crisis writing, it would now occupy a position similar to that of a number of other anonymous or nearly anonymous tracts circa 1679–82. But the *First Treatise* is made to occupy something of the role of prologue to the *Second Treatise* in the 1689 edition; and we know that the great fame of Locke as political theorist grew from the *Second Treatise* (which was frequently printed separately from the *First Treatise*). This was a work triumphantly free of caviling and animadversion, a work of timeless propositions and effects repeatedly, self-consciously, and artfully conjured. Just as the *First Treatise* reveals rhetorical self-awareness about its role in deflating a powerful if vapid and harmful tract, so the *Second Treatise* too must be considered for its rhetorical stamp and style: neutrality to the point of translucence, generality to the point of ahistoricity. The vigorous topical engagement that the *First Treatise* shares with so many of the Exclusion Crisis tracts, poems, and pamphlets is missing from the *Second;* in its stead we discover elevation above polemic, a deliberative neutrality of manner. Like Dryden, Locke denies partisanship and disclaims polemical argument, and he would have understood Dryden's intentions in doing so in the preface to *Absalom and Achitophel.* For Locke's neutrality and generality of manner in this radical, inflammatory, and highly partisan tract serve the same purpose as Dryden's prefatory gestures. Both aimed at and both achieved the elevation of poetry and philosophy, categories at once gratifying and advantageous for the partisan laureate and the apologist of resistance theory and dissolution of government.

It is difficult to overestimate the partisan pressures under which both Dryden and Locke worked. As laureate and man of letters, Dryden was a famous and targeted figure; he had a very public past as a writer, a past that his detractors would not let him either forget or deny. Though Locke wrote without the pressures of a published life, he would have been aware of the vulnerabilities of such a life from his relations with Shaftesbury, and he might well have been suspected of deep partisan commitment to the programs as well as the theories of government shared by Exclusionist Whigs. There is little in the *First Treatise* with its exegetical method that could have been construed as treason, but that was not the case with the philosophical *Second Treatise.* Could a contemporary have read Locke's chapter on the dissolution of government or the appeal to heaven without seeing in them a call to arms as the appropriate response to the long train of abuses committed by Charles II and foreseen, to even more ruinous effect, under a Catholic successor? But the rousing of passions, the denunciation of tyranny, and the trumpeting of heroic endeavor were not among Locke's aims in the *Second Treatise*.

Laslett describes the work as "the authoritative statement of Anglo-Saxon political assumptions, the supreme literary expression of English history and English constitutional development."[45] If only to judge from its exalted life in eighteenth- and nineteenth-century political thought, it would indeed be surprising to discover that Locke's work was without literary distinction. But students of the work, though they have carefully and brilliantly elucidated the sources and legacies of *Two Treatises*, have had little to say about its expressiveness. Indeed, if we compare *Two Treatises* with *Leviathan*, Clarendon's *History of the Rebellion*, or *Areopagitica*, what is most striking about Locke's prose is its transparency, its lack of personal voice, its distance from the damaging, brilliant, and scurrilous writing of the late seventeenth century. The Exclusion Crisis produced not only an unusual volume and variety of political writing—squibs, pamphlets, portraits, epics, comedies, tragedies, and sermons—but writing of a very high quality. And while we might easily allow the presence of *Two Treatises* among the literary masterpieces of the Exclusion Crisis, we need to mark its difference from the writing that surrounded and precipitated that crisis. Most simply, it seems to lack all reference, direct or indirect, to the events and personalities of Exclusion. Is there any piece of writing produced during Exclusion that so completely avoids its events, that so utterly ignores the personnel of the crisis? It may be an exaggeration to say that the Exclusion Crisis was a crisis of language, of narration, scandal, libel, and defense, but Exclusion Crisis literature is dominated by a swirl of rumor, accusation, and artifice, by blasts of condemnation and claims of libel.[46] *Two Treatises* may have been a tract for the times, but it was utterly and determinedly not of the times. Not only was Locke aware of this distance: he invented it. He chose for his Exclusionist tract the idiom of first principles and global generalizations; he wrote, as did Hobbes in the midst of pamphlets and petitions, a language not of political crisis but of the science of politics. He chose a syntax of long, capacious sentences within the bland rhythms and repeated folds of which there was sufficient room to all but hide the authorial voice. The *Second Treatise* is larded with principles and careful definitions, with balanced parallels, discriminations, and distinctions. But it is foremost a piece of writing as anonymous and impersonal as an author might effect.

The whole of *Two Treatises* is, in fact, a denial of personality. The Exclusion Crisis teemed with personality and personal revelation; its texts are crowded with character; praise and abuse make up the bulk of Exclusion Crisis verse. The genius of the crisis is indeed the genius of character. Locke stakes out a territory as far from this center as he could find. Here one might encounter self-evident truths, but not a shred of the congested and abusive satires written against the court, the Whig grandees, the London radicals, or the mob. Locke's tract offers something of the timelessness and impersonality of the dictionary. His chapters begin with definitional gestures: "The State of War is...," "the fundamental law of nature is...," "the great and chief end therefore, of Mens uniting into Commonwealths is...," "the Legislative Power is...," "Tyranny is..."; and so we are marched through an elevated register of political theorems. But if abstractions and theorems were the only method of *Two Treatises,* they would offer an even odder engagement with Exclusion than the one already acknowledged. Although much of the texture of the *Second Treatise* is studied neutrality, at some moments we can watch Locke skating toward the present tense of the crisis and hinting at the crucial relations between the tumultuous present and the realm of theory in which much of the work studiously maintains its existence. These passages provide a telling encounter with that other masterpiece of Exclusion, *Absalom and Achitophel.* Though dominated by the contested and abusive present, Dryden's poem reaches toward the lofty and the universal at scattered moments, just as *Two Treatises* reaches, on rare occasion, toward the historical and the particular. Though exactly opposite in overall effect, these works come into suggestive proximity at both ends of the rhetorical spectrum.

We might assume that the detailed discussion of concubines and inheritance in the *First Treatise* (I.123) would be conducted with more than a casual or theoretical interest in a chapter that calls itself "Who Heir?" The Exclusion Crisis was, after all, a crisis of inheritance. Locke pursues his inquiry through various combinations of claimants to a throne:

> I go on then to ask whether in the inheriting of this Paternal Power, this Supreme Fatherhood, The Grand-Son by a Daughter, hath a Right before a Nephew by a Brother? Whether the Grand-Son by the Eldest Son, being an Infant, before the Younger Son a Man and able? Whether the Daughter before the Uncle? or any other Man, descended by a Male

Line? Whether a Grand-Son by a Younger Daughter, before a Grand-Daughter by an Elder Daughter? Whether the Elder Son by a Concubine, before a Younger Son by a Wife? From whence also will arise many Questions of Legitimation, and what in Nature is the difference betwixt a Wife and a Concubine? (I.123)

The final clause poses a question that more than one politician had asked of the "concubines" of the king in the years since his marriage. We have seen how Dryden enters this debate at the opening of *Absalom and Achitophel*. No one could have spoken of concubines, legitimacy, and authority in 1681 without a precise awareness of the circumstances of Exclusion. But close and suggestive as Locke's discussion is, he does not directly resolve the conflict between the claims of a legitimate collateral line and an illegitimate son. In fact, just as Locke's discussion seems to veer closest to the circumstance of 1681, it skirts away from those particulars to propose other "Questions of Legitimation": "Whether the Eldest Son being a Fool, shall inherit this Paternal Power, before the Younger a wise Man? And what Degree of Folly it must be, that shall exclude him? ... Whether the Son of a Fool excluded for his Folly, before the Son of his wise Brother who Reign'd?" (I.123). Perhaps Locke is engaged in a comic allegory in which the duke of York plays "the Son of a Fool" and Monmouth "the Son of his wise Brother," but the heat of Exclusion does not burn very close to the surface of the text, even within this quite tempting and entertaining set of topics. The most striking moments of polemical excitation glitter in the *Second Treatise* in Locke's discussion of passive obedience, of tyranny, and, especially, of the dissolution of government.

In the chapter boldly titled "Of the State of War," we encounter the most directly polemical thrust of the *Second Treatise*. Having begun the treatise with derivations from first principles, with an encomium to reason, justice, and charity, and with invocations of the "one Omnipotent, and infinitely wise Maker" (II.6), Locke proceeds in the next chapter to a discussion of war. What interests him, however, is not war between nations, or international diplomacy, or even "passionate and hasty" actions, but something more specific, what he calls a "sedate setled Design," a declaration by "Word or Action" of one man to gather another "into his Absolute Power" (II.16, 17). As Locke develops his argument, we once again discover the state of nature hovering at the margins of *Two Treatises*. But while that state is defined in the second chapter as "Reason" itself, it becomes in the third chapter something quite different. Now we read that the "Fundamental Law of Nature" is self-defense, a right men apparently have whenever they discern that "sedate setled Design" of "Absolute Power" (II.16, 17). Indeed, such an assertion of absolute power is a declaration of civil war, for "he that in the State of Society, would take away the Freedom belonging to those of that Society or Common-wealth, must be supposed to design to take away from them every thing else, and so be looked on as in a State of War" (II.17). The language, with its emphasis on self-defense, settled and declared designs, slavery, and absolutism, is resonant with Exclusion; the rather curious insistence on "setled Design" looks like a specific reference to Whig versions of royal policy and royal behavior, while slavery and self-defense fit neatly the contemporary idiom of passive obedience. By making self-defense the "Fundamental Law of Nature," Locke enters contemporary discussion of passive obedience, contending against the oaths that all officeholders, clergymen, and university students had sworn, "never to raise arms against the sovereign."

There is a yet more sharply engaged element in Locke's discussion of "the State of War": such a state exists where we discern the settled design of tyranny, where force is used, and where we find "no common Superior on Earth to appeal to for relief" (II.19). Here the language is tuned to a high rhetorical pitch: where men are subject to force or "a declared design of force" without appeal, there they are subject to "Enmity, Malice, Violence, and Mutual Destruction" (II.19). When there is no appeal to justice, no remedy for state violence, where remedy is denied "by a manifest perverting of Justice, and a barefaced wresting of the Laws... though by hands appointed to administer Justice, it is still violence and injury, however colour'd with the Name, Pretences, or Forms of Law" (II.20). Where such a state exists, "War is made upon the Sufferers, who having no appeal on Earth to right them, they are left to the only remedy in such Cases, an appeal to Heaven" (II.20). Locke reaches unusual rhetorical heights here, far removed from the analytical discriminations, the abstractness and generalities, that dominate most of the *Second Treatise*. Perhaps, as Laslett suggests, much of this chapter belongs to 1689 rather than 1679, the "appeal to Heaven" nearly a direct reference to the invitation to the Prince of Orange.[47] But there is nothing in Locke's discussion of slavery, violence, and the "barefaced wresting of the Laws" that does not equally belong to the arsenal of Whig arguments against the prospect of Roman Catholic monarchy or that had not been charged against Charles II—against, that is, his packing of juries, manipulations of the law, and invasion of liberties in the early 1680s.

The subtle attack on passive obedience through an elevation of self-defense into the "Fundamental Law of Nature" could not have been missed or misunderstood in a political culture in which such obedience was exalted into a matter of nearly divine principle and trumpeted from pulpits not only in January 30 sermons, but in sermons preached regularly on various scriptural texts. The pitch of Locke's language here, as in the discussion of tyranny and the dissolution of government at the close of the *Second Treatise,* seems fixed to move and persuade. The collocation of violence and injury, the attack on the perversion of justice, the smearing accusations of deceit and artifice—this is exactly the polemic so steadily deployed in the pamphlets, broadsides, and satires aimed against the government in Exclusion. Whether Locke meant to rouse and inflame or to justify and exculpate, the rhythms of these paragraphs are hurried and ardent; they are meant to participate not in the long moment of political theory but in the shorter perspective of revolutionary action.[48] And though Locke does not often indulge in such direct persuasion, he is fully capable of playing on that polemical instrument. The importance and vitality of the idiom are registered, among other places, in Dryden's poem with its deliberate incantation of law and the disinterested administration of justice. The role of justice in the rhetoric of Dryden's poem must be understood as directly responsive to arguments like those Locke makes in "Of the State of War."

The rhetorical stakes are again high where we might expect them to be, in Locke's discussion in chapter 18: "Of Tyranny." The chapter falls into two parts; the first was clearly composed during Exclusion, and the second, again like the second half of chapter 3, might belong to the postrevolutionary months. The first half concerns us here, especially its introductory paragraph:

> As Usurpation is the exercise of Power, which another hath a Right to; so Tyranny is the exercise of Power beyond Right, which no Body can have a Right to. And this is making use of the Power any one has in his hands; not for the good of those, who are under it, but for his own private separate Advantage. When the Governour, however intituled, makes not the Law, but his Will, the Rule; and his Commands and Actions are not directed to the preservation of the Properties of his People, but

the satisfaction of his own Ambition, Revenge, Covetousness, or any other irregular Passion. (II.199)

Here and at a few other points in the chapter we can hear Locke directly and passionately stirring the waters. "Tyranny" and "arbitrary government" were slogans of the Exclusion cause, shorthand for a train of associations that linked the Stuart court with popery, with Gallic collusion through rumors of secret treaties, and with foreign dominion and slavery. Could the intimation of "irregular Passion" have discovered anyone more obvious than Charles II? Scandal and irregular passion were satiric commonplaces since early in the Restoration; they were at the center of Marvell's polemical program in his *Last Instructions;* and now once again they would play a vivid role in a crisis over succession understood by many to have been wrought by the king's promiscuity. The collocation of sexual passion, ambition, revenge, and greed recurs at the close of the next paragraph, where Locke claims that "the difference betwixt a King and a Tyrant... consist[s] only in this, That one makes the Laws the Bounds of his Power, and the Good of the Publick, the end of his Government; the other makes all give way to his own Will and Appetite" (II.200). The argument pointedly and deftly meant to join the accusation of tyranny and arbitrary government that circulated during the Exclusion Crisis against the potential injury of a Catholic court with the present designs of a government driven by the appetites and passions of this king.

Appetite and extravagance had been the signature of Charles II's reign from its earliest days; now late in his reign they are thrust in the form of bitter satire and high-minded theory against corruption and tyranny. Locke's carefully orchestrated paragraph moves from distinctions in its opening sentence, through juxtapositions of "Law" and "Will," to the collocation of ambition, revenge, covetousness, and other irregular passion. The dialectic of appetite and the law made a particularly vivid display against the kingship of Charles II. It was exactly this dialectic that Dryden aimed to disarm in his high-minded discourse on the "law" and his own exposition of the civic meaning of passion. By insisting, at the beginning of *Absalom and Achitophel,* on the prominence of the law and by insinuating this vocabulary into the mouth of the king himself at the poem's close, Dryden actively engaged in the discourse of the law. He realized, of course, what Locke's paragraph makes clear: that aligning the language of the law with the king's reign and rewriting the history of his appetites were essential polemical maneuvers. Passion and excess had come to be synonymous with the court and with the person of the monarch; there was no combating these matters through denial. That much all the players in this drama would have to acknowledge. But the alignment of appetite and passion with tyranny and with the rule of arbitrary will was not the only geometry this topic might allow.

The opening of Dryden's poem is an exposition of appetite that insistently aligns it with public welfare; and here the patriarchal argument was crucially useful. The importance of putting appetite and the law into happy conjunction under monarchy is even more clearly evident once we have seen how passion and arbitrary government could be wielded as synonyms. Not only does Dryden realign the idioms, so that appetite and the law are insistently conjoined; he threads the terms through the whole of the poem so that generosity and abundance become synonymous with loyalty, while penury, meanness, and denial are made nearly to define rebellion. Dryden's handling of appetite argues, in fact, the opposite to those associations one reads out of the language of passion, appetite, and the will in Locke's remarks on tyranny.

The juxtaposition of Dryden and Locke on passion and tyranny heightens our awareness of just how carefully defended is the portrait of appetite in *Absalom and Achitophel;* it should also remind us of how caustic and how highly charged was Locke's collocation of these terms. No one reading Locke's manuscript in 1681 or his printed text in 1689 could have doubted that the history of monarchy and appetite in the seventeenth century could best be written from the annals of Charles II's reign. It was a history recorded by more than one of the king's courtiers and concubines,[49] a history that emphasized just how political was the body politic of this monarch. Of course, corruption and sensuality as political topics have long histories, but appetite and the private will had one especially prominent referent in the later seventeenth century. We are familiar with the theme of bland merriment in popular histories of Charles II's reign, but the late 1670s found nothing bland and rather little gaiety in his court. Appetite and arbitrary government were highly charged words in the political lexicon, and Locke handles them as instruments of polemical encounter that might be thrust against Stuart "tyranny," not in an analytical mode but rhetorically and polemically, to persuade and to inflame. Appetite and arbitrary will might be wielded as justification for the appeal to heaven and in defense of the dissolution of government, the last resort for a people oppressed by "a long train of Abuses, Prevarications, and Artifices, all tending the same way" (II.225). This was a language embedded in Whig polemic, and it shows us how closely aligned, even in this text of insistent philosophical purport, first principles might be with the devices of political persuasion. And where might such an appeal to "the People" end?

> They cannot but feel, what they lie under, and see, whither they are going; 'tis not to be wonder'd, that they should then rouze themselves, and endeavour to put the rule into such hands, which may secure to them the ends for which Government was at first erected; and without which, ancient Names, and specious Forms, are so far from being better, that they are much worse, than the state of Nature, or pure Anarchy; the inconveniencies being all as great and as near, but the remedy farther off and more difficult. (II.225)

Locke's subject is revolution; his indictment is brought against a regime denominated by appetite, abuse, and deceit; and his remedy is to argue that in 1681 England should recognize that it had devolved to that state of nature known more accurately under the name of tyranny. The language combines caution and provocation; indeed, the passage performs a delicate balancing act between the two. And as Locke moves toward the explicit invocation of civil war as the condition provoked by—and the remedy for—Stuart absolutism, he wavers between the impersonal and the inflammatory. Such remedy is an "endeavour to put the rule into such hands, which may secure to them the ends for which Government was at first erected"; but Locke does not leave the argument at this distance. He glosses "endeavour" first as "the state of Nature" and then as "pure Anarchy." The embrace of anarchy is as close to a direct call to armed resistance as Locke comes in the *Second Treatise,* and while he cannot quite face the boldness of calling for war on the king, the embrace of anarchy is clear-eyed and forceful. It is exactly the point that the narrator of *Absalom and Achitophel* makes in his unmasking of peace as "War in Masquerade" (752) and that David himself addresses in his sharp condemnation of factious crowds and brutal rage, the cold and bloody artifice of civil war. In invoking that memory, Dryden had the clear rhetorical advantage; Locke skillfully manipulates the idioms of abuse under which a people will long suffer, but in the condemnation of Locke's solution, Dryden's poem won the rhetorical day. Although 1681 veered close to civil war, neither the Exclusion Crisis nor the arms later introduced by the Prince of Orange were sufficient to translate civil society into a state of nature with its voluntaristic consequences.

The structure of the *Second Treatise* is intended to argue from definitions and first principles to political action. General arguments and first principles occupy its initial chapters; the middle sections address the forms of the commonwealth; and the last four chapters handle, with increasing rhetorical fervor, the matters of conquest, usurpation, tyranny, and the dissolution of government. One could imagine a structure for the *Second Treatise* that worked in reverse fashion, beginning with the dissolution of government, displaying its remedy in an argument that would ascend from the particulars of the state of anarchy through the proper constitution of the polity to first principles. But Locke is cautiously aware of persuasion, and the structure of *Two Treatises* descends from abstractions to remedies. His was a solution with a nearly universally contemned memory, and while the provoking of dissatisfaction with the government was hardly novel in 1681, Locke's remedy for such dissatisfaction was both unusual and inflammatory in the extreme. As Locke recognizes in his discussion of the dissolution of government, societies are slow to change, reluctant to acknowledge faults and to shift foundations:

> People are not so easily got out of their old Forms, as some are apt to suggest. They are hardly to be prevailed with to amend the acknowledg'd Faults, in the Frame they have been accustom'd to. . . . This slowness and aversion in the People to quit their old Constitutions, has, in the many Revolutions which have been seen in this Kingdom, in this and former Ages, still kept us to, or, after some interval of fruitless attempts, still brought us back again to our old Legislative of King, Lords and Commons. (II.223)

The *Second Treatise* aims to provoke the nation "To change Foundations, cast the Frame anew" (*Absalom and Achitophel*, 805). Small wonder, then, that Locke should have chosen the language of first principles and imagined a state of nature not as the primordial past in the long chronology of patriarchy extending from Adam to the court of Charles II, but as a synchronous condition to which a state might always and happily resolve itself. Locke's analytical generalities; like Dryden's layered histories, are not indifferent idioms; they are part of the deeply resourceful polemic of these works and this moment. The distance from civil society to the state of nature is much easier to cross if the bridge does not have to span the history of civilization.

6 Representing the Revolution:
Don Sebastian and
Williamite Panegyric

On October 28, 1688, the Prince of Orange and fifteen thousand troops set sail for England; they were turned back by storms, but a successful expedition arrived at Tor Bay on November 5, the eighty-third anniversary of the Gunpowder Plot. So began a remarkable series of events whose provenance and meaning were contested from the moment of the prince's arrival. The character of William's intervention, the nature of James's retreat, the role of the revolution in securing the Protestant faith and parliamentary freedom: all were vigorously debated in the Convention that met in January 1689 and in the months and years following the coronation of William and Mary. The events of 1688/89 were regretted and denounced by those who remained loyal to James II; they also provided materials for constructing the story of the progressive foundation of political liberty, what we have come to know as the Whig interpretation of history. That story has come under revision and attack: historians are now as likely to argue the revolution's conservative character. Some suggest that the term *revolution* itself is a misnomer for the events of the late fall and winter of 1688/89;[1] and one among them has recently argued the unruffled continuity of patriarchalism, deference, and divine-right ideology for the whole of the late seventeenth and eighteenth centuries.[2] However contested and revised, the events of 1688/89— among them the first edition of Locke's *Two Treatises of Government* and the creation of an English Bill of Rights—remain fixed as moments and texts of the highest importance in Anglo-American political history.

Yet if we look to the ways in which literary culture reflected and enacted the revolutionary moment, we might be surprised by the indifference of the literary record to the fact of the revolution. The standard histories of English literature, even studies of Augustan writing, hardly acknowledge the events of these months. And there is some justification for their silence. It is hard to think of a political crisis in this century so unremarked in literary form. The literary response to earlier political change and crisis is remarkable: Shakespeare meditating on the accession of James I in *Macbeth;*[3] Marvell worrying the relations between power and justice in 1649; Milton entering the whirlwind of national debate in 1659 with *The Readie and Easie Way;* or the subtleties and provocations of Exclusion displayed in *Venice Preserv'd* and *Absalom and Achitophel.* And we might well expect a literature of substantial energy and art to emerge in the months following William's intervention. But a reading of the cultural record produces few analogues to these masterpieces.

I want to speculate on the reasons for literary silence, partly for what that silence reveals of this revolution and partly for what it suggests about the cultural absorption of 1688. Both issues involve us in thinking about the character of the revolution, its representation, and what effect the political habits of the revolution—habits of obliqueness and innuendo—had on the literary imagination. In turn, I want to examine the revolution through its only literary masterpiece, *Don Sebastian;* and retrospectively, I want to consider the shadow that this revolution cast over one of the great achievements of late seventeenth-century literature: the translation of Virgil that Dryden published in 1697. The success of *Don Sebastian,* popular and aesthetic, raises questions about the force and identity of Jacobite ideals and values in the midst of the revolution; the *Virgil* allows us to consider the fate of heroic literature in a culture committed by 1697 to a European destiny and to a commercial revolution that for the next century and beyond fueled the creation of an empire.

On the eve of the revolution and directly in its aftermath we might assume that the work of literature would have been obvious and extensive. The events of 1688 were in need of defense, interpretation, and celebration. A Horatian ode on the landing at Tor Bay might have represented the complexity and anxiety of the moment, calibrated the fluidity of events, the possibilities of subversion, the moral and ethical consequences of political action, the dangers of resistance and passivity. Slightly more than a year before the revolution we have an example of a literary text that does exactly this kind of work. *The*

Hind and the Panther expresses the great sense of danger and instability that marked James's last year. What Dryden communicates in this intricate and evasive work is the difficulty of achieving political credibility for a monarch much in need of credibility and explanation. A fair amount of its energy is expended in arguments for the rectitude and high-mindedness of the regime. But the poem suggests other facts about James's rule: the anxiety of those charged with its defense, the precariousness of its political and religious aims. Obliqueness and fright run through the poem, and its defensiveness conveys an idea of how significant must have been the resistance to James's monarchy by the middle of 1687.

The revolutionary enterprise found no such expression or exaltation. The only great literary text of the revolution, and it comes almost a year after William's landing at Tor Bay, is a tragedy in blank verse that exalts the high courage and principles, not of the leaders of the revolution, but of the monarch who had fled his country and was by then pawn and dependent of Louis XIV. Rather than a revolutionary text, Dryden's *Don Sebastian* is a reactionary creed: it argued not the high-mindedness of the revolution, but the terms in which its apologetics might be resisted; it celebrated not the preservation of liberties, but the cultural resources that could be summoned on behalf of a deposed and discredited regime.

Perhaps it was merely an accident of literary history that the former laureate should have been trapped in his Roman Catholicism and Jacobitism in 1689; that the greatest exponent and exemplar of high culture in the 1690s should have been an adherent of Stuart monarchy and Stuart policy; and that the closest student of his art, Alexander Pope, should also have been a Catholic and Jacobite, and in his first major work, *Windsor-Forest,* should have identified himself as an acolyte of Stuart monarchy. Was it, however, solely chance that high culture should have been so firmly attached to Stuart monarchy, and that the revolution should have been attacked in cultural terms as boorish, illiterate, and dull;[4] that William's first laureate was Thomas Shadwell, dunce of *Mac Flecknoe;* and that the Williamite epic should have been Blackmore's *Prince Arthur* rather than Dryden's *Virgil?*

In fact the bonds between the Stuart court and literary culture are deep and complex in this century. Restoration panegyrists insistently linked the return of Stuart monarchy with the revival of arts and letters.[5] The patronage and production of high culture in the decades following the Restoration are impressive, not least so under James II.

But it is to simplify the sources of that productivity to suggest that wit and luxury were the exclusive model, precondition, or main support of literary art. We should not forget that Milton's epics were products of the first years of the Restoration, or that Bunyan and Baxter could hardly have found the court a source of inspiration. Clearly, both patronage by and resistance to the court play significant roles in Restoration culture. The sudden disappearance of the center of that patronage with the flight of James II must have been a source of some consternation in 1688. Yet not only did the patronage system itself continue—and often in the same hands—but new patrons emerged on the market together with a gathering force of patronage deployed for specifically political aims and purposes in the 1690s. The sudden flurry of new editions of Milton's works following the revolution suggests the increasing role of party politics in the formulation of literary canons.[6] But the Whiggish co-option of Milton argues more than a politicized canon, for republication, translation, and adaptation are more characteristic of the 1690s than is literary invention, a fact about the decade that returns us to the center of the problem, the literary silence surrounding the revolution.

Not all was silence, however. One of the most revealing texts of the revolution is the set of debates engaged in by members of the Convention that settled the crown on William and Mary.[7] Those who have studied the language of the Convention have noted the detailed and careful exchanges surrounding the choice of words for describing James's absence and William's presence in England. The scrupling over language had an immediate and important political rationale. On the correct choice of words rested a cornerstone of the revolution. For if the debates could satisfy the conscience of those who had sworn allegiance and passive obedience to James II, the revolution might be swiftly secured. Hence the careful deliberation over a vocabulary that would neutralize and pacify, that would suggest James's abandonment of the throne, its subsequent vacancy, and William's entry into England as an effort to secure and preserve parliamentary liberty. The deliberation was an effort at discovering a way of representing the revolution that would cause the least disturbance to the civic fabric, that would raise the fewest qualms, legal scruples, and ethical anxieties. Such a discovery was made in the language of vacancy and abdication.[8] Some regarded the debates as exercises in hypocrisy or self-delusion, but the efforts to fix a neutralizing vocabulary were successful. The nation as a whole allowed the revolution without hesitation. It helped, of course, that James had conducted an increasingly vigorous campaign to install his religion and coreligionists and secure the throne for Roman Catholicism in perpetuity, and the revolution was accompanied by a flood of anti-Catholic propaganda.[9] But the linguistic activities of the Convention should not be underestimated in calculating the success of the revolution.

In the story told by these debates we find not only a neutralizing and pacifying vocabulary but also a language that suggests the remarkable passivity of the nation. This is a revolution not of heroic endeavor and godly militancy but of deep impassivity and retreat, not a civil insurrection but a revolution effected by conspiracy and secret invitation. William was blown across the channel by a Protestant wind, the nation sat passively obedient (or disobedient, as the case may have been), and James withdrew from office.[10] To cast the nation as victim at once of Jesuit machination and Protestant redemption clears the people of complicity in both Roman Catholic intrigue and Dutch usurpation. And such passivity is to be found not only in the debates but everywhere in the verse celebrating the deliverance. For the nation to have played a passive, if willing, role in the rescue means that some of the scrupling over passive obedience can be put to rest and that a de facto acceptance of William and Mary can be taken as the route of least political resistance. Passive obedience was a banner that flew high over the camp of nonjurors and Jacobites; it was an idiom of considerable moral capital and authority.[11] National passivity allowed the mysteries of providence to wipe clear the crimes of rebellion and abjuration of oaths. So long as the revolution was acquiesced in rather than effected, the politics of conspiracy and rebellion could be eased into the principle of happy deliverance. If we miss Old Testament ethical vigor and moral urgency in the language of this Protestant revolution, if we are surprised by the supineness of this foundation of liberty, we need to be aware that the civil wars remained part of the context of any constitutional change in the seventeenth century. It was James's father, after all, who had gone to the block, and some of those who had witnessed the execution would still have been alive at the time of the revolution.

If the revolution of 1688 is glorious in part because it is bloodless, cultural silence may have been one of the minor expenses incurred along the passive way. Not that the conventional effort is entirely absent, but it seems hampered, confused in its handling of themes, caught out for an idiom, a language of revolutionary exaltation, nervously suspended between the claims of conscience and expediency. A respectable amount of verse was in fact produced, although by comparison with the Restoration (a comparison that panegyrists tactfully avoid), the amount of celebratory verse is surprisingly small. And though the quality of writing is lower than what we would expect even for corporate and occasional exercises—university volumes from Oxford and Cambridge as well as showpieces by individual entrepreneurs—the panegyrics taken as a whole have an interesting story to tell about the engagement of high culture with this revolution. What becomes immediately clear from the body of this verse is that both the character of the revolution and the ways in which it was represented work against the creation of a heroic idiom for 1688. Not simply that the events of the revolution were indeed bloodless, that the reigning monarch fled the country in fear, but also that the revolution was hardly the result of a national effort. This revolution was deliverance from outside and above, a providential revolution wrought by a foreign prince governing a former military and current commercial rival, stadholder of a nation that had effected a tremendous national humiliation in 1667. This prince was now chosen by a mysterious providence to spare a luckless people from the miseries of "popery and slavery"; a Dutchman was needed to rescue the virgin from the dragon's jaws.[12] The language of deliverance allows large sway for providential readings of this event, and sermon after sermon as well as nearly every panegyric celebrates the unpredictable and miraculous ways of providence. Although we need to allow that the conventions of panegyric include such elevation and agency, this heavenly rescue was effected by neither a martial hero nor a fearsome god. Zeal and enthusiasm were figures not welcome in this Protestant recovery; while miraculous, the revolution was no leveling or overturning but a victory of piety and moderation.

From the central fact of national passivity and acquiescence there seems to be no escape. Nor perhaps was one wanted. Quite consistently in the panegyrics, the nation is depicted as confused, unhappy, reluctant, and recumbent. England lies wasted and dismal; justice has withdrawn; the laws lie broken and trampled; the nation is prey to insulting foes.[13] The rescue is effected, however, not by arms but by "looks."[14] This revolution is a triumph of virtue, its hero praised not for martial valor but for prudence, his breastplate stamped with "Truth and Love."[15] Although more than one of these pieces nervously acknowledges conquest and invasion, even usurpation, those disagreeable idioms are transformed, pacified, Europeanized.[16] Indeed, some of the offending vocabulary drifts from the point where it might most cogently or immediately be applied to quite different targets; the panegyrics tell us of "usurping France . . . invading English rights";[17] more than once kingship by blood and immutable divine right are elided for merit and *salus populi:*

> Kings differ not from Men of baser blood,
> But in the Godlike Pow'r of doing Good,
> When some brave Spirit did the rest outshine,
> The Ancients bad him reign, and thought his Race divine;
> That being inthron'd, as in his proper sphere
> The lustre of his Worth more sparkling might appear:
> For Objects are not seen by being nigh,
> But plac't at a fit distance from the eye.[18]

The theory of divine-right kingship and the sanctity of lineal descent are here traded wholesale for kingship of the common good. In this account the optics of godlike ascendancy are simply a device to enhance political prestige; divine-right kingship is a trick of public relations rather than immutable civic or sacred truth.

One panegyrist mixes theories of kingship in order to account for and give credibility to William's unexpected and perhaps illegitimate presence in the kingdom:

> No dull Succession sanctifies his Right,
>   Nor Conquest gain'd in Fight,
>   But o're the Peoples minds, and there
> Does Right Divine Triumphantly appear.
>   The mind, impassible and free,
> No Pow'r can Govern, but the Deity;
> Hower'e o're Persons, and o're Fortunes, may
>   A bold Intruder sway;
>   The Right Divine is by the People giv'n,
> And 'tis their Suffrage speaks the mind of Heav'n.[19]

This odd mixture of providentialism, election, *jus divinum,* and contract dismisses lineal descent and conquest only to rescue divine right from the language of contract and donation. What we have here is not an exercise in high-strung ambiguity and paradox, but an irresolute and contradictory mixing of constitutional idioms. The lines, colored ever so slightly by a Miltonic rhetoric, suggest an absence of theory and a failure of idioms—heroic, legal, dynastic—by which one might indeed figure the meaning of the revolution or the person of its hero.

It is not difficult to understand this reluctance to allow succession, since the son-in-law and nephew displacing the father-in-law and uncle could hardly claim much protection from that model. Nor is the shyness over conquest hard to grasp. Conquest as a source of legitimacy carries a heavy price. What is worth observing about a number of these efforts is the very difficult and indeed contradictory circumstance into which the revolution, and its consented-to representation, delivered those who would vindicate the event and its principal actors. Miraculous redemption and business-as-usual are difficult points of view to argue simultaneously. I have not touched on the many references to William as savior of religion and the law, dwelling rather on the difficulties of model, office, and legitimating language because not only redemption but also continuity had to be addressed. While the rhetoric of liberty and property is frequently and on occasion energetically deployed, the circumstance of the revolution, the nature of William's entry, the very real as well as useful passivity of the nation, and the ambiguity of James's status created a troubled circumstance for a literature of heroism and high principles. It was a difficult task to adjudicate such a language in this revolution; but 1688 was not without parallels, analogues, and types that might explain the happy conquest.

It helped, of course, that the landing at Tor Bay took place on November 5, and that 1688 was the hundredth anniversary of the English triumph over international Catholicism. The defeat of Marian persecution, Elizabeth's glorious reign, and the humiliation of the Spanish Armada are precursors and predictors of William's Protestant triumph. But the defeat of the Armada, the centerpiece of such analogues, had its own mildly subversive subtext: 1588 was an English triumph over threatened foreign invasion; 1688 was a triumphant foreign invasion and routing of an English monarch. The ironies of the analogy are partly hidden under the shadow of its more happy application, but they could hardly have been invisible in a literature that everywhere allows, indeed embraces, passivity. And the problem of claiming an English identity both for the revolution and for its resistance was a real difficulty. In fact, what seems to be at the center of the revolution is absence: a throne that lies vacant, a king who has disappeared in the night, a people reluctant to act in defiance of or on behalf of William's entry. That set of circumstances—literal and metaphoric—suggests some of the difficulty encountered by those who might have produced a heroic literature of the revolution.

The highest forms of literature are then either in difficulty or in the hands of an opposition, but there is another literary mode— satire—not quite so fallow. I want to exclude for the moment some satiric forms that lie close to popular literature: broadside and lampoon. That public response belongs to a different category from that of high culture. But 1688 does not go unnoticed in the traditional forms of satire, where both Roman Catholic rapacity and Dutch boorishness and usurpation form topics of steady interest not only in 1688 but throughout the coming decade. Though the modern edition of that volume of *Poems on Affairs of State* covering the years 1688–1697 runs to more than six hundred pages and concerns itself with works that might be thought of as literature, the whole of William's reign has often been dismissed as "one of the dullest decades in the history of English literature."[20] In his commentary on the formal verse satires, W. J. Cameron remarks their narrowness of vision, the redundancy of personal attacks, the reductiveness of their caricature.[21] Although we would expect and indeed hope for such bluntness and hardness in lampoon and broadside (and there the reductiveness is not only imposed by formal demands—brevity and speed remarking the alliance to jingle and litany—but is also part of their attraction), the traditional appeal of satire also includes complexity, disinterestedness, and commentary from beside or above the fray. These qualities are more often absent from than characteristic of the satires of 1689 and after. Elsewhere I have suggested that fable and translation are particularly characteristic of and brilliantly practiced in this decade because so much about its public and political life seemed contingent, transient, and unstated.[22] The debates in the Convention can be read as an emblem of such uncertainty; they suggest as well that obliqueness and indirection follow from such a circumstance. Fable and translation offered the direct protection of cover and indirection in the expression of political aims and principles (and a number of writers in this century were caught holding difficult or embarrassing positions after a shift of power had taken place). In addition, and more expressively, fable and translation are indicators of the mood and circumstance of the whole culture. The political and intellectual uncertainty and obliqueness of the 1690s were hardly propitious for the growth of satire, which can happily flourish as opposition. But for such an opposition, values and limits must be fixed as a point of reference, and moral and civic ideals need to be taken for granted rather than newly charted with each shift of the political tide. The first years of the Restoration were ideal for such panegyric and satire; moral and political landmarks were visible, celebrated, idealized even if not adhered to. Such a case can be made well into the 1680s; the 1690s seem by contrast a moment of high political and cultural uncertainty; and that uncertainty communicated itself to satirists—indeed, to all who undertook literary venture. It was a circumstance in which fable, translation, and a drama of masking and innuendo would thrive.

Let me sharpen the case slightly. The events of 1688/89 might well be read as a revolution of compromise and collusion. Rather than a trumpeting of high ideals—the provision of a new social and political order—protection and retrenchment were its aims. This was a moment in the political culture when wary hesitation and cool distance marked much of the behavior of the political nation. Out of this circumstance, and more, out of disappointment, bitterness, and no little sense of irony came the literary masterpiece of the revolution, *Don Sebastian*, a play whose aesthetic and popular success must raise questions about the force of Jacobite and nonjuring sentiments in the 1690s. The popular success of the play in 1689 is particularly puzzling, for the fall of that year was a time when both the former laureate and his former master were under savage attack.

What, then, was the play articulating? For one thing, it is a feast of dramatic conventions and devices, of heroic rhetoric and high ideals, of double plots, concealed identities, hidden morals, interlocking rings, incestuous longings, and spurned honor. It is a play whose conventions Dryden knew well how to handle, and their somewhat nostalgic display in *Don Sebastian* must have provided a good deal of pleasure for those with a taste for heroic drama. But rather more was at stake for the former laureate than shuffling a familiar if brilliant hand of dramatic conventions. Dryden wanted very much to enter the public debate over the revolution, and he wanted to enter it on his own ground, in forms of which he was a master, with conventions and codes whose meaning he might shape, with a language whose resonance he might control. *Don Sebastian* gave him a format that could provide not only artistic and financial rewards, but also a means of vindicating his personal and political honor while minimizing the damage of his religious conversion and exposing the hypocrisy of the revolution, the bankruptcy of its ideals, the hollowness of its slogans.

In its own way, *Don Sebastian* is as steady and sharply directed a political argument as are the laureate's satires of the 1680s, but it is conducted in so different a set of circumstances that its very articulation has been denied and ignored in favor of what is read as timeless and universal in the work.[23] Needless to say, there is much that is timeless and universal in a play that announces a literary ancestry including Virgil, Statius, and Sallust. But we also need to recognize that the high ground of literary affiliation and literary history was itself a crucial vantage point for Dryden after 1688. The play steadily entertains and arranges a set of political issues so that eternal verities might be argued out of a historically potent and particular set of political events, positions, platforms, and claims. This is a play that is in steady colloquy with the arguments posed in defense of the revolution. The aim of that colloquy is to embarrass and debase the revolution and assert the heroic and tragic character of a Catholic prince vanquished by a cruel and usurping infidel. There is some irony in the fact that the very success of *Don Sebastian* as timeless literary masterpiece argues Dryden's ability to cover the polemical with claims of high principles, to soften and universalize difficult particulars, to divert attention away from polemical values and political conclusions that were fixed in the revolutionary moment. But first and foremost *Don Sebastian* is a piece of very high culture indeed.

Tragedy is the genre of this play, and it is so announced in bold letters that cross the title page. Under this rubric, we are invited to contemplate conquest, usurpation, betrayal, and retreat as the very stuff of high art. Generic identification not only elevates the materials of 1688 to a high pitch but lends them a particular interpretation, for *Don Sebastian* centers on a flawed but majestic hero whose fall was not a cowardly flight but a tragic inevitability, a reversal cruel and ironic, beyond comprehension, and following from sins concealed in distant generations. Such tragedy cannot be averted, particularly in the realm of politics, and the pattern of conquest, betrayal, and retreat is given tragic dignity by the play. Thus are the principles of the drama imagined, and thus is the fate of the conquered portrayed. Altitude and dignity are the argument not only of genre but also of the prefatory materials that accompanied the printed play.

Don Sebastian was dedicated to Philip Sidney, third earl of Leicester. The dedication to Leicester allowed Dryden to do several interesting things; most obviously, the long and deep connections of that family with literature and patronage are themselves a claim to aristocratic privilege and protection.[24] At one point in the dedication Dryden poses as Spenser to Leicester's Sidney. But a more elaborate argument about politics and art is folded into the dedication, for not only were the Sidneys aristocratic patrons; they were a family with republican associations, nowhere more shockingly asserted than in the execution of Philip's brother Algernon for complicity in the Rye House Plot. The third earl of Leicester had himself been a "zealous republican," counselor of Cromwell as well as member of Cromwell's "House of Lords."[25] Since 1660 he had lived in retirement, having put away politics in favor of patronage, wit, and art. But Leicester's political career could not have been entirely absent from Dryden's mind, nor could Dryden have been unaware of the important role that Leicester's younger brother, Henry, earl of Romney, played in the Glorious Revolution.[26] This dedication is, then, a claim to protection from a patron of Whiggish principles and republican lineage.

There is yet a more complex argument developed in the dedication about such a patron's significance, and that argument is twofold. First, Dryden notes—indeed, dwells on—the virtues of the retired life that his patron exemplifies and that are extended through analogy to the Roman aristocrat and patron Titus Pomponius Atticus. That analogy allows Dryden to play Cicero to Leicester's Atticus, giving ample scope to the dignity and moral virtues of patron and protégé. Both Roman figures exemplify the meaning of retirement from politics:

> What a glorious Character was this once in Rome; I shou'd say in Athens, when in the disturbances of a State as mad as ours, the wise Pomponius transported all the remaining wisdom and vertue of his Country, into the Sanctuary of Peace and Learning. But, I wou'd ask the World, (for you, My Lord, are too nearly concern'd to judge this Cause) whether there may not yet be found, a Character of a Noble Englishman, equally shining with that illustrious Roman? Whether I need to name a second Atticus; or whether the World has not already prevented me, and fix'd it there without my naming?[27]

Dryden's quotation from Cicero's letters at the close of the dedication ("Be pleas'd therefore, since the Family of the Attici is and ought to be above the common Forms of concluding Letters, that I may take my leave in the Words of Cicero to the first of them" [15:64]) sharpens the appropriation of Cicero's exile as a figure for his own condition after the revolution, the analogy suggesting that Dryden's dislocation bore no faint resemblance to Cicero's purge. Both sets of figures, Roman and English, have turned away from the turmoil and disappointments of politics toward contemplation, self-knowledge, charity, and constancy. Moreover, this motif, the retreat from politics, is crucial to the play, which closes as its hero departs for voluntary exile. Such a theme is, of course, a way of thinking about the circumstance of James II, that exemplar of piety and virtue who was cultivating self-knowledge in the gardens of Louis XIV.

One additional argument may be drawn out of the dedication to Leicester. Not only does the noble aristocrat retreat from politics to practice contemplation and self-knowledge; he is also to be found exercising patronage without regard to partisan affection. Such an exercise of patronage exemplifies a principle that allows a Jacobite to benefit from patronage irrespective of politics, and, moreover, expresses the true principles of patronage and thus articulates a whole system of moral, familial, and civic ties. Leicester's patronage is an example of the fullest meaning of charity and constancy not despite Dryden's political principles but because of them. The application of this ideal of patronage and charity to national politics is not difficult to make. The subjects of constancy and beneficence are repeatedly examined in the play, in the behavior of its principals, in the comic inversions, in the relations of subject to sovereign, in the inconstancy of the mobile. Those who have shunned and betrayed the former laureate are practicing a brutality very much exemplified by the acts of betrayal and usurpation depicted within *Don Sebastian* and presumably visible everywhere since the revolution. The dedication to Leicester argues the meaning of charity and constancy on the local and the national levels. The play suggests the eternal verities of such an argument, and it intimates how such verities might be seen in the events of the months before the staging of the work in November 1689.

Perhaps because the dedication is laid at the feet of a republican aristocrat, Dryden can dare the arguments he indulges, nor could the principles of charity and constancy be faulted. Indeed, the high-minded display of such principles is steady throughout the play, and while they have not only a sustained moral but also a sharp polemical meaning, the application of such materials to personal and national politics in 1688 was not simple. Dryden was quite aware of the potential applications from the play, and he both invites and shields the play from them. Part of the shield is to be found in the very complexity of materials within the play, the unsteady system of analogies and parallels, proximities and disparities, that defeats any simple allegorical arrangement and, in part, is meant to discourage historical applications.[28] This is, moreover, an important argument of the preface, which suggests in other ways how generic issues insulate the play from too easy a political reading. For in this preface the playwright insists that the substance of his work is pure fiction. Many poems and plays of this century are eager to appropriate the honorific of history, to marshal its qualities, to claim significance through veracity. But Dryden's argument in the preface to *Don Sebastian* is quite the opposite:

> As for the story or plot of the Tragedy, 'tis purely fiction; for I take it up where the History has laid it down.... declaring it to be fiction, I desire my Audience to think it no longer true, than while they are seeing it represented....
> I must likewise own, that I have somewhat deviated from the known History, in the death of Muley-Moluch, who, by all relations dyed of a feaver in the Battel, before his Army had wholly won the Field; but if I have allow'd him another day of life, it was because I stood in need of so shining a Character of brutality, as I have given him. (15:67–68, 70)

The intermixing of comic scenes, subplots, hidden identities, and delayed discoveries enlarges the scope of Dryden's claim that the play is pure fiction. And to those resources we must add the quite ostentatiously fictional element of the plot: the discovery of incest committed between hero and heroine. Whatever applications we might be invited to make from the play, no one was suggesting that incest was a crime either contemplated or committed by James II or William III. There might be a slight titillation in the fact that William III was both James's son-in-law and nephew, but the charge of incest is one of the few not leveled against William in the satiric literature of the 1690s, where just about every other natural and unnatural vice is charged to his person.

The preface aims, then, to situate the play within the realms of romance, pathos, and tragedy; it shields the play against too quick an application by having us contemplate its politics philosophically as well as historically. And it has one additional and rather important argument to make about the character of the work: its lineage and its author's position within that lineage. The literariness of the work is underscored by the argument about fiction; it is also very much the subject of the discussion of technique. The play, Dryden confesses, came after a long absence from the theater; it is rather too long for the stage, a fact that he learned from the opening night. And yet as a printed work its beauties and proportions are everywhere visible. Indeed, Dryden claims that this tragedy surpasses "any of my former Tragedies. There is a more noble daring in the Figures and more suitable to the loftiness of the Subject; and besides this some newnesses of English, translated from the Beauties of Modern Tongues, as well as from the elegancies of the Latin" (15:67). Those who have read the work, among them the earl of Dorset, think it "beyond any of my former Plays" (15:71). Dryden both commends its qualities and gives his readers the terms in which they are to appreciate the play. He is also insistent on the tradition to which this work belongs, the line of writers in which he might claim a position: Euripides and Sophocles, Lucan, Sallust, and Corneille—these are Dryden's models and peers.

The preface closes with a quotation from Virgil which recalls the use of Cicero at the end of the dedication and forms part of a complex, defensive, and rather delicate argument about literary identity and moral authority in a changing and hostile political world.[29] The exalted literary tradition and the lofty literary character of his work both shield Dryden from some of the dangers of a hostile political world and give him an authority to speak of its character and values. This may strike us as naïve or wishful, but the high-mindedness of the work must have been part of its immediate success. Both Dryden's prefatory writing and the highly wrought, self-conscious character of the play suggest that he knew quite well what the polemical values of altitude were, what protection they might offer, and what argumentative advantage they allowed. The invocation of high culture, even the explicit denial of historical accuracy and intent, offered a polemical advantage; it was one of the few that Dryden could easily claim after 1688.

Part of the polemical argument of *Don Sebastian* is, then, the connection between high culture and the values of the play: the meaning of principles, the nature of oaths, the quality of honor, the uncertainties of fate. The play also provides explicit political materials and arguments that it would harness to the loftiness of its enterprise; they not only suggest the abstract polemical situation of the work, but also indicate how it is doing business with the claims made on behalf of the revolution and its settlement. Dryden's handling of themes and plots, of verbal and dramatic idioms, is in fact an excellent guide to the polemics of the revolution.

Any writer choosing the Portuguese king for his subject had, by the late seventeenth century, a wealth of histories and legends among which to sift. The centerpiece of the histories was a sixteenth-century king of Portugal, a Catholic gallant who entertained fantasies of a glorious reign dedicated to military triumphs in the cause of his religion, a mystic and fanatic.[30] This history intersects Moroccan politics in the battle of Alcazarquivir, which closed an ill-fated campaign that Don Sebastian had conducted on behalf of a slighted heir to the Moroccan throne—merely one incident in a saga of political and familial intrigue and treachery, fratricide, assassination, and rival claims to the throne. In fact, Moroccan history, the immediate background to Dryden's play, might itself be taken as an emblem of divided ruling houses, conquests, and usurpations. Don Sebastian's military crusade resulted in his own death and the destruction of the Portuguese army, a defeat followed by years of decline and domination by Spain, and the growth of the Sebastian legend, which held that the king had not died in battle but would one day return from exile to claim his throne.

It is not difficult to see what this history of political mayhem, Catholic gallantry, and Sebastianist hopes for an exiled prince might have offered Dryden in 1689. The parallels are so obvious that it may be surprising Dryden chose to dramatize the legend at all. A version of the story dramatized by Philip Massinger had been suppressed on political grounds in 1631,[31] and though we do not know if Dryden was aware of this, he must have been aware of the parallels to be drawn out of his subject in 1689, parallels that he orchestrates, complicates, and heightens. He must also have known of the danger of doing so, and we have seen some of the steps that he took both to excite the applications and to distance himself from them, to dehistoricize and neutralize the politics of the legend while allowing the obvious inferences to be drawn. He not only indulged these parallels and applications; he wove so complex a system of such parallels that their variety and number are slightly dizzying. If, for a moment, we take 1688 to be the center of *Don Sebastian*—a proposition that Dryden and some of his explicators would vigorously contest—we are offered parallels to English politics from both Moroccan and Portuguese history, and these are mixed and indulged in scenes of straight fiction and scenes based on history. What the multiplicity suggests is that revolution, usurpation, exile, and retreat are something like the inevitable conditions of politics, a conclusion amply illustrated in all the histories drawn on and implied by the play.

Such a display of confusion and revolution leads us to understand that good men are forced by tragic circumstances beyond their control and understanding to retreat from the turbulence of politics and to embrace stoic retirement. Self-knowledge, charity, and beneficence alone are beyond the reach of political revolution, which is, after all, simply an instrument of blind fate. Several examples illustrate this pattern: Philip, earl of Leicester, and his Roman counterpart, Titus Pomponius Atticus; the former laureate and his Roman pattern, Cicero; the Don Sebastian of history and the Don Sebastian of Dryden's play, who closes the work with renunciation and retreat; and of course James II, who is following such a pattern of retreat and piety at St. Germain. To abjure empire, to hold property and power in moral contempt, suggests the final example of piety and elevation: Christ of the Gospels. Dryden may not explicitly draw all the analogies, but the materials for constructing such a pattern and abstracting such a meaning from the play and its legends are obviously there. Given such a design, we can see how the dedication, preface, and the play itself might be read as a thematically linked and continuous text pointing a repeated stoic moral, one quoted from Cicero and Virgil and expressed by the hero himself:

> The world was once too narrow for my mind,
> But one poor little nook will serve me now;
> To hide me from the rest of humane kinde.
> . . . .
> A Scepter's but a play-thing, and a Globe
> A bigger bounding Stone.
>
> (V.i.547–55)

Politics is the prime example and inevitable stage of such instability: crowns and empires are slippery things; conquest and usurpation simply beget more such; once a rent is made in the fabric of bonds, oaths, and gratitude, the state unravels. Political activism is clearly not Dryden's aim in *Don Sebastian*, but the consoling moral of endless fluctuation is repeatedly drawn in dramatic colloquy over such topics as title, empire, conquest, providence, and fate. Although William and Mary have been crowned, James has been deposed, and his laureate dispossessed, the victory is but a momentary variation in the larger scheme of instability and change. It is hardly surprising, given the moral and political comfort of such a philosophy, to find Dryden translating Lucretius in the 1690s; if not with a vengeance then certainly with some pleasure Dryden embraced the Lucretian flux in *Fables*, a moral and political consolation already obvious to him in 1689.

. The histories that form the background to *Don Sebastian* provide both frame and consolation. The play itself engages more directly than the preface in polemical work, although we ought not to underestimate the polemical value in Dryden's handling of the large frame of providential histories. Providential rescue was a theme crucial to a revolution that argued the divine right of providence as a handsome alternative to the divine right of kings. Dryden is careful to engage that theme at various moments in the play so that we have both a general devaluation of the politics of providence and a rather more specific refutation of providential arguments applied to conquest and tyranny within the play itself. Indeed, rather than lift the play above the revolution, such philosophical material situates *Don Sebastian* in the midst of that great political event, steadily engaging the themes, the principles, the banners, and the catchwords of the revolution and its apologetics. The attack is aimed at the theory of the revolution and its language, at the claims of necessity and high-mindedness, at the character of its principles. *Don Sebastian* steadily inspects the rationale of the Glorious Revolution, the action of the rabble and its political and religious leaders, the slogans of popery and slavery, property and religion. Through comic scenes that slight the principles of the revolution, through soliloquy that heightens non-juring values, through a steady examination and deflation of such terms as *title, slavery, conquest, tyranny*, and *sovereignty*, Dryden offers an alternative reading of the revolution, its justification, its rhetoric, and its principal actors. In this light we see 1688 not as the high-minded and selfless rescue of religion, property, and the law from the hands of a reckless and bigoted innovator, but as an act of political betrayal motivated by greed, argued with lies, a revolution that everywhere revealed the cupidity, cowardice, and moral indifference of the nation.

The polemical engagement that I have been describing takes place in several ways. Most abstractly, the play spins out philosophical and moral principles: the universe is in flux; providence is inscrutable; title is mere vanity; only an indifference to the things of this world can guarantee nobility of character and purity of soul. Less abstractly, the main characters in the play are allowed through language and circumstance to suggest, often in momentary, fleeting, and partial ways, the principal figures of the revolution. The Moroccan shereef, a bloody tyrant, martial and heroic yet cruel and morally indifferent, flits in and out of focus as William III. The hapless, noble, and stoic Don Sebastian—"a Man, / Above man's height, ev'n towring to Divinity. / Brave, pious, generous, great, and liberal: / Just as the Scales of Heaven that weigh the Seasons, / He lov'd his People, him they idoliz'd. . . . His goodness was diffus'd to human kind" (I.i.101–9); "no other / Cou'd represent such suff'ring Majesty" (I.i.342–43)—offers us an idealized James, a portrait that may strain credulity and was obviously intended as flattering suggestion rather than careful delineation. A virtuous princess loyal to her murdered father and to her brother's ghost, who upbraids her father's nephew, a man who seized the father's throne, is clearly an inversion of Mary. And there is a set of secondary characters whose actions suggest momentary analogy with either the principal actors or the circumstances of the revolution.[32]

Dryden also fits out the debates and exchanges in the play with a set of political idioms that was crucial to the Williamite representation of 1688. For example, playing out a scene in which real slaves are bought and sold at market, the drama literalizes the meaning and conditions of slavery in a manner intended to puncture and ridicule the political uses of that word. The steady cry of "popery and slavery" was crucial to the rhetoric of the revolution; *Don Sebastian* insists that *slavery* is a word that has, first of all, a literal meaning and a political provenance; slavery is the direct result of conquest, and the Catholic slaves in this play are bought and sold at the whim of a conquering infidel. By literalizing the word and depicting slavery as the result of military conquest and by suggesting that conquest is indeed the condition of William's triumph, that retreat and retirement acknowledge such conquest, Dryden uses a set of political circumstances implacably to argue the meaning of national conquest: the people are now quite literally slaves of a conqueror, to be bought and sold at his whim. The scenes and colloquies that analyze slavery as language and condition have the effect first of insisting on root definitions and political preconditions. No one argued that James had taken the throne by conquest; many were troubled by the title of conqueror as it applied to William. This was a crucial issue, and by linking conquest and slavery in both comic and serious scenes, Dryden entered the debate, argued its language, and suggested that the most important political consequence of conquest was slavery.

And so it is with other crucial words of the revolution. Repeatedly, characters in this play examine and debate the word *title*, always to its detriment as fixed indicator of the virtue of proprietary right: "Thou wouldst have Titles, take 'em then, Chief Minister, First Hangman of the State" (I.i.65–66); "By what title, / Because I happen'd to be born where he / Happen'd to be a King?" (I.i.86–88). Not only is this a philosophical disquisition on the relations of words and things; it seems a direct commentary on the debates over title in the Convention. Dryden's argument that title is mere cipher, that qualities of honor and sovereignty are more deeply fixed than the language denominating those terms, is at once philosophical and political. None should fool themselves into believing that the mere application of title would legitimate the deposing of James II and the installation of William and Mary in his stead. Nor was Dryden the only one to raise such scruples; the nature and meaning of title was an issue of some significance in the wake of the revolution, and scrupling over the language with which to denominate the persons and events of 1688/89 was a subject of long-standing debate.

Dryden entered this particular debate quite early and staked out the Jacobite position with apparent ease. Having himself lost the laureateship, he was in no mood to be overawed by title, to allow that a mere shift of name would confer authority and preeminence. This was at once a personal, political, and philosophical argument, and it is part of the interest of this play that several venues can be simultaneously engaged, that the complexity and varied applications of political and linguistic issues can be handled through the different modes of the work: tragic, comic, satiric, and ironic. The importance of the comic to the tragic action in *Don Sebastian* is nowhere better seen than in the variety of polemical tones that the two modes allowed; balance and disinterest suggested by the comic writing strengthen the pathos and philosophical elevation that define such topics as fate, providence, fortune, and title.

Scenes of mistaken identity, accidental appearance, and displaced lovers play out in a comic vein the rather portentous political and philosophical arguments of *Don Sebastian*. Fate itself, the comic scenes argue, is hardly a source for the authority or virtue of either action or agency. Thus the lottery scene in the first act, in which the fates of hero and heroine are supposedly decided, is covered by whim and accident. That debunking of fate and fortune is followed by repeated scenes of accidental and mistaken action and identity that alone seem to determine turns of plot and fortune. Arguments that based the revolution on analogy with 1588 or likeness with other Protestant redemptions are engaged in specious polemic; justification by providence is an argument made from whimsy dressed as legitimating divinity.

Dryden also understood the power of images of mob rule and civil anarchy in treating of the revolution. Both in scenes of high principle and in episodes of ridicule and burlesque, he derides the clergy and the mufti, who are seen alike as bent on profit and self-promotion, who willfully incite riot and tumult, who play on the greed of the multitude and the chimera of consensual politics to ride the crest of revolution to new heights of property and power. The repeated image of mob rule stalks the play, as does the suggestion of a physics of revolution run toward chaos and destruction. The politics of fear was well understood by publicists both for and against the revolution, and indeed, those defending the revolution had a rather more immediate arsenal of images with which to conjure rape, murder, and plunder. But figures of political tumult and social leveling were still forcefully to be deployed in 1688, and the evocation of the revolutionary mob as "A Million strong of Vermine ev'ry Villain: / No part of Government, but Lords of Anarchy, / Chaos of Power, and priviledg'd destruction" (I.i.145–47) must have been potent in the months following the revolution. Exclusion had been defeated in part through the association of Whiggery and the good old cause; and this play manages scenes of mob instability to excite the meaning of the revolution as social dismemberment. Once conquest and tumult were embraced, the play argues, all stood in danger: "when Kings and Queens are to be discarded, what shou'd Knaves do any longer in the pack?" (IV.iii.169–70). The language neatly combines the figure of chance—politics as gaming—with the argument that revolutions, once begun, are difficult to control; all parties should have an interest in social stability. This revolution, the play argues, is a dangerous unhinging of social and political order.

Certainly self-interest as an engine of the revolution played an important role in the rhetoric of those who regretted 1688, and Dryden displays his mastery of the topic. In an extremely witty scene (IV.iii) where the mufti excites opposition to tyranny and absolutism—

charges repeatedly hurled against James—he mingles self-interest, fantasies of a glorious national history, and religious hokery in order to rouse mob allegiance. The mufti's speech is riddled with ironies, nowhere more tellingly expressed than in his "three P's: Self-Preservation, our Property, and our Prophet" (IV.iii.111). These are, of course, a debased and ridiculed version of the slogans of 1688. And while we can find the invocation of a people's right to self-defense in the contemporary pamphlet literature, not all those who embraced the revolution were eager to raise the standard of self-preservation with its Hobbesian overtones. Dryden repeatedly takes aim at this principle, contrasting self-preservation as low self-interest with the bonds of nature, family, and society. By fixing self-interest as the first principle of the revolution, he aims to expose greed and cowardice as its driving force. As Antonio, a character who comically plays out the role of thief and principal of the new order, admits: "Not very heroick; but self preservation is a point above Honour and Religion too" (III.ii.233–34). This from a character who cheats his father-in-law by stealing his daughter and using his property to found a new regime. The application to English politics is not simply obvious: it seems willfully so.

Indeed, the whole handling of property as a principle of the revolution is extremely imaginative in the play. The topic allowed Dryden to debase the motives of the rabble as plunder and tumult and simultaneously to undercut the rhetoric of the revolutionary settlement. The steady reach in *Don Sebastian* is for the moral high ground, and nowhere does this reach allow Dryden more play than in his handling of property as a motive for the revolution. Property addressed in various terms was indeed part of the apologetic rhetoric of 1688, but it was not a principal term, mainly, I think, because it was not very heroic matter. Sensing the vulnerability of the term, Dryden exploited its weakness as moral and social principle. This exploitation allowed him to arrange the political principles of the play so that property and self-interest and "our holy Mahomet" (IV.iii.108) vindicate 1688; and trust, loyalty, and the bonds of family and society suffer defeat. The old ties of family and society are intended as a foil against which the poet can display the politics of plunder and property. If one might begin the argument that the revolution was theft, and property its mainspring, then the authority of the entire action is undercut. From property spring the violation of familial bonds, social disorder, and the contempt for duty, trust, and gratitude; 1688 was a revolution driven by appetite, contemptuous of the polity, fixed in a brave new world of opportunism, craft, and greed.

Don Sebastian has more to argue than the hollowness of revolutionary principles and more ways of arguing that theme than I have suggested. What wants observing is how thoroughly the apologetics of the revolution are engaged, how carefully structured, scene by scene, is this high drama of the Sebastian legend. The play was taking part in a contest for moral and cultural authority, and Dryden brought to that contest not only his gifts as a stylist of the heroic drama, his keen ear for political rhetoric, but also an understanding of how historical romance could be used to orchestrate a political argument. The matter of Don Sebastian allowed Dryden to indulge in a brilliant display of hints, allusions, and innuendo; it also allowed him to construct an allegory of moral principles, and in such a construction he holds the winning hand. Honor and obligation, loyalty and gratitude, the spare soulfulness of Atticus and Cicero—these are the properties of a Jacobite position. Needless to say, such a conclusion did not altogether fit the public perception either of the Jacobite cause or of the playwright himself.

For whom did Dryden think he was writing this play in the summer and early fall of 1689? In the preface he argues that he was forced back to the stage by financial need; one could think of any number of topics, themes, and histories that might have offered more promise of wide popularity in 1689 than *Don Sebastian*. Yet what is most puzzling is not this apparent contradiction—one would have thought that a more grateful audience could have been discovered in the antechambers of St. Germain than on London's commercial stage—but the actual success of the play in 1689 and thereafter. This is not a play of opaque and occult politics. Of course, an audience might always ignore or deny the applications, but the idioms of the revolution are so clearly handled that it would have taken not simply a willing suspension of disbelief to ignore or elide the politics, but an active denial of much of the language of the play to achieve an apolitical reading. It might well be that the philosophical materials of *Don Sebastian*—and they are elegantly displayed in both dedication and text—are more immediate and attractive for us than are its politics. But for contemporaries, the political currents would have been extremely difficult to ignore. That the politics of 1688 are provided with an overlay of philosophical meaning not only makes them more attractive but also deepens their argumentative coherence. Philosophy, as Locke so well understood, gives politics altitude and dignity, and those are among the principal polemical aims of *Don Sebastian*.

To whom, then, could such a play have appealed? Could the portraits and arguments of *Don Sebastian* have flattered an audience, some of whose members had not simply accommodated the revolution but embraced it? What might they have seen in its exposition of revolutionary folly and greed, its condemnation of the new political morality, its debasement of the rhetoric of the revolution? I have no certain answer to this puzzle, but we might think that the political and moral values that this play celebrates—gratitude, loyalty, honor, trust, beneficence—could not have been willingly abandoned by the nation in its rapid acquiescence to a convenient revolution. Although Dryden was in control of the action and language of his play, he could not entirely regulate its reception and understanding. One might imagine an audience that both endorsed the revolution and proclaimed its allegiance to the values that this play honors. Dryden might hope to deny an audience this ground, but the embrace of paradoxes is not easy to regulate, nor can the playwright insist on scrupulous self-knowledge among his audience. The success of the play does not inevitably argue the acceptance of Dryden's polemical intentions; one might indeed embrace the principles of *Don Sebastian* while regretting the politics of its author and the misbehavior of James II. So eager was the political nation to deny the revolutionary character of 1688/89, so anxious was it to underscore the continuity with, indeed the return to, ancient principles, to argue James as aberration, that it might go to the theater, witness a production of Dryden's play, and vigorously assent to the values of *Don Sebastian* without conceding the playwright's application of those principles. In fact, the success of *Don Sebastian* seems to me rather interesting evidence of the continuity of political values, or at least of the moral and psychological advantages for Dryden's audience in professing such a continuity of values and forms.

Although politics in the months following the flight of James and the installation of William and Mary were sufficiently fluid to allow for both the ironies of Dryden's play and his audience's suspension of political disbelief, it would not have been surprising had the revolutionary settlement finally silenced Dryden. *Don Sebastian* turned out, however, to be not a valedictory work but the prologue to a remarkable decade for the former laureate. And while assassination plots, associations, and rumors of Jacobite invasion complicated the fabric of political culture throughout the 1690s, the revolutionary settlement did not remain suspended in ironies and suspicion. Running a literary shop on Jacobite and nonjuring sentiment proved more than adequate for the invention of *Don Sebastian,* but could it remain so after the Battle of the Boyne, after William's European campaigns, and after the financial revolution that enabled William to prosecute the war against France? I want to reflect briefly on this issue by way of the literary masterpiece of the 1690s, Dryden's translation of Virgil.

Dryden had hoped all his life for a circumstance in which to cultivate epic; now opposition, financial need, and political reversal had, ironically, allowed him such an opening.[33] The analogy with Milton in the 1660s may take some edge off the strangeness of Dryden's coming to epic at this moment in his career, but the comparison should not too quickly deprive us of a sense of incongruity, the dissonance between the argument of epic and the circumstance of Virgil's translator. Dryden's own sense of their incommensurability was quite sharp; as he observed in the postscript to his translation: "What Virgil wrote in the vigour of his Age, in Plenty and at Ease, I have undertaken to Translate in my Declining Years: strugling with Wants, oppress'd with Sickness, curb'd in my Genius, lyable to be misconstrued in all I write."[34] We need to allow for the poet's familiar defensive gestures, but we should also honor their likelihood, the real as well as strategic distance between what Dryden saw as his own position and what he imagined of Virgil's intimacy with the court of Augustus Caesar and with the project of empire. The potential uses of Virgil to celebrate William's consolidation of rule and success on the Continent must have seemed too obvious to comment on, but the fate of Virgil in this decade was not to celebrate the investment in empire but to regret its coming. That the *Aeneid* could not wholly be made to obey this imperative must have been clear, perhaps to no one more than to Dryden, who had earlier assimilated Virgil to the imperial ambitions of Stuart Restoration. The force and poignancy of Dryden's translation came neither from its confidence in the triumphs of war nor from its complaint against invasion and conquest, but rather from the negotiation that Dryden had to make between regret and ambition, between justice and fate. And that negotiation opened the space not only for his translation but more broadly for literary culture in this decade.

If Dryden's translation of Virgil were wholly the remnant of an age that was out, it would serve as a powerful nostalgic emblem; but his

Virgil was more than an act of Jacobite piety. Making an English Virgil in the 1690s allowed Dryden to regret "usurpation"; it also forced him to recast the invasion, to mediate his understanding of the revolution, to accommodate both himself and the events of 1688/89 to a larger frame. Reminiscent of the political and moral dilemma Marvell had faced more than forty years before, the issues surrounding this Stuart demise might be understood in terms of a clear political calculus:

> Though Justice against Fate complain,
> And plead the antient Rights in vain:
>> But those do hold or break
>> As Men are strong or weak.[35]

What Marvell warily acknowledges in the *Horatian Ode*, however, Dryden heightens and celebrates in his rendering of Virgil's *fatum*. Translating Virgil enabled Dryden to plead the ancient rights, but it also allowed him to acknowledge the mysteries of fate and the ambiguities of fortune. Dryden discovered in the ample folds of Virgil's epic a way of coming to terms with the past and the present by acknowledging his regret over the unsteadiness of politics and by assimilating his ambitions not wholly to a political cause but to the immortality of verse.[36]

The Works of Virgil might also be seen to anticipate the circumstance of heroic literature in the years to come, when epic repeatedly took shelter in translation, nostalgia, and parody. There is indeed a prophetic irony in Virgil's celebration of imperial Rome turned against the foundations of British empire. Nor would that irony seem merely Jacobite regret, for Great Britain's age of military, commercial, and colonial triumph steadily resisted epic construction. Dryden's Virgil, Pope's Homer, and *The Dunciad*—none could be mistaken for imperial celebration. Perhaps *Robinson Crusoe*, that allegory of acquisition and empire, augurs a new day. But the formulation of a new cultural order was accomplished neither in the midst of the revolution nor in the years of William's rule. Comprehending the revolution, charting its cultural implications, and untangling its rhetoric were difficult tasks, and it is not surprising that the muses were reluctant to speak in 1688. They were, I think, uncertain of what to say and what forms to say it in.

From that perspective, both the silence surrounding the revolution

and the florescence of Jacobite culture in the years following James II's
political demise seem to have their own logic. The Glorious Revolution, we have often been told, ushered in the dullest decade in English
literature; although this is not altogether just, it was a difficult decade
for literary invention. Given the perplexity of values and events, the
embarrassment and silence over the revolution, it is not surprising
that the greatest literary achievements of the 1690s should have been
in translation. For the former laureate, the revolution no doubt provoked deep anxiety, a literal and figurative dislocation, but it also
allowed a remarkably productive late phase, an elevation above or at
least a bittersweet reconciliation with politics and empire. We might
recall again the analogy with Milton after the collapse of the protectorate: two epic poets struggling with dislocation; indeed, the analogy
suggests an unexpected symbiosis between exile and epic endeavor.
Perhaps the analogy can be argued in another way as well, for what
is striking about the 1690s is not only the career of its dispossessed
laureate but the ways in which it seems to echo the 1650s.

The demise of James II was not a regicide, but both the 1650s and
the 1690s began in the wake of revolution, and their years were
crossed by political crises, by the turbulence of conspiracy and the
threat of invasion. They were also decades of public moral regulation
and political suspicion, of literary caution and indirection. In this
regard it is striking that the two English Virgils from the seventeenth
century should stand as such clear temporal markers, John Ogilby's
published in 1649 and John Dryden's in 1697, and that the cult of
Aesop—editions, translations, and adaptations—flourished in such
similar ways during these decades. Dryden did not plan his *Fables* so
that the political culture of the 1690s might be crowned with an anthology of translations and fables, of epic fragments, pastorals, and
romances, but that does not gainsay its paradigmatic force. *Fables* is
crossed by a network of topical allusions, and these help us locate one
of the sites where the poet was at work; but the topical is merely one
axis of the political, and neither its deepest nor its most crucial. Other
thematic and formal idioms—indeed, aesthetic theory itself—provide
the structures through which the literary articulates the political. Milton understood that politics was aesthetics as he prepared to answer
the *Eikon Basilike* at midcentury; Dryden must have sensed, in 1700,
that translation and metamorphosis were political acts, that elevation
above the fray was still a political geography.

Conclusion

I began *Lines of Authority* hoping to raise questions about Restoration culture: where, for example, might we locate its borders, what defined its character, what constituted the relations between its political and imaginative modes, and where might those relations best be studied? One conclusion that I have drawn here is the necessity of fixing the climacteric of the later seventeenth century not in the ceremonies of renewal at 1660 but in the turbulence of civil war. Situating the Restoration within the long memory of the civil wars allows us to see the ties between the political experience at midcentury and the polemical modes of the later decades. More important, it reveals the integrity of politics and culture through all the decades and imaginative modes of this century. Within that new configuration, 1660 remains a point to be meditated on—a moment, paradoxically, of recovering and forgetting the past—but best understood in relation to the decade of political experimentation that preceded and the years of hectic partisanship that followed. There was good reason for those who battled Exclusion to cry " '41 is come again"; we need, however, to see the importance of that argument not only to the polemics of the 1680s but to the whole of imaginative culture in the later seventeenth century.

Politics informs all the decisions and delicate assays of literary work in this world. Milton wrote devastating attacks on poetry in *Eikonoklastes;* he refuted whole genres and systems of literary imagination, and in that work he was clearly obeying polemical design. But Milton's grand essay on pastoralism in *Paradise Lost* and Walton's nostalgic anthology of Jacobean lyric in *The Compleat Angler* are, I suggest, equally to be understood within the compass of political art. By following the life of individual genres across these decades, by observing, for example, the career of heroic literature from the epic theater of the 1660s to Dryden's translation of Virgil in the 1690s, or by contemplating the transformations of pastoral from the solacing gardens of Lord Fairfax's estate, across the harsh polemical terrain of *The Last Instructions* where pastoral repose is so affectingly poised against court corruption, into the gardens of stoic retreat that Dryden glimpsed at Leicester House, we come to appreciate the contestative force and the polemical expressiveness of all the literary materials within the frame of this half century.

On both sides of this frame, in the fields of Penshurst or the groves of Windsor Forest, georgic and pastoral articulated not only complex patronage relations but a clear system of social values. And yet, I want to insist, when such literary systems as epic and pastoral were carried through the force field of civil war, they emerged brilliantly charged, freighted with convictions and urgencies quite different from those that animated literary forms before the civil wars and after the wars had passed from living memory.

The range of polemic is, then, part of my theme, but just as important is the vibrancy of political argument across and among all the genres of the period: pamphlet and pastoral, political meditation and panegyric, satire and epic, philosophical treatise and tragedy. I have tried to suggest this range and quality of expression by allowing the reach of polemic to cross from one site of contest to another, from the most clearly marked points of contest—the openly repudiatory gestures of *Eikonoklastes* or the brilliant and scurrilous portraiture of *The Last Instructions* and *Absalom and Achitophel*—to the middle ground of public genres—the schemes of apocalyptic praise in *The First Anniversary* or the elaborate and self-conscious literary machinery of *Annus Mirabilis*—to the abstractions and syntactical neutralities of Locke's *Second Treatise*. Nor have we finished our work when we have tracked the signs of contest to the less obvious haunts of the civic muse. We need to extend our inquiry to other sites: the literary defense and critical essay, the lyric gestures of the drinking song, the fields of heroic love and tragic romance. Centering the aesthetic within the political, a geometry that was second nature to those who wrote the politics and the imaginative literature of the later seventeenth century, allows us to appreciate the contestative force of its literature and the complex ways in which the aesthetic performed and transformed the political.

Pope and Swift went to school here; they learned the shape of a polemical world and how to wield its instruments. But the stakes had begun to change by the close of the seventeenth century. A sea change took place when the civil wars had to be reconstituted wholly as secondary effect. Dryden knew this was about to happen, and he shows his hand wistfully in the lyrics he wrote for *The Secular Masque;* Swift too understood that the stakes were shifting when he wrote the *Battle of the Books,* as did Pope when he invented a triumphant epic not of empire but of dullness. There is no regretting the astonishing diminutions of *The Dunciad;* but the apocalypse that Pope imagined was very different from the one that Marvell hoped might suffuse the world and transform time at the close of *The First Anniversary.* No one was yawning when the angel of the commonweal stirred the healing waters in 1654 or when, at the height of Exclusion, Locke allowed himself to imagine the dissolution of civil society. Dullness is one kind of cultural demise; civil war, quite another.

The shadows of that conflagration fell across all the decades that remained of this century. The fear of the past haunted not only politics but political theory as well, not only polemical programs but also lyric and epic poetry. As Dryden and Locke knew, and as Algernon Sidney and Stephen College discovered, theirs was a dangerous world in which to cultivate politics and aesthetics, nor was it always possible to distinguish between the two. Nor is it difficult to think that such a past is best recovered by imagining a world where they were constituted as a whole.

Notes

Introduction

All quotations from seventeenth-century texts follow the original spelling, capitalization, and punctuation; italics, however, have been removed.

1. This topic has been more thoroughly explored for early modern France than for England; see, for example, Robert Darnton, "Reading, Writing, and Publishing in Eighteenth-Century France: A Case Study in the Sociology of Literature?" *Daedalus* 100 (1971): 214–56; François Furet and Jacques Ozouf, *Reading and Writing: Literacy in France from Calvin to Jules Ferry* (Cambridge: Cambridge University Press, 1982); Roger Chartier, *The Cultural Uses of Print in Early Modern France,* trans. Lydia G. Cochrane (Princeton: Princeton University Press, 1987); and *The Culture of Print: Power and the Uses of Print in Early Modern Europe,* ed. Roger Chartier, trans. Lydia G. Cochrane (Princeton: Princeton University Press, 1989). For work on literacy in early modern England, see Lawrence Stone, "Literacy and Education in England, 1640–1900," *Past and Present* 42 (February 1969): 69–139; David Cressy, *Literacy and the Social Order: Reading and Writing in Tudor and Stuart England* (Cambridge: Cambridge University Press, 1980); Margaret Spufford, *Small Books and Pleasant Histories: Popular Fiction and Its Readership in Seventeenth-Century England* (Athens: University of Georgia Press, 1981); Keith Thomas, "The Meaning of Literacy in Early Modern England," in *The Written Word: Literacy in Transition,* ed. Gerd Baumann (Oxford: Clarendon Press, 1986), 97–131; Lisa Jardine and Anthony Grafton, " 'Studied for Action': How Gabriel Harvey Read His Livy," *Past and Present* 129 (November 1990): 30–78; and Tessa Watt, *Cheap Print and Popular Piety, 1550–1640* (Cambridge: Cambridge University Press, 1991). For a cogent review of the debate over literacy and its implications for literary reading, see J. Paul Hunter, *Before Novels: The Cultural Contexts of Eighteenth-Century English Fiction* (New York: W. W. Norton, 1990), chap. 3, "Readers Reading," 61–88.

2. John Milton, *Paradise Lost. A Poem in Twelve Books* (London, 1678), Osborn Collection, pb 9, Beinecke Library, Yale University.

3. *The Poems of John Dryden*, ed. James Kinsley, 4 vols. (Oxford: Clarendon Press, 1958), 3:1015–16, lines 496–511.

4. *The Conspiracy of Aeneas & Antenor* (London, 1682), Osborn pb 68; *Poems, &c. Written upon several Occasions, And to Several Persons: By Edmund Waller* (London, 1686), Osborn Collection, pb 66; Samuel Garth, *The Dispensary: A Poem in Six Canto's* (London, 1699), Osborn 71; John Dryden, *The Duke of Guise* (London, 1687), Folger Library copy, D2208; James Tyrrell, *Patriarcha Non Monarcha. The Patriarch Unmonarched* (London, 1681), Folger Library, 146555.

5. *Satyr Unmuzzled* (London, 1680), lines 11–22; text from *Poems on Affairs of State: Augustan Satirical Verse, 1660–1714*, ed. George deF. Lord et al., 7 vols. (New Haven: Yale University Press, 1963–1975), 2:209–10.

6. Pope's annotations are recorded in *Poems on Affairs of State*, 2:209–16.

7. *Cobbett's Complete Collection of State Trials*, 33 vols. (London, 1809–1826), 9 (1682–1684): 821.

8. *Cobbett's Complete Collection of State Trials*, 9:915.

1. Poetics

1. The nature, sources, and growth of partisanship in the years leading to and encompassing the English civil wars are subjects of intense debate, but see Anthony Fletcher's comment: "It is right to look to the early years of Charles I's reign for the beginning of that 'mutual commerce of fear' which we have to understand if we are to explain why political deadlock ended in war.... [P]olitical debate was conducted in emotional and often highly dramatized terms. Gossip and rumour fanned the flames of crisis. Normally sane and balanced men became the prisoners of their own fears and imaginings" (*The Outbreak of the English Civil War* [London: Edward Arnold, 1981], xxix–xxx). On the growth of faction and conflict as constant themes after 1640, see John T. Evans, *Seventeenth-Century Norwich: Politics, Religion, and Government, 1620–1690* (Oxford: Clarendon Press, 1979); and Ann Hughes, *Politics, Society, and Civil War in Warwickshire, 1620–1660* (Cambridge: Cambridge University Press, 1987), 289: "A more permanent consequence of the Civil War and its aftermath was probably the politicisation of local government.... The Civil War forced into prominence a more overt, if very crude, polarisation between the malignants and the well-affected, the wicked and the honest, godly 'party'. At the higher levels of local government, the letters of the major generals abound with this kind of rhetoric." On county division, godly fear, and anti-Catholic rioting in the localities, see William Hunt, *The Puritan Moment: The Coming of Revolution in an English County* (Cambridge, Mass.: Harvard University Press, 1983). Conrad Russell, *The Causes of the English Civil War* (Oxford: Clarendon Press, 1990) and *The Fall of the British Monarchies, 1637–*

1642 (Oxford: Clarendon Press, 1991), argues the opposite position and claims that polarization and division flowed from Scotland. See Derek Hirst's review of Russell's *Fall of the British Monarchies* and *Unrevolutionary England, 1603–1642* (London: Hambledon Press, 1990) in the *Times Literary Supplement,* June 7, 1991, 4.

On division as an artifact of the first years of peace, see Mark Kishlansky, "The Emergence of Adversary Politics in the Long Parliament," *Journal of Modern History* 49 (1977): 617–40; and the response by Derek Hirst, "Unanimity in the Commons, Aristocratic Intrigues, and the Origins of the English Civil War," *Journal of Modern History* 50 (1978): 51–71. On legitimation of opposition, see Mark Kishlansky, *Parliamentary Selection: Social and Political Choice in Early Modern England* (Cambridge: Cambridge University Press, 1986).

On literature and polarization, see Thomas N. Corns, ed., *The Literature of Controversy: Polemical Strategy from Milton to Junius* (London: Frank Cass, 1987), 1–5; T. N. Corns, W. A. Speck, and J. A. Downie, "Archetypal Mystification: Polemic and Reality in English Political Literature, 1640–1750," *Eighteenth-Century Life* 7, no. 3 (1982): 1–27; and W. A. Speck, "Political Propaganda in Augustan England," *Transactions of the Royal Historical Society,* 5th ser., 22 (1972): 17–32.

2. The recovery of the civic from within the imaginative texts of Renaissance literature and the negotiation of social, political, and economic issues within Renaissance imaginative literature—what has loosely been known in the United States as the new historicism and in the United Kingdom as cultural materialism—have now themselves become the object of political study, contextualization, and demystification. The coherence and stability of this contribution to cultural study can be gauged both by the anthologizing of essays under its rubrics and by the volume of essays devoted to its methods. In the first instance, see, for example, Jonathan Dollimore and Alan Sinfield, eds., *Political Shakespeare: New Essays in Cultural Materialism* (Ithaca: Cornell University Press, 1985); Kevin Sharpe and Steven N. Zwicker, eds., *Politics of Discourse: The Literature and History of Seventeenth-Century England* (Berkeley and Los Angeles: University of California Press, 1987); Stephen Greenblatt, ed., *Representing the English Renaissance* (Berkeley and Los Angeles: University of California Press, 1988); and Heather Dubrow and Richard Strier, eds., *The Historical Renaissance* (Chicago: University of Chicago Press, 1988). For work on the methods of new historicism, see Louis Montrose, "Renaissance Literary Studies and the Subject of History," *English Literary Renaissance* 16 (1986): 5–12; Jean E. Howard, "The New Historicism in Renaissance Studies," *English Literary Renaissance* 16 (1986): 13–43; Alan Liu, "The Power of Formalism: The New Historicism," *ELH* 56 (1989): 721–71; and H. Aram Veeser, ed., *The New Historicism* (New York: Routledge, 1989).

This is not intended as a checklist of the new historicist Renaissance, but works of note appearing over the past decade include Stephen Greenblatt, *Renaissance Self-Fashioning: From More to Shakespeare* (Chicago: University of

Chicago Press, 1980); Louis Montrose, "A Poetics of Renaissance Culture," *Criticism* 23 (1981): 349–59 (review of *Renaissance Self-Fashioning*); Jonathan Goldberg, *James I and the Politics of Literature* (Baltimore: Johns Hopkins University Press, 1983); David Norbrook, *Poetry and Politics in the English Renaissance* (London: Routledge and Kegan Paul, 1984); Frank Whigham, *Ambition and Privilege: The Social Tropes of Elizabethan Courtesy Theory* (Berkeley and Los Angeles: University of California Press, 1984); Leah Marcus, *The Politics of Mirth: Jonson, Herrick, Milton, Marvell, and the Defense of Old Holiday Pastimes* (Chicago: University of Chicago Press, 1986); and Michael C. Schoenfeldt, *Prayer and Power: George Herbert and Renaissance Courtship* (Chicago: University of Chicago Press, 1991). See also the essay collections, Claude J. Summers and Ted-Larry Pebworth, eds., *"The Muses Common-Weale": Poetry and Politics in the Seventeenth Century* (Columbia: University of Missouri Press, 1988); and Andrew Gurr, ed., volume 21 of *The Yearbook of English Studies: Politics, Patronage, and Literature in England, 1558–1658* (London: Modern Humanities Research Association, 1991).

3. On the political, radical, and topical Shakespeare, see Jonathan Dollimore, *Radical Tragedy: Religion, Ideology, and Power in the Drama of Shakespeare and His Contemporaries* (Chicago: University of Chicago Press, 1984); Dollimore and Sinfield, eds., *Political Shakespeare;* Leah Marcus, *Puzzling Shakespeare* (Berkeley and Los Angeles: University of California Press, 1988); and Annabel Patterson, *Shakespeare and the Popular Voice* (Oxford: Basil Blackwell, 1989).

On political and polemical implications of lyric, see Kevin Sharpe, "Cavalier Critic? The Ethics and Politics of Thomas Carew's Poetry," in *Politics of Discourse,* ed. Sharpe and Zwicker, 117–46; and Kevin Sharpe, *Criticism and Compliment: The Politics of Literature in the England of Charles I* (Cambridge: Cambridge University Press, 1987), 265–301. On royalist uses of romance, see Annabel Patterson, *Censorship and Interpretation: The Conditions of Writing and Reading in Early Modern England* (Madison: University of Wisconsin Press, 1984), 159–202; Paul Salzman, *English Prose Fiction, 1558–1700: A Critical History* (Oxford: Clarendon Press, 1985), 110–76; and Lois Potter, *Secret Rites and Secret Writing: Royalist Literature, 1641–1660* (Cambridge: Cambridge University Press, 1989), 72–112.

4. On the growth of political opposition in early Stuart politics, see Kevin Sharpe, ed., *Faction and Parliament: Essays on Early Stuart History* (Oxford: Clarendon Press, 1978); and Richard Cust and Ann Hughes, eds., *Conflict in Early Stuart England: Studies in Religion and Politics, 1603–1642* (London: Longman, 1989).

5. See the collection of civil war ballads in H. E. Rollins, ed., *Cavalier and Puritan: Ballads and Broadsides Illustrating the Period of the Great Rebellion, 1640–1660* (New York: New York University Press, 1923); and Natascha Würzbach, *The Rise of the English Street Ballad, 1550–1650,* trans. Gayna Walls (Cambridge: Cambridge University Press, 1990), 24–26, 236–41.

6. For critical and biographical work on Marvell, Dryden, and Milton

which has been especially responsive to the role of polemic within the literary career, see, for example, Hilton Kelliher, *Andrew Marvell: Poet and Politician, 1621–78* (London: British Museum Publications, 1978); Warren L. Chernaik, *The Poet's Time: Politics and Religion in the Work of Andrew Marvell* (Cambridge: Cambridge University Press, 1983); and Conal Condren and A. D. Cousins, eds., *The Political Identity of Andrew Marvell* (Aldershot: Scolar Press, 1990).

The biographical and critical work on Dryden includes George McFadden, *Dryden: The Public Writer, 1660–1685* (Princeton: Princeton University Press, 1978); James Anderson Winn, *John Dryden and His World* (New Haven: Yale University Press, 1987); and David Bywaters, *Dryden in Revolutionary England* (Berkeley and Los Angeles: University of California Press, 1991).

On Milton, see Keith Stavely, *The Politics of Milton's Prose Style* (New Haven: Yale University Press, 1975); Christopher Hill, *Milton and the English Revolution* (New York: Viking Press, 1977) and *The Experience of Defeat* (New York: Viking Press, 1984); Andrew Milner, *John Milton and the English Revolution* (London: Macmillan, 1981); Thomas N. Corns, *The Development of Milton's Prose Style* (Oxford: Oxford University Press, 1982); Mary Ann Radzinowicz, "The Politics of *Paradise Lost*," in *Politics of Discourse*, ed. Sharpe and Zwicker, 204–29; David Loewenstein and James Grantham Turner, eds., *Politics, Poetics, and Hermeneutics in Milton's Prose* (Cambridge: Cambridge University Press, 1990); Michael Wilding, *Dragons Teeth: Literature in the English Revolution* (Oxford: Clarendon Press, 1987), esp. 7–88, 232–58; and Thomas Healy and Jonathan Sawday, eds., *Literature and the English Civil War* (Cambridge: Cambridge University Press, 1990), esp. Thomas N. Corns, " 'Some rousing motions': The Plurality of Miltonic Ideology" (110–26).

7. On the politicization of pastoral, romance, and fable, see Patterson, *Censorship and Interpretation*, passim; and more recently Patterson's "Fables of Power," in *Politics of Discourse*, ed. Sharpe and Zwicker, 271–96; *Pastoral and Ideology: Virgil to Valéry* (Berkeley and Los Angeles: University of California Press, 1987), chap. 3; and *Fables and Power: Aesopian Writing and Political Theory* (Durham, N.C.: Duke University Press, 1991). On politics and Renaissance genre, see the essays in part 3, "Genre, Politics, and Society," in Barbara Kiefer Lewalski, ed., *Renaissance Genres: Essays on Theory, History, and Interpretation*, Harvard English Studies, vol. 14 (Cambridge, Mass.: Harvard University Press, 1986); Potter, *Secret Rites*, chap. 3, "Genre as Code"; and David Norbrook, "Marvell's 'Horatian Ode' and the Politics of Genre," in *Literature and the English Civil War*, ed. Healy and Sawday, 147–69. On the uses of history in seventeenth-century poetry, see Achsah Guibbory, *The Map of Time* (Urbana: University of Illinois Press, 1986), 231–40; and Gerald MacLean, *Time's Witness: Historical Representation in English Poetry, 1603–1660* (Madison: University of Wisconsin Press, 1990), esp. 44–61.

On the polemical significance of collections of civic verse, see the unsigned "Preface" to *State Poems ... Now carefully Examined with the Originals, and Published without any Castration* (London, 1697): "In short the said State-Poems, and this Continuation thereof, make a Compleate Collection of all that are valuable in that nature, for these forty years; and is the best Secret History of our late Reigns, as being writ by such great Persons as were near the Helm, knew the Transactions, and were above being brib'd to flatter, or afraid to speak truth."

8. Peter Burke, "A Survey of the Popularity of Ancient Historians, 1450–1700," *History and Theory* 5 (1966): 135–52, has examined the frequency of editions and translations of the Roman historians in the English Renaissance. On the political uses of Tacitus's *Annals* and *Histories,* see, for example, M. F. Tenney, "Tacitus in the Politics of Early Stuart England," *Classical Journal* 37 (1941): 151–63; Else-Lilly Etter, *Tacitus in der Geistesgeschichte des 16. und 17. Jahrhunderts* (Basel: Helbing & Lichtenhahn, 1966); Kenneth Schellhase, *Tacitus in Renaissance Political Thought* (Chicago: University of Chicago Press, 1976); and Steven N. Zwicker and David Bywaters, "Politics and Translation: The English Tacitus of 1698," *Huntington Library Quarterly* 52 (1989): 319–46. See, allied to this theme, Kevin Sharpe, "The Foundation of the Chairs of History at Oxford and Cambridge: An Episode in Jacobean Politics," *History of Universities* 2 (1982): 127–52 (rpt. in Sharpe's *Politics and Ideas in Early Stuart England: Essays and Studies* [London: Pinter Publishers, 1989], 207–29).

More work needs to be done, however, on the political significance and frequency of editions and translations of classical poets at midcentury. Attention has been paid to some authors; see, for example, John Emperor, *The Catullian Influence in English Lyric Poetry, 1600–1650* (1928; rpt. New York: Octagon Books, 1973); Joanna Martindale, "The Response to Horace in the Seventeenth Century (with Special Reference to the *Odes* and to the Period 1600–1660)" (D. Phil. thesis, Oxford, 1977); the chapters on Horace (86–147) and Juvenal (148–81) in Paul Hammond's *John Oldham and the Renewal of Classical Culture* (Cambridge: Cambridge University Press, 1983); Lee Pearcy, *The Mediated Muse: English Translations of Ovid, 1560–1700* (Hamden, Conn.: Archon Books, 1984); the remarks on Lucan in MacLean's *Time's Witness,* 26–44; and, more generally, George deForest Lord, *Classical Presences in Seventeenth-Century English Poetry* (New Haven: Yale University Press, 1987). But other classical poets have been neglected. Not enough attention has been paid, for example, to Lucretius: John Evelyn published a translation of book 1 of *De rerum natura* in 1656, Thomas Creech published a Lucretius in 1682, and Dryden translated selections in *Sylvae* (1685), on which see Paul Hammond, "The Integrity of Dryden's Lucretius," *Modern Language Review* 78 (1983): 1–23. Nor have the political uses of Virgil at midcentury been sufficiently studied. Donald Wing's *Short-Title Catalogue* shows us how much attention Virgil received during the 1650s: Latin editions were published in 1650, 1657, 1658, 1661, 1663, 1664, and 1667, and editions of the Ogilby translation were issued in 1649, 1650, 1654, and 1665; *The Destruction of Troy* was published in 1656; James Harrington's *Essay upon two of Virgil's Eclogues and two Books of his Aeneis,* in 1658; Edmund Waller and Sidney Godolphin, trans., *The Passion of Dido,* in 1658; and John Boys's *Aeneas His Descent into Hell,* in 1661.

9. This topic has received very little attention; it would be useful to have a comparative study of the successive issues and editions of such authors as Carew, Cartwright, Cleveland, Cotton, Cowley, Davenant, Donne, Herbert, Herrick, King, Sidney, Spenser, and Waller. The classic study of republication is A. B. Worden's introduction to his edition of Edmund Ludlow, *A Voyce from the Watch Tower,* Camden Society, 4th ser., vol. 21 (London: Royal Historical Society, 1978). On John Toland as late seventeenth-century biographer and editor of Milton, see Stephen H. Daniel, *John Toland: His Methods, Manners, and Mind* (Kingston and Montreal: McGill-Queen's University Press, 1984), 60–63, 212–13; and cf. Bernard Sharratt, "The Appropriation of Milton," in *Essays and Studies, 1982,* ed. Suheil Bushrui (London: John Murray, 1982), 30–44.

More work also needs to be done with the republication of originally polemical items like *London's Flames Reviv'd . . . Now humbly offered to the Considerations of all True Protestants* (London, 1689), an antipapal account of the Fire of London republished as part of the propaganda in 1689; and Robert Ferguson, *The Design of Enslaving England Discovered in the Incroachments Upon the Powers and Privileges of Parliament, by K. Charles II. Being a New corrected Impression of that Excellent Piece, intitled. A Just and Modest Vindication of the Proceedings of the Two Last Parliaments of King Charles the Second* (London, 1689).

10. On the circulation of manuscript and printed materials, see Brice Harris, "Captain Robert Julian, Secretary to the Muses," *ELH* 10 (1943): 294–309; George deF. Lord et al., eds., *Poems on Affairs of State: Augustan Satirical Verse, 1660–1714,* 7 vols. (New Haven: Yale University Press, 1963–1975), 1:xxxii–xlii; Paul Hammond, ed., *John Wilmot, Earl of Rochester: Selected Poems* (Bristol: Bristol Classical Press, 1982), xxv–xxvi; Harold Love, "Scribal Publication in Seventeenth-Century England," *Transactions of the Cambridge Bibliographical Society* 9 (1987): 130–54; and Arthur Marotti, "Patronage, Poetry, and Print," *Yearbook of English Studies* 21 (1991):1–26.

On the history of publication by subscription, see Sarah L. C. Clapp, "The Beginnings of Subscription Publication in the Seventeenth Century," *Modern Philology* 29 (1931): 199–224; and F. J. G. Robinson and P. J. Wallis, *Book Subscription Lists: A Revised Guide* (Newcastle upon Tyne: Harold Hill & Son, 1975).

11. On press regulation, see J. Walker, "The Censorship of the Press during the Reign of Charles II," *History* 35 (1950): 219–38; Frederick Seaton Siebert, *Freedom of the Press in England, 1476–1776: The Rise and Decline of Government Control* (Urbana: University of Illinois Press, 1952); Timothy Crist, "Government Control of the Press after the Expiration of the Printing Act in 1679," *Publishing History* 5 (1979): 49–77; Patterson, *Censorship and Interpretation,* passim; Philip Hamburger, "The Development of the Law of Seditious Libel and the Control of the Press," *Stanford Law Review* 37 (1985): 661–765; and

Christopher Hill, "Censorship and English Literature," in *Collected Essays of Christopher Hill*, vol. 1, *Writing and Revolution in Seventeenth-Century England* (Brighton: Harvester Press, 1985), 32–71.

On the book trade, see D. F. McKenzie, "The London Book Trade in the Later Seventeenth Century" (Sandars Lectures, 1976); see also Robin Myers and Michael Harris, eds., *Economics of the British Booktrade, 1605–1939* (Cambridge: Chadwyck-Healey, 1985). In addition to the McKenzie lectures, the work of an older generation of biographers of seventeenth-century publishers provides us with some access to this history: H. A. Plomer, *A Dictionary of the Booksellers and Printers . . . 1641–1667* (London: Bibliographical Society, 1907); George Kitchin, *Sir Roger L'Estrange: A Contribution to the History of the Press in the Seventeenth Century* (London: Kegan Paul, Trench, Trübner, 1913); Leona Rostenberg, "Nathaniel Thompson, Catholic Printer and Publisher of the Restoration," *The Library*, 5th ser., 10 (1955): 186–202; and Kathleen Lynch, *Jacob Tonson, Kit-Cat Publisher* (Knoxville: University of Tennessee Press, 1971).

12. On the literary defense, see Margaret W. Ferguson, *Trials of Desire: Renaissance Defenses of Poetry* (New Haven: Yale University Press, 1983); and Daniel Javitch, *Poetry and Courtliness in Renaissance England* (Princeton: Princeton University Press, 1978), 100–104. The defenses themselves can still most easily be consulted in Joel Spingarn, ed., *Critical Essays of the Seventeenth Century*, 3 vols. (Oxford: Clarendon Press, 1908–1909).

13. On poetry as a site for literary criticism and on the development of seventeenth-century verse arts of poetry, see Randall Current, "The Curious Art: A Study of Literary Criticism in Verse in the Seventeenth Century" (Ph.D. diss., University of California at Los Angeles, 1972).

14. Michael Mann, *The Sources of Social Power*, vol. 1, *A History of Power from the Beginning to* A.D. *1760* (Cambridge: Cambridge University Press, 1986), makes some interesting connections between rhetorical and literary forms and governance and politics in the ancient world. See, for example, his discussion of the impact of Athenian-style democracy on the choice of Greek literary forms, and the popularity of dialogues and rhetoric (207), or his remarks on the literary content of Roman education and the Romans' obsession "with their language, its grammar, and its style, and with the connections of these to literacy and to historical texts dealing with the growth of Roman power. Hence also their concern with rhetoric, the art of communication and debate. This also had a practical connection to the legal system and to the aristocratic profession of jurist. But we must still ask why this professional training was in rhetoric, not statute or case law (like our own). The answer lies in the importance of literate but mnemonic communication in giving *morale* to the ruling class of the empire, giving them common access to the stock of cultural knowledge and reinforcing their cultural solidarity through communal reading and debating activities" (314).

The application of these issues to cultural politics in mid-seventeenth-century England seems both obvious and important. The civil wars and the political crises that followed throughout the rest of this century were struggles over religion, economics, social control, and political ascendancy, but they were also controversies over the control of texts and culture. The importance of the links between art and empire acknowledges the significance of the dominating elite culture, poetry first and foremost, but history, rhetoric, and classical texts as well.

15. *The Poems of John Dryden,* ed. James Kinsley, 4 vols. (Oxford: Clarendon Press, 1958), 1: 215, line 4, preface to *Absalom and Achitophel.*

16. On the gradual liberation of the aesthetic, see Michael McKeon, "Politics of Discourses and the Rise of the Aesthetic in Seventeenth-Century England," in *Politics of Discourse,* ed. Sharpe and Zwicker, 35–51.

17. Citations are to the text of Sir Philip Sidney, *The Defence of Poesy,* edited by Katherine Duncan-Jones in *Sir Philip Sidney* (Oxford: Oxford University Press, 1989); references are given by page number in parentheses in my text.

18. See Duncan-Jones, ed., *Sir Philip Sidney,* viii–ix.

19. On the afterlife of the *Defence,* see Dennis Kay, "Introduction: Sidney— A Critical Heritage," in *Sir Philip Sidney: An Anthology of Modern Criticism,* ed. Kay (Oxford: Clarendon Press, 1987), 3–41; and Jackson Boswell and H. R. Woudhuysen, "Some Unfamiliar Sidney Allusions," in *Sir Philip Sidney: 1586 and the Creation of a Legend,* ed. J. van Dorsten, D. Baker-Smith, and Arthur F. Kinney (Leiden: E. J. Brill/Leiden University Press, 1986), 221–37.

20. *The Poems of John Milton,* ed. John Carey and Alastair Fowler (London: Longmans, 1968), 344.

21. On Milton's engagement with the heroic drama, see Jackson I. Cope, "*Paradise Regained:* Inner Ritual," *Milton Studies* 1 (1969): 51–65; and Steven Zwicker, "Milton, Dryden, and the Politics of Literary Controversy," work in progress.

22. Dryden's twinning of poetry and history is exemplified in the preface to *Annus Mirabilis;* on the uses of history in the preface, see Steven N. Zwicker, *Politics and Language in Dryden's Poetry: The Arts of Disguise* (Princeton: Princeton University Press, 1984), 40–43. In the debate between poetry and history, Thomas Sprat gives the laurels to history for verisimilitude; see Sprat's dedicatory letter to Walter Pope, *The Plague of Athens* (London, 1667), A3^r–A3^v: "Though it must be said, that the Historian had a vast advantage over the Poet; He having been present on the place, and assaulted by the disease himself, had the horror familiar to his Eyes, and all the shapes of the misery still remaining on his mind, which must needs make a great impression on his Pen and Fancie. Whereas the Poet was forced to allow his foot-steps, and onely work on that matter he allow'd him. This I speak, because it may in some measure too excuse my own defects: . . . besides only writing by an Idea of that which I never yet saw, nor care to feel, (being not of the humor of the Painter in Sir Philip Sidney, who thrust himself into the midst of a Fight, that he might the better delineate it.) Having, I say, all these disadvantages,

and many more, for which I must onely blame my self, it cannot be expected that I should come near equalling him, in whom none of the contrary advantages were wanting."

23. See John Sitter, *Literary Loneliness in Mid-Eighteenth-Century England* (Ithaca: Cornell University Press, 1982).

24. Cf. David Underdown, *Pride's Purge: Politics in the Puritan Revolution* (Oxford: Clarendon Press, 1971), 174: "For the seventeenth century the modern term 'public opinion' obviously has little meaning. Nevertheless, in a vague and indefinite way, public opinion existed and could not be ignored. It could be artificially stimulated, as had been shown by earlier petitioning campaigns. Both sides recognized its importance, and the chorus of pamphlets and sermons reached a climax in the weeks between the Purge and 30 January. There was no shortage of argument or information in London, as the rival presses thundered forth their angry rhetoric." On political culture, see Tim Harris, *London Crowds in the Reign of Charles II* (Cambridge: Cambridge University Press, 1987), 14–35.

25. The *Catalogue of the Pamphlets, Books, Newspapers, and Manuscripts Relating to the Civil War, the Commonwealth, and Restoration, Collected by George Thomason, 1640–1661* [By G. K. Fortescue], 2 vols. (London: British Museum, 1908), suggests something of the density of this textualized world. See also Rüdiger Ahrens, "The Political Pamphlet: 1660–1714," *Anglia* 109, no. 1/2 (1991): 21–43; the "Chronological Index" to *British Newspapers and Periodicals, 1641–1700,* comp. Carolyn Nelson and Matthew Seccombe (New York: Modern Language Association of America, 1987), 622–94; and Thomas N. Corns, "Publication and Politics, 1640–1661: An SPSS-based Account of the Thomason Collection of Civil War Tracts," *Literary and Linguistic Computing* 1 (1986): 74–84. On prints and print culture during this period, see Alexander Globe, *Peter Stent: London Printseller circa 1642–1665* (Vancouver: University of British Columbia Press, 1985).

26. Edward, earl of Clarendon, *The History of the Rebellion,* ed. W. Dunn Macray, 6 vols. (Oxford: Clarendon Press, 1888), 1:456.

27. *OED,* s.v. "Animadversion."

28. See Lyman Ray Patterson, *Copyright in Historical Perspective* (Nashville: Vanderbilt University Press, 1968); Siebert, *Freedom of the Press in England;* and McKenzie, "The London Book Trade."

29. See Joseph Loewenstein, "The Archaeology of Miltonic Genius," forthcoming.

30. We need to know more about this subject; the primary bibliographical tool is Samuel Halkett and John Laing, *Dictionary of Anonymous and Pseudonymous English Literature,* ed. James Kennedy, W. A. Smith, and A. F. Johnson, 7 vols. (Edinburgh and London: Oliver and Boyd, 1926–1934).

31. The Osborn Collection in the Beinecke Library of Yale University contains a number of manuscript anthologies from this period; see esp. Osborn b 111, "Loyal Poems," a collection of manuscript poetry of the most pronounced Jacobite sentiment, bound in leather, stamped with the royal

cipher "J. R.," and once owned by Sir Robert Strange, brother-in-law of Andrew Lumisden, secretary to Prince Charles Edward, the Young Pretender. William J. Cameron cites Percy Dobell's speculation that the anthology was made for James II in his exile; see *Poems on Affairs of State*, vol. 5, *1689–1697*, ed. William J. Cameron, 531; see also the *Index of English Literary Manuscripts*, vol. 2, *1625–1700*, pt. 1, comp. Peter Beal (London: Mansell Publishing, 1987), 483.

32. For the circumstances of publication see Mary Edmond, *Rare Sir William Davenant* (New York: St. Martin's Press, 1987), 103–20.

33. William Davenant, *Preface* to *Gondibert*, in *Critical Essays of the Seventeenth Century*, ed. Spingarn, 2:9–10; subsequent parenthetical volume and page references are to Spingarn's text.

34. The lament over the decline of wit is widespread in the 1650s; see, e.g., the preface to *The Floating Island: A Tragi-comedy, Acted before his Majesty at Oxford, Aug. 29, 1636* (London, 1655), A2^r: "Were this translated into Latin or Italian, it would be greatful to foreign Wits; and if it find lesse welcome, 'tis because there is not so much true wit among us as was or ought to be. It is not now inscribed to any for Protection."

35. On Davenant, Hobbes, and English neoclassicism, see Cornell Dowlin, *Sir William Davenant's "Gondibert," Its Preface, and Hobbes's Answer: A Study in English Neo-Classicism* (Philadelphia: University of Pennsylvania Press, 1934); D. Judson Milburn, *The Age of Wit, 1650–1750* (New York: Macmillan, 1966), 93–97, 130–32; and Irene Simon, *Neo-Classical Criticism, 1660–1800* (London: Edward Arnold, 1971), 15–16.

36. Thomas Hobbes, *Answer to Davenant's "Preface" to "Gondibert,"* in *Critical Essays of the Seventeenth Century*, ed. Spingarn, 2:58–59; subsequent parenthetical volume and page references are to Spingarn's text.

37. See Allan Pritchard, ed., *The Civil War* (Toronto: University of Toronto Press, 1973), 4–5.

38. Abraham Cowley, *Preface* to *Poems* (London, 1656), in *Critical Essays of the Seventeenth Century*, ed. Spingarn, 2:77; subsequent parenthetical volume and page references are to Spingarn's text.

39. See, for example, "The Preface" to *The Psalter of David: With Titles and Collects according to the matter of each Psalme* (London, 1646), A4^v–A5^r: "It was my custome long since to secure my selfe against the violences of Discontents abroad . . . in my bookes and my retirements: But now I was deprived of both them, and driven to a publicke view and participation of those dangers and miseries which threatened the Kingdome, and disturbed the evennesse of my former life. I was therefore constrained to amasse together all those arguments of hope and comfort, by which Men in the like condition were supported; and amongst all the great examples of trouble and confidence, I reckon'd King David one of the biggest, and of greatest consideration. For considering that he was a King, vexed with a Civill Warre, his case had so much of ours in it, that it was likely the devotions he used might fit our turne, and his comforts sustaine us."

40. The touchstone for art throughout Thomas Sprat's *Life and Writings of Cowley* (London, 1668) is the term *wit;* it appears a dozen times within the compass of the short essay, an epithet whose aim is to vindicate the politics and the style of Cowley, to offer a model of political loyalty and literary excellence—a literary intelligence pliant, variable, sudden, and expressive.

41. *Wit and Loyalty Reviv'd In a Collection of some smart Satyrs in Verse and Prose on the late Times. By Mr. Abraham Cowley, Sir J. Berkenhead, and the Ingenious Author of Hudibras, &c.* (London, 1682); the printer, W[alter] Davis, issued a number of other royalist pieces during Exclusion.

42. *Wit and Loyalty Reviv'd,* unpaginated prefatory leaves.

43. *Wit and Loyalty Reviv'd,* unpaginated prefatory leaves.

44. *The Poems of John Dryden,* ed. James Kinsley, 4 vols. (Oxford: Clarendon Press, 1958), 1:46, lines 98–107.

45. See "wit" in John Aden, ed. and comp., *The Critical Opinions of John Dryden: A Dictionary* (Nashville: Vanderbilt University Press, 1963), 277–79.

46. See Keith Thomas's review of Roy Porter's *Mind-Forg'd Manacles* (London: Athlone Press, 1987) in the *Times Literary Supplement,* December 4–10, 1987, 1340.

47. Thomas Sprat, *The History of the Royal Society* (London, 1667), 431; subsequent references are given by page number in parentheses in my text.

48. For the continuing polemical vitality of wit, dullness, and sobriety, see the satires against William and Mary in volume 5, *Poems on Affairs of State,* ed. William J. Cameron, passim.

49. On wit as weaponry, see John Oldham's "Prologue" to the *Satires upon the Jesuits,* quoted from volume 2 of *Poems on Affairs of State,* ed. Elias F. Mengel, Jr.: "For who can longer hold? when ev'ry press, / The bar and pulpit too, has broke the peace? / When ev'ry scribling fool at the alarms / Has drawn his pen, and rises up in arms? / . . . 'Tis pointed satire and the sharps of wit / For such a prize are th'only weapons fit" (19–20).

50. On the growth of libel and invective, see also *Short Dull Remarks, Upon the Long Dull Essay upon Poetry* (London, 1683), 3–4: "In the Worlds dawn, when Man by Nature taught, / Resented Wrongs, they boldly told, and fought; / So Cain no Libel on his Brother threw, / But spar'd the tender Fame of him he slew. / Scorn and malicious laughter had no name, / Some kindly pardon'd, bravely some o'recame. / But when the Earth, beneath the Waters shrunk, / Thou wanton God wert with the Deluge drunk; / And then it was vile Laughter did'st Inspire / In Satyrists, who still profane thy Fire. / In that same Age Curs'd Ham began to Mock, / (That shameful off-spring of so Rich a stock) / And since, most sing, to prove they're angry grown, / The just Reverse of what should make it known."

51. See headnote and text, Elias F. Mengel, Jr., ed., *Poems on Affairs of State,* 2:425–31.

52. See Jonas Barish, *The Antitheatrical Prejudice* (Berkeley and Los Angeles: University of California Press, 1981), 155–90, 221–55; and the Ordinance for the Utter Suppression and Abolishing of All Stage-Plays, February 11,

1647/48, in *Acts and Ordinances of the Interregnum, 1642–1660,* ed. C. H. Firth and R. S. Rait, 3 vols. (London: HMSO, 1911), 1:1070–72.

53. See, e.g., *An Essay Towards a General History of Whoring* (London, 1697); *A Help to a National Reformation* (London, 1700); *Reflexions upon the Moral State of the Nation* (London, 1701); Josiah Woodward, *An Account of the Progress of the Reformation of Manners* (London, 1701).

2. The King's Head and the Politics of Literary Property: The *Eikon Basilike* and *Eikonoklastes*

1. Citations to the *Eikon Basilike* are to the edition prepared by Philip A. Knachel (Ithaca: Cornell University Press for the Folger Shakespeare Library, 1966), abbreviated here as *EB;* citations to *Eikonoklastes* are to the *Complete Prose Works of John Milton,* ed. Don M. Wolfe et al., 8 vols. (New Haven: Yale University Press, 1953–1982), vol. 3, *1648–1649,* ed. Merritt Y. Hughes (1962), 335–601, abbreviated here as *E;* page references to both appear in my text in parentheses. On the significance of Milton's additions to the second edition, see Keith Stavely, *The Politics of Milton's Prose Style* (New Haven: Yale University Press, 1975), 84–86, 90.

2. The standard bibliography is Francis F. Madan, *A New Bibliography of the Eikon Basilike of King Charles I* (Oxford: Oxford Bibliographical Society Publications, n.s. 3, 1949). On the phenomenal publishing history of the first year in the face of "the whole apparatus of state control of the press," see Thomas N. Corns, "Milton's Prose," in *The Cambridge Companion to Milton,* ed. Dennis Danielson (Cambridge: Cambridge University Press, 1989), 194.

3. The issue of authorship is treated by Madan, *A New Bibliography,* 1–2; the most recent contributors to the discussion include Richard Helgerson, "Milton Reads the King's Book: Print, Performance, and the Making of a Bourgeois Idol," *Criticism* 29 (Winter 1987): 1–2, 9; Lois Potter, *Secret Rites and Secret Writing: Royalist Literature, 1641–1660* (Cambridge: Cambridge University Press, 1989), 170–73; and Robert Wilcher, "What Was the King's Book For? The Evolution of *Eikon Basilike,*" *Yearbook of English Studies* 21 (1991): 218–28.

4. For the publishing history of *Eikonoklastes,* see volume 3 of the *Complete Prose Works of Milton,* 147–50.

5. Reference to *Eikonoklastes* in the contemporary literature can be followed in John T. Shawcross, comp., *Milton: A Bibliography for the Years 1624–1700* (Binghamton, N.Y.: Medieval and Renaissance Texts and Studies, 1984). See also William R. Parker, *An Exhibit of Seventeenth-Century Editions of Writings by John Milton* (Bloomington, Ind.: Lilly Library, 1969), items 26–27 (unpaginated); Parker notes that at least 103 copies survived the public condemnation.

6. Partisan struggles over the interpretation and application of Scripture

were legion in these years. In the polemic generated by the *Eikon Basilike* one controversialist justified his own commentary by noting that even Scripture is subject to exegesis: "Is it not enough that so rare a temple should be destroyed, but that all his thoughts must perish. But I undervalue the Sun too much, to think it can be prejudic'd by such a fog; and should think my self guilty of the same fault, in proving the sun-shine by the light of my candle; but that my boldness takes its rise from this observation, that Comments have been written upon the Scriptures" (*Eikon e Piste* [London, 1649], A3^r).

7. See M. Dorothy George, *English Political Caricature: A Study of Opinion and Propaganda*, 2 vols. (Oxford: Clarendon Press, 1959), 1:34–36.

8. There is no full bibliography of responses to the execution, but on January 30 sermons, see Helen W. Randall, "The Rise and Fall of a Martyrology: Sermons on Charles I," *Huntington Library Quarterly* 10 (1947): 135–67. On the associations of Charles I with the drama and on the afterlife of the execution as polemic and art, see, variously, Nancy Klein Maguire, "The Theatrical Mask/Masque of Politics: The Case of Charles I," *Journal of British Studies* 28 (1989):1–22; John Kenyon, *Revolution Principles: The Politics of Party, 1689–1720* (Cambridge: Cambridge University Press, 1977), 61–82; Potter, *Secret Rites and Secret Writing*, 156–207; Donald T. Siebert, "The Aesthetic Execution of Charles I: Clarendon to Hume," in *Executions and the British Experience from the Seventeenth to the Twentieth Century: A Collection of Essays*, ed. William B. Thesing (Jefferson, N.C.: McFarland, 1990), 7–27; and Gerald MacLean, *Time's Witness: Historical Representation in English Poetry, 1603–1660* (Madison: University of Wisconsin Press, 1990), 214–19.

9. On the *Eikon Basilike* as "performance" rather than literary text, see Helgerson, "Milton Reads the King's Book," 9.

10. See R. Malcolm Smuts, *Court Culture and the Origins of a Royalist Tradition in Early Stuart England* (Philadelphia: University of Pennsylvania Press, 1987), passim; Oliver Millar's catalog, *The Age of Charles I: Painting in England, 1620–1649* (London: Tate Gallery, 1972); Millar's essay, "Van Dyck in London," in *Anthony van Dyck*, ed. Arthur K. Wheelock, Jr., Susan J. Barnes, and Julius S. Held (Washington, D.C.: National Gallery of Art, 1990), 53–58; Michael Brennan, *Literary Patronage in the English Renaissance* (London: Routledge, 1988), 188–90; and J. C. Robertson, "Caroline Culture: Bridging Court and Country?" *History* 75 (October 1990): 388–416.

11. See Stephen Orgel, *The Illusion of Power: Political Theater in the English Renaissance* (Berkeley and Los Angeles: University of California Press, 1975), 77–87; and, of course, Milton in *Eikonoklastes*.

12. Cf. Sir Henry Wotton's praise of Charles I as patron and collector: "But the most splendid of all your entertainments, is your love of excellent Artificers, and Works: wherewith in either Art both of Picture and Sculpture you have so adorned your Palaces, that Italy (the greatest Mother of elegant Arts) or at least (next the Grecians) the principall Nursery may seem by your magnificence to be translated into England" (*Reliquiae Wottonianae* [London,

1651], 158–59). On Charles I's collection of paintings, see Oliver Millar, ed., *The Inventories and Valuations of the King's Goods, 1649–1651*, Walpole Society, 43 (1972).

13. See Kevin Sharpe, *Criticism and Compliment: The Politics of Literature in the England of Charles I* (Cambridge: Cambridge University Press, 1987), 1–53; Annabel Patterson, *Marvell and the Civic Crown* (Princeton: Princeton University Press, 1978), 59–68; and David Norbrook, "Marvell's 'Horatian Ode' and the Politics of Genre," in *Literature and the English Civil War*, ed. Thomas Healy and Jonathan Sawday (Cambridge: Cambridge University Press, 1990), 148–49.

14. See John Phillips, *The Reformation of Images: Destruction of Art in England, 1535–1660* (Berkeley and Los Angeles: University of California Press, 1973), 195–98; and, more recently, Ernest Gilman, *Iconoclasm and Poetry in the English Reformation: Down Went Dagon* (Chicago: University of Chicago Press, 1986), 40; and cf. Millar, *Inventories and Valuations of the King's Goods;* on the dispersal of the picture collection, see also *The Diary of John Evelyn*, ed. E. S. de Beer, 6 vols. (Oxford: Clarendon Press, 1955), 2:549: "Bellcan shewd us an excellent Copy of his Majesties Venus Sleeping, & the Satyre, with other figures; for now they had plunderd sold & dissipated a world of rare Paintings of the Kings & his Loyall Subjects."

15. For a guide through the intricacies of this problem, see the review article by Kevin Sharpe, "Culture, Politics, and the English Civil War," *Huntington Library Quarterly* 51 (1988): 95–135. On the aesthetic taste and refinements of some of those who supported Parliament, see Robertson, "Caroline Culture," 414–15.

16. See George, *English Political Caricature*, 1:34–36; as George points out, the frontispiece was itself the subject of commentary, exegesis, and controversy.

17. Cf. [F. H.], *An Elogie, and Epitaph* (n.p., 1649), stanza 12: "The Arts in him conspired to erect / A lasting fabrick to eternity, / Whose concave did containe the true effect / Of the most absolute ACADEMIE: / Had ye observ'd, this Mirour did present / The Sciences in an EPITOMIE; / Or rather 't seem'd they had beene onely sent / From him to borrow light and dignity."

18. Milton was clearly sensitive to the capacity of the *Eikon Basilike* as monument; see, e.g., "And the Kings admirers may heer see thir madness to mistake this Book for a monument of his worth and wisdom, when as indeed it is his Doomsday Booke" (*E,* 382). On elegy and monumentalism, see, e.g., the "Dedication" to Princess Elizabeth in John Quarles, *Regale Lectum Miseriae* (1649), A2ᵛ: "Madam, I am confident that I may, without adulation say, that your Royall Fathers death, gave a life to Vertue. And as we have a sufficient cause to deplore the absence of his Person, so we have an undeniable reason to rejoyce for the presence of his perfections, which will build everlasting Pyramids in the hearts of those, which were his loyall Subjects."

The preface to [Peter Heylyn], *Bibliotheca Regia, Or the Royal Library, containing A Collection of such of the Papers of His Late Majesty King Charls* (London

1659), *2ʳ, yields a set of interesting metaphors for the king's writings as mangled body parts: "It is reported of Medea, that when she fled with Jason, and the rest of the Argonauts, from the Court of her Father, whom she had robbed of his Treasures...she caused her young brother Absyrtus, whom she took along with her, to be wickedly murdered, scattering all the way she went with his broken bones: And this she did unto this end...that if her Father should pursue her, he might be totally imployed in gathering up the fragments of that mangled body, and thereby give her opportunity to escape his hands. The like hath happened unto me, who being in the persute of other studies, have been diverted by taking up such Pieces of his Majesty the late King Charles, as have escaped the rack and ruines of these times."

19. Ben Jonson, "On My First Sonne," *Ben Jonson*, ed. C. H. Herford and Percy and Evelyn Simpson, 11 vols. (Oxford: Clarendon Press, 1925–1952), 8:41; see the commentary of Joshua Scodel, *The English Poetic Epitaph: Commemoration and Conflict from Jonson to Wordsworth* (Ithaca: Cornell University Press, 1991), 92–103.

20. On the material and political bodies of the king, see Ernst H. Kantorowicz, *The King's Two Bodies: A Study in Mediaeval Political Theology* (Princeton: Princeton University Press, 1957).

21. *An Elegie upon the Death of King Charls* (London, 1649[?]), brs.

22. *The Subjects Sorrow*, 23.

23. [Charles I] *Reliquiae Sacrae Carolinae, The Works of that Great Monarch and Glorious Martyr King Charles the Ist* (Hague, Printed by SAM: BROWNE, [1648]), [Part One], 96.

24. *An Apologetick for the sequestered clergy of the Church of England. Disclaiming and detesting the late Unnatural, Presumptuous, Unparallel'd and Antichristian Proceedings, against the Honor and Life of the Best of Kings, Our most Dear and Dead Soverign Lord and King. St. Charls the Martyr. Printed at New-Munster in the year of Confusion* (1649), 1.

25. *Caroli* (London, 1649), 11. One of the most frequently used rhetorical devices for describing the king's execution is the drawing and denying of parallels; see, for example, *A Faithful Subjects Sigh* (London, 1649), 1: "Old Time! I challenge thee to match but this / Most horrid Treason, and from thy Abisse / Of Monuments, and darke Lethean Cell / Where Monsters sleep, draw one to Parallel / The English Rebell; rake Hell and extract / From thy worm-eaten blinde Records, an Act / So black, So Hellish; as, when Charls now slaine, / Was past by Subjects on a Soveraigne." See also Fabian Philipps, *King Charles the First, no Man of Blood: But a Martyr for his People* (London, 1649), 66: "The light of Israel is put out; and the King, Lawes, Religion, and Liberties of the People murthered, an action so horrid, and a sinne of so great a magnitude, and complication as if we shall aske the daies that are past, and enquire from the one end of the Earth to the other, there will not bee found any wickednesse like to this great wickednesse, or hath been heard like it."

26. The Davidic parallel was frequently used for Charles I; one of the

more interesting examples is to be found in the frontispiece engraving to *Il Davide Perseguitato. Written in Italian by The Marquesse Virgilio Malvezzi: And done into English by Robert Ashley* (London, 1647), which shows Charles I as David playing the harp and holding a shield on which is written, "The Lord is my Shield." Psalm 105:15 is quoted at the bottom of the engraving: "Touch not my Anointed. / And do my Prophets no harme." The book was published in Italian in 1637 and translated before 1641, the year Ashley died. The program for the engraving must have been the invention of the book's royalist publisher, Humphrey Moseley. For further discussion of *Il Davide Perseguitato*, see Potter, *Secret Rites*, 161; Potter's book came to my attention after I had completed work on this chapter.

Although royalists claimed special rights to King David's book of Psalms, parliamentarians used the Davidic parallel for both Fairfax and Cromwell; see, for example, John Maudit, *The Christian Souldiers Great Engine, Or the Mysterious and Mighty workings of Faith, discovered in a Sermon Preached before the Lord General in Oxford, May 20, 1649* (Oxford, 1649), ¶2ᵛ: "I could not make you better provision on so short warning, then Ahimelek did for that same David, setting before you and your Captaines a little Shew-bred, & to bring you forth Goliahs sword, and the Armes of the old Warriers, which hang up in the Sanctuary."

27. James I, "The Epistle Dedicatorie," *A Meditation upon The 27. 28. 29. Verses of the XXVII. Chapter of S. Matthew; or a paterne for a Kings inauguration. Written By The Kings Maiestie* (London, 1620).

28. See, e.g., Henry Leslie, *The Martyrdome of King Charles, or his conformity with Christ in his sufferings* (The Hague, and re-printed at London, 1649); or J. W., *King Charles I. his imitation of Christ. Or the parallel lines of our Saviours and our kings sufferings; drawn through fourty six texts of Scripture* (London, 1649).

29. [Walter Montague], *Jeremias Redivivus; Or, An Elegiacall Lamentation on the Death of our English Josias* ([London?], 1649), title page.

30. Leslie, *Martyrdome of King Charles*, 12; or see *A Faithful Subjects Sigh*, 5: "A Truer Symbole of our Christ then now / Ne're suffered since; then surely for His sake / Some lamentable change thou ought'st to make, / O're our most Gracious Soveraign now dead, / By His owne People (base Jewes) Martyred: / And 'twixt two Theeves too, Crucified, which were / The INDEPENDENT and the PRESBYTER."

31. In 1649 a play was published called *Love In it's Extasie: Or, the large Prerogative. A kind of Royall Pastorall written long since, by a Gentleman, Student at AEton* (London, 1649). In the preface, "To the Reader," the anonymous editor or presenter of the text observes of its publication, "Did the Stage enjoy its former lustre, this would have lien still neglected and forgotten: but since those pastimes are denied us wherein we saw the soule and genius of all the world lye contracted in the little compasse of an English Theater, I have thought fit amidst a number of more serious pieces to venture this in publike. You may be confident there lyes no Treason in it nor State invective, (The common issues of this pregnant age)."

32. *The Famous Tragedie of King Charles I* ([London], 1649), A3ʳ.

33. *The Electra of Sophocles: Presented to her Highnesse The Lady Elizabeth; with an Epilogue, Shewing the Parallel in two Poems, The Return, and the Restauration* (The Hague, 1649), ¶2ᵛ–¶3ʳ.

34. [Robert Brown], *The Subjects Sorrow: Or, Lamentations Upon the Death of Britaines Josiah King Charles* (London, 1649), 16.

35. Cf. [F.H.], *An Elogie, and Epitaph,* 2: "But he in Lamb-like sufferings hath wrought / More then Herculian conquest o're your rage, / Though with the deare price of his blood y'have bought / England th'Aceldama; your dreadfull stage, / Whereon y'have acted such a tragedy, / Nero had wept, had he but lived to see."

36. Quoted from *The Poems and Letters of Andrew Marvell*, ed. H. M. Margoliouth, 3d ed. rev. Pierre Legouis with E. E. Duncan-Jones, 2 vols. (Oxford: Clarendon Press, 1971), 1:92–93, and see notes to lines 53–58 (299–300); cf. Blair Worden's comment on the execution as theater, "Andrew Marvell, Oliver Cromwell, and the Horatian Ode," in *Politics of Discourse: The Literature and History of Seventeenth-Century England,* ed. Kevin Sharpe and Steven N. Zwicker (Berkeley and Los Angeles: University of California Press, 1987), 171.

37. Indeed, so fitted is the theatrical metaphor to the person and event that both the king's elegists and those responsible for his execution understood its propriety; cf. John Cook, *King Charls his Case* (London, 1649), 5, with its reference to the trial of the king as "the most comprehensive, Impartial, and Glorious piece of Justice, that ever was Acted and Executed upon the Theater of England."

38. Cf. Humphrey Chambers, *A Motive to Peace and Love. Delivered in a Sermon at Pauls* (London, 1649), 6.

39. An Act against Unlicensed and Scandalous Books and Pamphlets, in *Acts and Ordinances of the Interregnum, 1642–1660,* ed. C. H. Firth and R. S. Rait, 3 vols. (London: HMSO, 1911), 2:245–46.

40. W. Ca., *A Sad and Serious Discourse Upon a Terrible Letter, Sent by the Ministers of the Province of London. To the Lord General and his Councel of War* (1648 [9]), A2ʳ: "When mouth Granadoes from Sion Colledge fly about with so much sacred Authority, and the fierce sons of Thunder tell us, they have obtained a Commission for fire and brimstone from Heaven; and all the Cyclops of the Province of London are summoned, to give up their stock of thunderbolts... Tis high time for all that are under the influence of this prodigeous meteor, to bespeak a covering, and ship themselves in the Ark of Innocence; that the deluge of the threatened storm might not irrecoverably sink them unto the bottomless pit of Presbyterian destruction."

41. "To my learned Friend on his apt choice and seasonable translation of Electra in Sophocles," *Electra of Sophocles,* Q4ᵛ.

42. See *Musarum Oxoniensium* (Oxford, 1643), B2ʳ–B2ᵛ: "For since the State in Civill Warres hath burn'd / Our silken Hoods have all to Scarfes been turn'd. / 'Mongst us there's scarce a verse, nay line, without / Charge to the

Front, to th' Reere, and Face about. / This Metamorphosis is strange, but wee / Embrace it, as we would our Liberty / Extorted from us by those hands, that steale / (If you'l beleeve 'em) for the Common weale."

See also Leonard Lichfield's verses, "The Printers Conclusion to Her Majesty" (D4ᵛ): "Presses of Old, as Pens, did but incite / Others to Valour; This It Selfe did fight: / In Ranks and Files these Letters Marshall'd stood / On Dismall Edg-Hill-day, yet 'twas not blood / They boaded by their Black, for Peace they sought, / And Teem'd with Pardons while the Rebells fought. / Yet those that found it on that Boysterous day / Tooke't for some Dread Commission of Arry; / And thought each Letter Theta, every Point / To give a Period to a Life or Joynt."

43. On the early chronological disruption, see Knachel's suggestion that chapter 7 refers to Henrietta Maria's earlier visit to Holland in 1642 (*EB*, 29); for the uses of past and present tense in the structure of the *Eikon Basilike,* see Wilcher, "What Was the King's Book For? The Evolution of the *Eikon Basilike*," *Yearbook of English Studies* 21:224–27.

44. Cook, *King Charls his Case,* 6.

45. For an analysis of the rhetorical structure of Milton's opening paragraph, see Janel Mueller, "On Genesis in Genre: Milton's Politicizing of the Sonnet in 'Captain or Colonel,' " in *Renaissance Genres: Essays on Theory, History, and Interpretation,* ed. Barbara Kiefer Lewalski (Cambridge, Mass.: Harvard University Press, 1986), 227–30.

46. "For in words which admitt of various sense, the libertie is ours to choose that interpretation which may best minde us of what our restless enemies endeavor, and what wee are timely to prevent" (*E,* 342).

47. Cf. [Robert Brown], *The Subjects Sorrow,* 20: "Neither may we here (as the constant Attendant, and sworne servant unto His Princely Prudence) but with wonder reflect upon His Kingly Eloquence, His flowing and (as Tacitus speakes of Augustus) King-becomming stile, sweet, pure, accurate, perspicuous, grave, full of copious facility, and elegant felicity without streined affectation, or servile and forced imitation: so that had He not some naturall difficulties in pronountiation, He would have beene approved as the best Orator, and perfect Master of Language (as he was of Reason) that ever Britaine yet bred."

48. See n14, above; and Keith Thomas, *Religion and the Decline of Magic* (London: Weidenfeld and Nicolson, 1971), 491.

49. See the Ordinance for the Utter Suppression and Abolishing of All Stage-Plays, in *Acts and Ordinances of the Interregnum, 1642–1660,* 1:1070–72.

50. Thomas N. Corns notes the suggestion of the "Mediterranean" literary tradition in Milton's linking of arcadias and romances (*The Development of Milton's Prose Style* [Oxford: Clarendon Press, 1982], 72). See, as well, Annabel Patterson on Milton's "critique of the morals, politics, and esthetics of the king and of romance tradition" (*Censorship and Interpretation: The Conditions of Writing and Reading in Early Modern England* [Madison: University of Wisconsin Press, 1984], 178–79).

51. Cf.: "But the matter heer considerable, is not whether the King, or his

Houshold Rhetorician have made a pithy declamation against Tumults" (*E*, 383); and "[the] corrupted and beleper'd...Clergie...some one of whose Tribe rather then a King, I should take to be compiler of that unsalted and Simonical praier annex'd" (*E*, 497).

52. Plagiarism is the immediate concern of *Eikon Alethine* (London, 1649), which denounces the authors of the *Eikon Basilike* as "lyars and forgers to the world" (A').

53. On Charles I's Second Folio Shakespeare, see T. A. Birrell, *English Monarchs and Their Books from Henry VII to Charles II* (The Panizzi Lectures, 1986) (London: The British Library, 1987), 44–46.

54. See Andrew Marvell, *An Horatian Ode*, lines 53–62, *The Poems and Letters of Andrew Marvell*, ed. H. M. Margoliouth, 3d ed. rev. Pierre Legouis with E. E. Duncan-Jones, 2 vols. (Oxford: Clarendon Press, 1971).

55. See Madan, *A New Bibliography*, 139–46; and Kenyon, *Revolution Principles*, 68–71.

56. When Milton returns to the issue late in *Eikonoklastes*, the use of David's Psalms has become straight-out plagiarism: "Had he borrow'd Davids heart, it had bin much the holier theft. For such kind of borrowing as this, if it be not better'd by the borrower, among good Authors is accounted Plagiarie" (*E*, 547).

57. Thomas Corns sees less tension here, suggesting that Milton's "suspicion of 'poetic' prose, while it serves his immediate purpose of blackening the image of the King, also accords well with the austerity of his own practice in 1649" ("Milton's Prose," *Cambridge Companion to Milton*, 194).

3. Hunting and Angling: *The Compleat Angler* and *The First Anniversary*

1. Citations are to Izaak Walton, *The Compleat Angler, 1653–1676*, ed. Jonquil Bevan (Oxford: Clarendon Press, 1983); and *The Poems and Letters of Andrew Marvell*, ed. H. M. Margoliouth, 3d ed. rev. Pierre Legouis with E. E. Duncan-Jones, 2 vols. (Oxford: Clarendon Press, 1971); page or line references appear in my text in parentheses.

2. On the sources and traditions, see Bevan's introduction to *The Compleat Angler, 1653–1676;* and Thomas Westwood and Thomas Satchell, *Bibliotheca Piscatoria* (London: W. Satchell, 1883).

3. On the rhetorical and political program of *The First Anniversary*, see John M. Wallace, *Destiny His Choice: The Loyalism of Andrew Marvell* (Cambridge: Cambridge University Press, 1968), 106–44; Steven N. Zwicker, "Models of Governance in Marvell's 'The First Anniversary,' " *Criticism* 16 (1974): 1–12; Annabel Patterson, *Marvell and the Civic Crown* (Princeton: Princeton University Press, 1978), 68–90; and Derek Hirst, " 'That Sober Liberty': Marvell's Cromwell in 1654," in *The Golden and the Brazen World:*

Papers in Literature and History, 1650–1800, ed. John M. Wallace (Berkeley and Los Angeles: University of California Press, 1985), 17–53.

4. Though we should distinguish the political sensibilities of royalists who remained in England from those of exiled courtiers, Walton's syncretic royalism would have appealed to a variety of royalist sympathies. On pastoralism and retirement in royalist literature and politics, see Maren-Sofie Røstvig, *The Happy Man: Studies in the Metamorphoses of a Classical Ideal, 1600–1700* (Oslo: Akademisk Forlag, 1954), 59–64; Satendra Khanna, "A Study of the Non-Satirical Poetry of Charles Cotton" (Ph.D. diss., University of California at Los Angeles, 1969); Earl Miner, *The Cavalier Mode from Jonson to Cotton* (Princeton: Princeton University Press, 1971), 232–37; Annabel Patterson, *Censorship and Interpretation: The Conditions of Writing and Reading in Early Modern England* (Madison: University of Wisconsin Press, 1984), 171–76; Anthony Low, *The Georgic Revolution* (Princeton: Princeton University Press, 1985), 221–95; and Lois Potter, *Secret Rites and Secret Writing: Royalist Literature, 1641–1660* (Cambridge: Cambridge University Press, 1989), 76, 158. See also Paul H. Hardacre, *The Royalists during the Puritan Revolution* (The Hague: Martinus Nijhoff, 1956).

The literature of royalist pastoralism includes *Il Pastor Fido . . . Newly Translated out of the Originall* (London, 1647); Mildmay Fane, *Otia Sacra* (London, 1648), including "My Countrey Audit," "Upon the Times," "To my Book, upon the second Part," "To Retiredness"; Clement Barksdale, *Nympha libethris, or The Cotswold Muse* (London, 1651); translations of *Anacreon. Bion. and Moschus* (London, 1651); the pastorals in Thomas Stanley's 1651 *Poems;* Christopher Wase's translation of *Gratii Falisci Cynegeticon. Or, a Poem of Hunting by Gratius the Faliscian* (London, 1654); *The Bucolicks of Baptist Mantuan* (London, 1656); *The Shepheards Kalender: Newly Augmented and Corrected* (London, 1656); John Evelyn, *An Essay on the First Book of T. Lucretius Carus De Rerum Natura* (London, 1656); and Evelyn's *Sylva* (London, 1664).

See especially Evelyn's *Essay on . . . Lucretius,* 100–102, with its argument about the politics of Lucretius and its suggestion that the English civil wars can be allegorized as Roman politics; or Richard Fanshawe's prefatory letter to the *Essay* (6–9), with its invocation of friendship and shared literary culture, and Fanshawe's obvious gesture of rural retreat in his signature from "Tankersley 27 Decemb. 1653."

5. On the problem of cultural styles, see the series of essays by G. E. Aylmer, "Collective Mentalities in Mid Seventeenth-Century England," *Transactions of the Royal Historical Society,* 5th ser., 36–39 (1986–1989), "I: The Puritan Outlook," "II: Royalist Attitudes," "III: Varieties of Radicalism," and "IV: Cross Currents: Neutrals, Trimmers and Others."

6. This is a topic that Rosalie L. Colie made particularly her own; see *"My Ecchoing Song": Andrew Marvell's Poetry of Criticism* (Princeton: Princeton University Press, 1970).

7. On the dating of *Upon Appleton House,* see Derek Hirst and Steven

Zwicker, "High Summer at Nun Appleton, 1651: Andrew Marvell and Lord Fairfax's Occasions," forthcoming, *Historical Journal.*

8. See John R. Cooper, *The Art of "The Compleat Angler"* (Durham, N.C.: Duke University Press, 1968), 138–65; Bevan, *The Compleat Angler, 1653–1676*, 15–33; and Timothy Edward Bollinger, who points out that Walton lifted some of the technical information in his book word for word from Leonard Mascall's *Booke of Fishing with Hooke and Line* (London, 1590) (Bollinger, "Levels of Meaning in *The Compleat Angler*" [Ph.D. diss., University of California, Riverside, 1975], 54–58).

9. See Cooper, *Art of "The Compleat Angler,"* 95; and Northrop Frye, *Anatomy of Criticism: Four Essays* (Princeton: Princeton University Press, 1957), 309–12.

10. On mixed genres in the English Renaissance, see Rosalie L. Colie, *The Resources of Kind: Genre–Theory in the Renaissance*, ed. Barbara K. Lewalski (Berkeley and Los Angeles: University of California Press, 1973); and Barbara Kiefer Lewalski, ed., *Renaissance Genres: Essays on Theory, History, and Interpretation* (Cambridge, Mass.: Harvard University Press, 1986), 5–6.

11. On this theme, see Hardacre, *Royalists during the Puritan Revolution*, 79–85. On royalist activism, see David Underdown, *Royalist Conspiracy in England, 1649–1660* (New Haven: Yale University Press, 1960).

12. See Bernard S. Horne, *The Compleat Angler, 1653–1967: A New Bibliography* (Pittsburgh: The Pittsburgh Bibliophiles, 1970).

13. See Miner, *Cavalier Mode*, 282–97; and cf. Sir Richard Fanshawe's dedication to his translation of Camões, *The Lusiad* (London, 1655).

14. Horne, *The Compleat Angler, 1653–1967: A New Bibliography*, 20.

15. On the social and political uses of mirth in Jacobean and Caroline England, see Leah Marcus, *The Politics of Mirth: Jonson, Herrick, Milton, Marvell, and the Defense of Old Holiday Pastimes* (Chicago: University of Chicago Press, 1986), esp. 1–23 and 140–68.

16. Cf. Evelyn's preface, "The Interpreter to Him that Reads," to his *Essay on . . . Lucretius*, A7ᵛ–A8ᵛ: "To the Scrupulous now, which are the last sort of persons I have promised to treat with, and shall endeavor to satisfie: They are such as seem greatly to declaim against our Author, as altogether Irreligious and Prophane; and therefore not fit (say they) to be so much as read or entertained amongst Christians. But if this be the sole and grand objection, I would likewise enquire, why those nicer and peevish spirits should at all approve, or in the least make use of any other Heathen Writer whatsoever. . . . No man, I hope, comes hither as a Spider, to swell his bag with poyson onely, when with half that pains, he may with the industrious Bee, store and furnish his Hive with so much wholesome and delicious Honey."

17. On sociability and contention, see Sir Percy Herbert, *Certaine Conceptions, or, Considerations of Sir Percy Herbert, upon the Strange change of Peoples, Dispositions and Actions in these latter times* (London, 1650), A2ʳ–A4ᵛ: "Having compiled this small Treatise, chiefly for the entertainment of my selfe and private family, consisting of morall and divine principles, collected according

to my severall conceptions, answerable to the distractions of these times...
of unnecessary and distasteful contentions, but also of most desperate quar-
rels, proceeding from dispositions too furious.... Women [have] grown im-
pudent, and the common People Atheistical; so may we perceive now, by a
strict enquiry, that at present the very Natures and Dispositions of most
Persons are changed into a certain kinde of strange Lunacy, or preposterous
Madness in their Actions, as if some ominous Revolution were yet to be made
in this Nation."

18. On sequestered royalism and antiquity, see Irene Coltman, *Private Men
and Public Causes* (London: Faber and Faber, 1962), 144n: "The riverside
quietism of the *Compleat Angler* was closely connected with the religious quietism of Bishop Sanderson, of Morley, Hammond and Chillingworth, who were
friends of Izaak Walton and of Viscount Falkland."

19. The classic essays on this subject are those of Renato Poggioli, *The Oaten
Flute: Essays on Pastoral Poetry and the Pastoral Ideal* (Cambridge, Mass.: Harvard
University Press, 1975), and Bruno Snell, "Arcadia: The Discovery of a Spir-
itual Landscape," in *The Discovery of the Mind: The Greek Origins of European
Thought*, trans. T. G. Rosenmeyer (Oxford: Basil Blackwell, 1953), esp. 292–
94.

20. On sequestration and change of lands, see Sir John Habakkuk, "The
Land Settlement and the Restoration of Charles II," *Transactions of the Royal
Historical Society*, 5th ser., 28 (1978): 201–22; and "The Rise and Fall of English
Landed Families, 1600–1800," *Transactions of the Royal Historical Society*, 5th
ser., 29 (1979): 187–207.

21. In tracing the reception of *The Compleat Angler* over the later seventeenth century, it is interesting to note the changes in Evelyn's diary entries
for Christmas and Epiphany (*The Diary of John Evelyn*, ed. E. S. de Beer, 6
vols. [Oxford: Clarendon Press, 1955]); during the interregnum, Evelyn carefully notes the holidays; see 3:185, for December 25 (1656): "I went to Lond,
to receive the B: Communion this holy Festival, at Dr. Wilds lodging, where
I rejoiced to find so full an assembly of devout & sober Christians"; and
December 26: "I invited some of my Neighbours & Tennants according to
Costome, & to preserve hospitality & Charity." After the Restoration, Evelyn
shows little interest in December 25, occasionally failing altogether to note
the holiday.

22. See *The Works of John Dryden*, ed. H. T. Swedenberg, Jr., et al., 20 vols.
(Berkeley and Los Angeles: University of California Press, 1956–), vol. 15,
Plays (1976), ed. Earl Miner, 60–61; and the discussion in Chapter 6, below,
of retirement in *Don Sebastian*.

23. See, allied to this theme, D. R. Woolf, "The 'Common Voice': History,
Folklore and Oral Tradition in Early Modern England," *Past and Present* 120
(August 1988):26–52.

24. Cf. "Minute Book of the Wirksworth Classis," *Journal of Derbyshire Ar-
chaeological and Natural History Society* 2 (1880): 157: "This day Mr John Wierd-
shall Minister of Bradley upon summons according to formal order before

the Classis; where it was Layd to his charge that he had (contrarie to the forme of Government established) admitted not onlie his own people p'miscuslie to the Sacrament of the Lords supper but also some others of Parish Wirkesworth who were not thought fitt to receive in their own Congregations"; and cf. *The Diary of Ralph Josselin, 1616–1683*, ed. Alan Macfarlane (London: Oxford University Press for the British Academy, 1976), 233, 235–36, on admission into the communion.

25. Cf. Mary Douglas, ed., *Constructive Drinking* (Cambridge: Cambridge University Press, 1987).

26. On the politics of the alehouse in the 1640s and 1650s, see Anthony Fletcher, *Reform in the Provinces: The Government of Stuart England* (New Haven: Yale University Press, 1986), 229–52; Peter Clark, "The Alehouse and the Alternative Society," in *Puritans and Revolutionaries*, ed. Donald Pennington and Keith Thomas (Oxford: Clarendon Press, 1978), 47–72; and Peter Clark, *The English Alehouse: A Social History, 1200–1830* (London: Longman, 1983), 177: "From the mid 1640s, however, as the war abated and county administration regained momentum, alehouses once more became a focus of magisterial attention. . . . Regulation had acquired a national dimension. As well as being determined to recover administrative ground lost during the upheavals of the Civil War, local authorities were anxious to prevent alehouses becoming social and political flashpoints in the critical economic conditions of the late 1640s. . . . With mounting antipathy between the Cromwellian regime and county landowners and with royalist risings in 1655, the Major-Generals were appointed to overawe the provinces and reassert the authority of the centre. Their reports to London demonstrate that action against alehouses was a high priority, partly because of the fear that they were hidey-holes of royalist traitors, and partly because as old Puritan *bêtes noires* their suppression would furnish clear proof of the godly credentials of the Major-Generals."

27. Cf. Michael Hechter, *Principles of Group Solidarity* (Berkeley and Los Angeles: University of California Press, 1987).

28. Cf. Sir William Waller, the parliamentary general and Presbyterian leader, *Divine Meditations Upon Several Occasions* (London, 1680), 146: "Of all recreations, Fishing is the most agreeable to contemplative Spirits, as being a sedate quiet sport; free from those clamours, and disturbances of the senses, which usually accompany other pleasures of the field; and not so ingrossing the mind, but that withal it is at a freedom to intertain it self with good thoughts."

29. See Austin Woolrych, *Commonwealth to Protectorate* (Oxford: Clarendon Press, 1982), esp. 316–18; and Eric C. Walker, *William Dell: Master Puritan* (Cambridge: W. Heffer, 1970), 137–67.

30. See, e.g., Richard Cody, *The Landscape of the Mind* (Oxford: Clarendon Press, 1969), 159–60.

31. Though see Richard Franck, *Northern Memoirs, Calculated for the Meridian of Scotland. . . . To which is added, The Contemplative and Practical Angler. Writ in the year 1658* (Edinburgh, 1821).

32. Though Horace gives an ironic inflection to the theme, the Second

Epode—translated at one end of the century by Jonson and at the other by Dryden—was one of its most familiar expressions.

33. Leah Marcus sees vestiges of cavalier sympathy in Marvell's handling of pastoral idioms in *Upon Appleton House:* "If the Cavaliers crowned themselves monarchs in order to salvage the image of kingship, Marvell adopted the role of king and high prelate to work himself out of the residual power those images continued to exert upon him" (*Politics of Mirth*, 258).

34. Mary Ann Radzinowicz has addressed this theme in an unpublished lecture, "The Proto-Internationalism of Milton and Marvell," delivered at the 17th Triennial Meeting of the International Association of University Professors at New York University, 1986; see also Michael McKeon, "Pastoralism, Puritanism, Imperialism, Scientism: Andrew Marvell and the Problem of Mediation," *Yearbook of English Studies* 13 (1983): 56–59.

35. See Sir Kenelm Digby, *Observations on the 22. Stanza in the 9th. Canto of the 2d. Book of Spencers Faery Queen* (London, 1644), 22–23: "In like manner, when a mans Actions are regular and directed towards God, they become like the lines of a Circle, which all meet in the Center, then his musick is most excellent and compleat, and all together are the Authors of that blessed harmony which maketh him happie in the glorious vision of Gods perfections. . . . Whereas on the contrary, if a mans actions be disorderly, and consisting of discords, (which is, when the sensitive part rebels and wrastles with the Rationall, striving to oppresse it) then this musick is spoiled, and instead of eternall life, pleasure and joy, it causeth perpetuall death, horrour, paine, and misery."

36. Annabel M. Patterson, *Hermogenes and the Renaissance: Seven Ideas of Style* (Princeton: Princeton University Press, 1970), 8, characterizes "the Seventh Idea, that of . . . Gravity," as "both a mighty style in its own right and . . . an ideal of total eloquence."

37. See Hirst, " 'That Sober Liberty,' " 27–29.

38. See Kevin Sharpe, "Cavalier Critic? The Ethics and Politics of Thomas Carew's Poetry," in *Politics of Discourse: The Literature and History of Seventeenth-Century England*, ed. Kevin Sharpe and Steven N. Zwicker (Berkeley and Los Angeles: University of California Press, 1987), 117–46; and Kevin Sharpe, *Criticism and Compliment: The Politics of Literature in the England of Charles I* (Cambridge: Cambridge University Press, 1987), chap. 1, "Culture and Politics, Court and Country," 1–53.

39. On the political and ideological significance of the 1645 volume, see Thomas N. Corns, "Milton's Quest for Respectability," *Modern Language Review* 77 (1982): 769–79; and Annabel Patterson, " 'Forc'd fingers': Milton's Early Poems and Ideological Constraint," in *"The Muses Common-Weale": Poetry and Politics in the Seventeenth Century*, ed. Claude J. Summers and Ted-Larry Pebworth (Columbia: University of Missouri Press, 1988), 9–22.

40. See James Turner, *The Politics of Landscape: Rural Scenery and Society in English Poetry, 1603–1660* (Cambridge, Mass.: Harvard University Press, 1979), 85–115.

41. On the apocalyptic elements in *The First Anniversary*, see R. I. V. Hodge,

Foreshortened Time: Andrew Marvell and Seventeenth Century Revolutions (Cambridge: D. S. Brewer, 1978), 106–13; and Margarita Stocker, *Apocalyptic Marvell: The Second Coming in Seventeenth-Century Poetry* (Athens: Ohio University Press, 1986), 15–23.

42. For a similar sense of the rhythm of Cromwell's apocalyptic urgency, and a strikingly similar critique of monarchy and corruption, see the preface to *Britannia Triumphalis* (London, 1654), A2ᵛ–A4ᵛ and 2–3, where we hear of a court "rejecting the more noble dictates of nature and grace, not atchieving any one enterprise, that might render them either feared abroad or loved at home."

43. The most famous conflation is Virgil's Fourth Eclogue; but Marvell's near contemporary John Milton knew very well how to manipulate the apocalyptic within the pastoral, as both *The Nativity Ode* and *Lycidas* demonstrate.

44. See Wallace, *Destiny His Choice*, 132–36.

45. On analogy and distinction, see Zwicker, "Models of Governance," 1–12.

4. The Politics of Pleasure: *Annus Mirabilis, The Last Instructions, Paradise Lost*

1. There is no complete bibliography of responses to the Restoration, but there are a number of resources, including *British Library Catalogue*, s.v. "Charles II, Miscellaneous"; *Catalogue of the Pamphlets, Books, Newspapers... Collected by George Thomason* [By G. K. Fortescue], 2 vols. (London: British Museum, 1908); Arthur E. Case, *A Bibliography of English Poetical Miscellanies, 1521–1750* (Oxford: Oxford University Press for the Bibliographical Society, 1935); Joseph Frank, *Hobbled Pegasus: A Descriptive Bibliography of Minor English Poetry, 1641–1660* (Albuquerque: University of New Mexico Press, 1968); and Gerald MacLean's unpublished "Check-list of English Poems on the Restoration Appearing in Printed Books during 1660." See also the series of articles by Carolyn A. Edie: "The Popular Idea of Monarchy on the Eve of the Stuart Restoration," *Huntington Library Quarterly* 39 (1976): 343–73; "Right Rejoicing: Sermons on the Occasion of the Stuart Restoration, 1660," *Bulletin of the John Rylands Library* 62, no. 1 (Autumn 1979): 61–86; and "News from Abroad: Advice to the People of England on the Eve of the Stuart Restoration," *Bulletin of the John Rylands Library* 67, no. 1 (Autumn 1984): 382–407.

2. For a more skeptical account of the reception of the Restoration, see Christopher Hill, *Some Intellectual Consequences of the English Revolution* (London: Weidenfeld and Nicolson, 1980), 3–6, 7–15; and Hill, *The Experience of Defeat* (New York: Viking, 1984), 151–53, 161–62; but see as well the corrective in Tim Harris, *London Crowds in the Reign of Charles II* (Cambridge: Cambridge University Press, 1987), 48–51, 60–61. Ronald Hutton provides a general narrative, *The Restoration: A Political and Religious History of England and Wales, 1658–1667* (Oxford: Clarendon Press, 1985), 125–80.

3. *The Diary of John Evelyn,* ed. E. S. de Beer, 6 vols. (Oxford: Clarendon Press, 1955), 3:246. Cf. the verse by G.V. from the Oxford anthology of panegyrics, *Britannia Rediviva* (Oxford, 1660), Ff2ʳ: "Our water laughs it self now into Wine, / Bacchus extends beyond his wonted line. / Fair May gave life, gives rule unto our King: / Needs must his future Reign be flourishing."

4. James Heath, *The Glories and Magnificent Triumphs of the Blessed Restitution of His Sacred Majesty K. Charles II* (London, 1662), 152.

5. Cf. *Calendar of State Papers, Venetian, 1661–1664,* 33:205 (November 3, 1662): "Besides this infamous libels are cast about the city almost every day and night against the king and Court, and especially in the palace of Whitehall, which shows the dissatisfaction of the people and the great licence which is taken. Indeed the discontent is general and everyone complains of the king and that he allows himself to be governed by ministers and cares for nothing, attending only to his hunting, his lusts and other amusements." See, as well, P. R. Seddon, "The Nottinghamshire Militia and the Defence of the Restoration, 1660–1670," *Transactions of the Thoroton Society of Nottinghamshire* 86 (1982): 79–88. On Venner's Rising, see Hutton, *The Restoration,* 150–52.

6. The young John Locke celebrated not only the king's divinity but his patriarchal political authority and its origins in the donation to Adam: "Kings are Gods here, but yet as 'tis above, / There is no heaven where there is no Love. / When the first man without a rivall stood / Possest of all, and all like him was good: / Heaven thought that All imperfect, till beside / 'T had made another self, and given a Bride: / Empire, and Innocence were there, but yet / 'Twas Eve made Man, and Paradise compleat" ("Crowns, Scepters, Thrones, & the whole state of Kings," in *Domiduca Oxoniensis* [Oxford, 1662], B1ᵛ–B3ᵛ).

7. See, e.g., Heath, *The Glories and Magnificent Triumphs.*

8. See, e.g., Richard Allestree's *Sermon Preached at Hampton-Court on the 29th of May 1662* (London, 1662), 31–32: "Vertue was out of countenance and practice, while prosperous and happy Villany usurp'd its name, while Loyalty, and conscience of oaths, and duty were most unpardonable crimes, to which nothing but ruine was an equal punishment; and all those guilts that make the last times perillous, Blasphemy, disobedience, truce-breaking and Treasons, Schisms and Rebellions, with all their dismal consequences and appendages, (for these are not single, personal crimes, these have a politick capacity), all these did not onely walk in the dress of piety, and under holy Masks, but were themselves the very form of Godliness, by which 'twas constituted and distinguished, the Signature of a party of Saints, the Constellation of their graces: And on the other side, the detestation of such hypocrisie made others Libertines and Atheists; while seeing men such holy counterfeits, so violent in acting, and equally engag'd for every false Religion, made them conclude there was none true, or in earnest. And all this was because we were without our King."

9. Some of the moral and literary complexity of that decade can be seen in its libertine literature; on this topic, see David Foxon, *Libertine Literature in*

England, 1660–1745 (New Hyde Park, N.Y.: University Books, 1965), 1–5; and Roger Thompson, *Unfit for Modest Ears* (Totowa, N.J.: Rowman and Littlefield, 1979), 4–6, 8–14.

10. Andrew M. Coleby, *Central Government and the Localities: Hampshire, 1649–1689* (Cambridge: Cambridge University Press, 1987), 55: "Under the Protectorate, the central government got involved in the systematic enforcement of moral reformation, during the rule of the major-generals."

11. See, e.g., George, earl of Berkeley, *Historical Applications and Occasional Meditations upon Several Subjects* (London, 1667), 64–65: "Our gracious Sovereign Charles the Second, whom I beseech God to blesse with a long and happy Reign: His sweet, obliging, mild disposition is more agreeable to the English temper then to any Nation whatsoever, our Climate being so justly famed for producing in all Ages so many good-natured people." On Charles II, see also Halifax's "Character," in *The Works of George Savile Marquis of Halifax*, ed. Mark N. Brown, 3 vols. (Oxford: Clarendon Press, 1989), 2: 484–505.

12. The Declaration can be consulted in *The Stuart Constitution, 1603–1688*, ed. J. P. Kenyon, 2d ed. (Cambridge: Cambridge University Press, 1986), 331–32; cf. An Act of . . . Indemnity and Oblivion (1660), in *Stuart Constitution*, ed. Kenyon, 339–44.

13. *An Humble Representation of the sad Condition of many of the Kings Party, Who since His Majesties Happy Restauration have no Relief, and but Languishing Hopes* (London, 1661).

14. Patronage at the court of Charles II still awaits its historian; but see Peter Skrine, "Court and Theatre in Restoration England," in *Europäische Hofkultur im 16. und 17. Jahrhundert*, ed. August Buck et al., 3 vols. (Hamburg: Hauswedell, 1981), 2:329–34.

15. *To the Kings Most Excellent Majesty. The Humble Petitionary Poem of Edmond Dillon, Esq.* (London, 1664), 2: "Much of these blessings now (like Manna) show'rs / On Albion, from Jehovah's azure Tow'rs / Dispens'd by You: since that auspicious time, / God made his Type, and lawful Steward climbe / The Widowed Throne; and in this Orphan-land, / Restor'd the Fathers Soveraign Command."

16. See Kevin Sharpe, "A Commonwealth of Meanings," in his *Politics and Ideas in Early Stuart England: Essays and Studies* (London: Pinter Publishers, 1989), 60–61; and Sharpe, "Cavalier Critic? The Ethics and Politics of Thomas Carew's Poetry," in *Politics of Discourse: The Literature and History of Seventeenth-Century England*, ed. Kevin Sharpe and Steven N. Zwicker (Berkeley and Los Angeles: University of California Press, 1987), 117–46.

17. An obvious example of the hopes for fertility can be found in the opening lines of Dryden's *Astraea Redux* with their emphasis on passion and marital bliss: "We sigh'd to hear the fair Iberian Bride / Must grow a Lilie to the Lilies side, / While Our cross Stars deny'd us Charles his Bed / Whom Our first Flames and Virgin Love did wed" (*The Poems of John Dryden*, ed. James Kinsley, 4 vols. [Oxford: Clarendon Press, 1958], 1:16, lines 17–20).

Cf. Henry Bold, "To His Sacred Majesty Charles the II. At His happy Return," *Poems Lyrique, Macaronique, Heroique* (London, 1664), 206: "May You live long and happy, to improve / In Strangers, Envy; in Your Subjects Love! / And marry'd may Your Computation run / Even, as Time, for every year a Son! / Until Your Royal Off-spring grow to be / The Hope, and Pride of all Posterity!"

18. See David G. Hale, *The Body Politic* (The Hague: Mouton, 1971); Sharpe, "A Commonwealth of Meanings," 63; and, more generally, on "the politics of love," Kevin Sharpe, *Criticism and Compliment: The Politics of Literature in the England of Charles I* (Cambridge: Cambridge University Press, 1987), 265–301. For earlier Caroline examples, see the verse in *Musarum Oxoniensium* (Oxford, 1638). On the meaning of royal fecundity, see the verse on the loss of a royal child at delivery, *Musarum Oxoniensium,* bb2^r: "Still may You thus goe on (Great Queene) and blesse / The King and People with Your fruitfulnesse"; and bb4^v: "And though the King hath lost some ballast, still / The ship is safe to recompence the ill. / Let no man murmure then, our Charles is seen / To goe and visit now his strengthning Queene. / O may shee still new joyes, and new unclose, / And never make him sad, but in her throes!"

At the Restoration, see Henry Bold, *A Poem Heroique:* "May his great Queen, in whose imperious Ey / Reigns such a world of winning Majesty / Like the rich Olive, or Falernian Vine, / Swell with more Gems of Cions Masculine; / And as her Fruit sprung from the Rose and Luce, / (The best of Stems Earth yet did ere produce) / Is ti'd already by a Sanguin Lace, / To all the Kings of Europes high-born Race; / So may they shoot their youthful Branches ore / The Surging Seas, and graff with evry shore. / May home-commerce and Trade encrease from far, / That both the Indies meet within his bar, / And bring in mounts of Coin his Mints to feed, / And Banquers (Trafics chief Supporters) breed, / Which may enrich Kingdoms, Court & Town, / And ballast still the coffers of the Crown."

19. As one panegyrist (R. West, student of Christ Church) argued in 1640, the queen's abundance was a political capacity, "as if your wise fertility / An extract were of all State Policie" (*Horti Caroini Rosa Altera* [Oxford, 1640], a3^v). See the poems on the marriage of Charles II and Catherine of Braganza in *Domiduca Oxoniensis;* for example, James Anglesey's "Upon the Queens Landing" (A1^v): "Great Prince! Whose Crowning frees the World from Shame; / Heav'ns have redeemed their Justice; Men their Fame: / Heav'n, that first gave, now does thy Crown Commend, / When glittring Triumphs in Chast Pleasures End"; and Richard Newport's "Proud of their present, the fair Lisbon dames" (A2^r): "The Patriarchs vessel, which about was hurl'd / Ore Growing Pines, when seamen were the world, / Strikes sayle to ours, though man-kind was its fare, / Since ours to rule 'em promises an Heir: / Whilst to our foes, our Nuptials are Alarms, / And Charles's pleasures dreadfull as his Armes."

20. *His Majesties Gracious Speech to the Lords and Commons* (London, 1661), 5–6.

21. See *An Humble Representation;* or Edmund Dillon, *To the Kings Most Excellent Majesty.* See also J. R. Jones, *Country and Court: England, 1658–1714* (Cambridge, Mass.: Harvard University Press, 1978), 131–36; Hutton, *The Restoration,* 136–37; Paul Seaward, *The Cavalier Parliament and the Reconstruction of the Old Regime, 1660–1667* (Cambridge: Cambridge University Press, 1989), 196–214; and S. K. Roberts, "Public or Private? Revenge and Recovery at the Restoration of Charles II," *Bulletin of the Institute of Historical Research* 59 (1986): 172–88.

22. Cf. *Calendar of the Clarendon State Papers,* vol. 5, *1660–1726,* ed. F. J. Routledge (Oxford: Clarendon Press, 1970), 278–79: "Latter [Edward Bagshaw] said London was highly discontented at the turning out of so many ministers from their livings . . . ; at the loss of Dunkirk to support which, with Tangier, the Parliament had increased the revenue; at the King's neglect of government for his mistresses; and that all was carried on by the Queen [Mother] and her cabal at Somerset House. . . . That there would be risings through the discontents of the people . . . and that the nation would rather be governed by those old Physicians than the upstarts now in the saddle."

23. See His Majesty's Declaration to All His Loving Subjects (excerpts in *Stuart Constitution,* ed. Kenyon, 379–82); and the debates in Parliament over uniformity and Indulgence, William Cobbett, *Parliamentary History of England,* 36 vols. (London, 1806–1820), 4:238–44, 260–65, 311–15. See also R. A. Beddard, "The Restoration Church," in *The Restored Monarchy, 1660–1688,* ed. J. R. Jones (London: Macmillan, 1979), 164–70.

24. An Act of . . . Indemnity and Oblivion: "And to the intent and purpose that all names and terms of distinction may likewise be put into utter oblivion, be it further enacted by the authority aforesaid that if any person or persons within the space of three years next ensuing shall presume maliciously to call or allege of, or object against any other person or persons, any name or names, or other word of reproach anyway tending to revive the memory of the late differences or the occasions thereof, that then every such person . . . shall forfeit and pay unto the party grieved . . . ten pounds" (*Stuart Constitution,* ed. Kenyon, 342). The lord chancellor spoke as early as 1660 on names, reproaches, and terms of distinction (Cobbett, *Parliamentary History of England,* 4:127).

25. Hutton documents the crises (*The Restoration,* 185–284).

26. See the proceedings in Anchitell Grey, comp., *Debates of the House of Commons from the Year 1667 to the Year 1694,* 10 vols. (London, 1769), 1:21ff.

27. The literary implications of this millenarianism were first suggested by Edward N. Hooker, "The Purpose of Dryden's *Annus Mirabilis,*" *Huntington Library Quarterly* 10 (1946): 49–67; and were thoroughly mapped by Michael McKeon, *Politics and Poetry in Restoration England: The Case of Dryden's "Annus Mirabilis"* (Cambridge, Mass.: Harvard University Press, 1975).

28. Thomas Moore, *Fornication Condemned. Marriage is honourable in all, and the bed undefiled; but whoremongers and adulterers God will judge* (London, 1667).

29. Richard Allestree, *A Sermon Preached before the King at White Hall on*

Sunday Nov. 17, 1667, "S. James IV.7. Resist the Devil and he will flee from you" (London, 1667).

30. See C. D. Chandaman, *The English Public Revenue, 1660–1688* (Oxford: Clarendon Press, 1975), 208; Hutton, *The Restoration*, 281–84; and Pepys, *The Diary of Samuel Pepys*, ed. Robert Latham and William Matthews, 11 vols. (Berkeley and Los Angeles: University of California Press, 1970–1983), 8:330 (July 12, 1667): "He heard my Lord Chancellor say to the King, 'Sir,' says he, 'the whole world doth complain publicly of treachery, that things have been managed falsely by some of his great ministers.' "

31. The large number of manuscript collections of verse satire from the later seventeenth century gives some idea of the extent of this work. For the major manuscript repositories in England and America, see the registers in the textual notes to *Poems on Affairs of State: Augustan Satirical Verse, 1660–1714*, ed. George deF. Lord et al., 7 vols. (New Haven: Yale University Press, 1963–1975).

32. Edmund Waller, *Instructions to a Painter*, in *Poems on Affairs of State*, ed. Lord, 1:20–33; subsequent reference is given by line number in parentheses in my text. The advice-to-painter genre in English was first documented by Mary Tom Osborne, *Advice-to-a-Painter Poems, 1633–1856: An Annotated Finding List* (Austin: University of Texas, 1949). The genre was subsequently studied by Warren Chernaik, *The Poetry of Limitation: A Study of Edmund Waller* (New Haven: Yale University Press, 1968), 188–94; Earl Miner, "The 'Poetic Picture, Painted Poetry' of *The Last Instructions to a Painter*," *Modern Philology* 63 (1966): 288–94; and Annabel Patterson, *Marvell and the Civic Crown* (Princeton: Princeton University Press, 1978), 111–74.

33. See Patterson, *Marvell and the Civic Crown*, chap. 3, "The Painter and the Poet Dare."

34. [Andrew Marvell], *The Second Advice to a Painter*, quoted from *Poems on Affairs of State*, ed. Lord, 1:39. For a summary of the debate over authorship and relevant bibliography, see Lord, ed., *Poems on Affairs of State*, 1:21 and note.

35. Rochester's satires provide the most brilliant printed source, but see, for a cross section, the satirical verse in Lord, ed., *Poems on Affairs of State*, vol. 1. The large number of extant manuscript copies suggests how widely circulated were such materials; see Lord, ed., *Poems on Affairs of State*, 1:xxxvii.

36. The satiric attacks on Clarendon can be consulted in volume 1 of Lord, ed., *Poems on Affairs of State*.

37. *Poems of John Dryden*, ed. Kinsley, 1:42, line 5; all subsequent citation to the text of *Annus Mirabilis* is to volume 1 of the Kinsley edition, line numbers given parenthetically in my text.

38. Valerie Pearl, *London and the Outbreak of the Puritan Revolution* (London: Oxford University Press, 1961), 38–44, 160–76; and G. S. De Krey, *A Fractured Society: The Politics of London in the First Age of Party, 1688–1715* (Oxford: Clarendon Press, 1985), 9–14.

39. *The Readie and Easie Way to Establish a Free Commonwealth*, in *Complete*

Prose Works of John Milton, ed. Don M. Wolfe et al., 8 vols. (New Haven: Yale University Press, 1953–1982), vol. 7, *1659–1660,* ed. Robert W. Ayers (rev. ed., 1980), 463.

40. See Ronald Hutton, *Charles II* (New York: Oxford University Press, 1989), 251.

41. Richard Allestree, *A Sermon Preached...Nov. 17, 1667.*

42. Citations are to *The Poems and Letters of Andrew Marvell,* ed. H. M. Margoliouth, 3d ed., rev. Pierre Legouis with E. E. Duncan-Jones, 2 vols. (Oxford: Clarendon Press, 1971) and given by line number parenthetically in my text.

43. See notes, *Poems and Letters of Andrew Marvell,* 1:351.

44. Pepys, *Diary,* 3:263 (November 22, 1662): "This day Mr. Moore told me that for certain the Queene Mother is married to my Lord St. Albans, and he is like to be made Lord Treasurer."

45. Legouis denies the explicitly sexual content of the figure. But whether we see the line as a reference to Jermyn's work as "pleasure salt," what Legouis calls "an obscene allusion to St. Albans' rumoured affair with Henrietta Maria," or, as Legouis would prefer, to a "Rabelaisian gird at the plenitude of the Ambassador's bottom" (*Poems and Letters of Andrew Marvell,* 1:351–52), the conflation of greed and physical excess is clear enough.

46. See *Poems and Letters of Andrew Marvell,* 1:352–53; and Pepys, *Diary,* 6:302 (November 17, 1665); 7:323 (October 15, 1666).

47. See *Poems and Letters of Andrew Marvell,* 1:352.

48. See John Dixon Hunt, *Andrew Marvell: His Life and Writings* (Ithaca: Cornell University Press, 1978), 159. Rosalie Colie is especially good on Marvell's literary adaptations of Ovid: see *"My Ecchoing Song": Andrew Marvell's Poetry of Criticism* (Princeton: Princeton University Press, 1970), esp. 159–61.

49. On the relation of private satisfactions to *res publica,* see J. G. A. Pocock, *Politics, Language, and Time* (New York: Atheneum, 1971; rpt. Chicago: University of Chicago Press, 1989), 88–89; and J. G. A. Pocock, *Virtue, Commerce, and History: Essays on Political Thought and History, Chiefly in the Eighteenth Century* (Cambridge: Cambridge University Press, 1985), chap. 2, "Virtues, Rights, and Manners," 37–50.

50. See John M. Wallace, *Destiny His Choice: The Loyalism of Andrew Marvell* (Cambridge: Cambridge University Press, 1968), 147; Hunt, *Andrew Marvell,* 152–53, 162; and John Kenyon, "Andrew Marvell: Life and Times," in *Andrew Marvell: Essays on the Tercentenary of His Death,* ed. R. L. Brett (Oxford: Oxford University Press, 1979), 21–22. But M. C. Bradbrook and M. G. Lloyd had already in 1940 seen in the portrait of the king a combination of outrage and "stinging personal satire" (*Andrew Marvell* [Cambridge: Cambridge University Press, 1940], 88–89).

51. For the outline of this pursuit, see Hutton, *Charles II,* 204; and C. H. Hartmann, *La Belle Stuart* (London: Routledge, 1924), 117.

52. See Richard Ormond and Malcolm Rogers, *Dictionary of British Portraiture,* 4 vols. (Oxford: Oxford University Press, 1979–1981), 1:117.

53. Hartmann, *La Belle Stuart*, 142; Pepys, *Diary*, 8:83 (February 25, 1667); and see John Evelyn's retrospective remarks on the portrait of Frances Stuart, duchess of Richmond, as Britannia in his *Numismata* (London, 1697), 27–28: "And yet has Monsieur Roti (Graver to his late Majesty Charles II.) so accurately express'd the countenance of the Dutchess of R[ichmond] in the Head of Britannia, in the Reverse of some of our Coin, and especially in a Medal, as one may easily, and almost at first sight, know it to be her Grace: And tho in smallest Copper, both for the Persons represented, and performance of the Artist, such as may justly stand in competition with the antient Masters; to name only those which he has made Medalions, Gold and Silver of the largest Volume."

54. HMC *Le Fleming*, p. 48, Newsletter of April 2, 1667: "Mrs. Stewart, now the Duchess of Richmond, continued at Whitehall till yesterday morning, when the King first learned that she was married, and then she immediately returned to Somerset House."

55. Wallace stresses the continuity of Marvell's loyalist principles by accepting as conviction Marvell's derisive and ironic handling of the scapegoating device of the king's evil ministers: "The usual fiction that his ministers were wholly responsible for his misrule was essential to Marvell's view of the English constitution and the nature of parliamentary government" (*Destiny His Choice*, 147).

56. *Britannia Rediviva*, Ff2^r.

57. Pepys, *Diary*, 8:355 (July 27, 1667).

58. *The Readie and Easie Way*, in *Complete Prose*, vol. 7 (rev. ed.), 422.

59. For a review of the biographical and critical issues in the sexual politics of Milton's career as pamphleteer, see Diane K. McColley, "Milton and the Sexes," in *The Cambridge Companion to Milton*, ed. Dennis Danielson (Cambridge: Cambridge University Press, 1989), 147–66; and Edward Le Comte, *Milton and Sex* (New York: Columbia University Press, 1978), 31–38.

60. See the essays in Michael Lieb and John T. Shawcross, eds., *Achievements of the Left Hand: Essays on the Prose of John Milton* (Amherst: University of Massachusetts Press, 1974); and Thomas N. Corns, ed., *The Literature of Controversy: Polemical Strategy from Milton to Junius* (London: F. Cass, 1987), especially Corns's "Introduction," 2–3, and Michael Wilding, "Milton's *Areopagitica*: Liberty for the Sects," 7–30.

61. *Poems of John Dryden*, ed. Kinsley, 1:104, line 1184.

62. A number of critics note Milton's suggestion of the vulnerability and prophetic fragility of the garden; see, especially, Michael Wilding, *Milton's "Paradise Lost"* (Sydney: Sydney University Press, 1969), 77–82.

63. *PL* 12.642; all citations to *Paradise Lost* are to the text in *The Poems of John Milton*, ed. John Carey and Alastair Fowler (London: Longmans, 1968). Subsequent references to book and line number are included parenthetically in my text.

64. On the pedagogical function of the classical analogies, see Joseph E. Duncan, *Milton's Earthly Paradise* (Minneapolis: University of Minnesota Press,

1972), 36: "[They] evoke images and feelings that enable the fallen imagination to pause and to struggle back to the one true lost paradise." See also Frank Kermode, "Adam Unparadised," in *The Living Milton,* ed. Frank Kermode (London: Routledge and Kegan Paul, 1960), 109; and A. Bartlett Giamatti, *The Earthly Paradise and the Renaissance Epic* (Princeton: Princeton University Press, 1966), 300 and 300n6.

65. There is a distinguished tradition of commentary on these lines; see, for example, William Empson, *Some Versions of Pastoral* (London: Chatto & Windus, 1935), 172–74; Christopher Ricks, *Milton's Grand Style* (Oxford: Clarendon Press, 1963), 125–26; and Louis L. Martz, *Poet of Exile* (New Haven: Yale University Press, 1980), 226–28.

66. For commentary on the literary sensuality of this scene, see Arnold Stein, *Answerable Style* (Minneapolis: University of Minnesota Press, 1953), 68–70; and John R. Knott, Jr., *Milton's Pastoral Vision* (Chicago: University of Chicago Press, 1971), 36–39.

67. On the function of garden labor in the moral economy of Eden, see Barbara K. Lewalski, "Innocence and Experience in Milton's Eden," in *New Essays on "Paradise Lost,"* ed. Thomas Kranidas (Berkeley and Los Angeles: University of California Press, 1969), 86–117, esp. 91–92.

68. On Milton's debts to Ovid, see Martz, *Poet of Exile,* passim; and Richard J. DuRocher, *Milton and Ovid* (Ithaca: Cornell University Press, 1985), 79–83. On Milton's earlier handling of the myth of Ceres and Proserpine, see Mary Loeffelholz, "Two Masques of Ceres and Proserpine: *Comus* and *The Tempest,*" in *Re-membering Milton: Essays on the Texts and Traditions,* ed. Mary Nyquist and Margaret W. Ferguson (New York: Methuen, 1987), 25–42.

69. *The Poems of John Milton,* ed. John Carey and Alastair Fowler, 616; cf. J. M. Evans's gloss on "steep wilderness," in *"Paradise Lost" and the Genesis Tradition* (Oxford: Clarendon Press, 1968), 248: "Although the poet stresses the beauty of the garden enclosed, we are never allowed to forget the threat of the encroaching wilderness."

70. On Milton's framing of marital bliss by "Satanic libido," see James G. Turner, *One Flesh: Paradisal Marriage and Sexual Relations in the Age of Milton* (Oxford: Clarendon Press, 1987), 260.

71. On the hymn to wedded love, see John Halkett, *Milton and the Idea of Matrimony* (New Haven: Yale University Press, 1970), 108–10; Peter Lindenbaum, "Lovemaking in Milton's Paradise," *Milton Studies* 6 (1974): 277–306; and Martz, *Poet of Exile,* 110–12.

72. On Milton's engagement with and regeneration of cavalier lyric in this passage, see William Kerrigan, *The Prophetic Milton* (Charlottesville: University Press of Virginia, 1974), 135–36. For a discussion of this passage in relation to the *Divorce Tracts* and other images of prelapsarian sex in *Paradise Lost,* see Turner, *One Flesh,* 233, and generally chap. 7, "Love Made in the First Age."

73. On authorship and dating, see J. W. Johnson, "Did Lord Rochester Write *Sodom?*" *Papers of the Bibliographical Society of America* 81 (1987): 119–53.

5. Paternity, Patriarchy, and the "Noise of Divine Right": *Absalom and Achitophel* and *Two Treatises of Government*

1. John Dryden's verse was *Heroique Stanzas* (1659); John Locke contributed verse in English and Latin to *Musarum Oxoniensium* (1654), the Oxford volume on the English victory in the Dutch wars.

2. Dryden's Restoration poem was *Astraea Redux* (1660); Locke contributed to the Oxford collection on the king's marriage, *Domiduca Oxoniensis* (1662).

3. *John Locke: Two Treatises of Government*, ed. Peter Laslett (Cambridge: Cambridge University Press, 1960), 35: "We shall assign the important part of the work of composition to the years 1679–80." Citations throughout are to this edition and are indicated in the text with roman numerals referring to the number of the treatise and arabic numbers referring to the paragraph number.

4. On the absorption of *Absalom and Achitophel* into contemporary political culture, see Hugh Macdonald, *John Dryden: A Bibliography of Early Editions and of Drydeniana* (Oxford: Clarendon Press, 1939), 223–31; *Dryden: The Critical Heritage*, ed. James Kinsley and Helen Kinsley (New York: Barnes and Noble, 1971), 128–35; and volume 6 of *Drydeniana* (New York: Garland Publishing, Inc., 1975).

On the circulation and early reception of *Two Treatises of Government*, see "Check-List of Printings, 1689–1956," in Laslett's edition, 121–29; M. P. Thompson, "The Reception of Locke's *Two Treatises of Government*, 1690–1705," *Political Studies* 24 (1976): 184–91; and John Dunn, "The Politics of Locke in England and America in the Eighteenth Century," in *John Locke: Problems and Perspectives*, ed. John W. Yolton (Cambridge: Cambridge University Press, 1969), 45–80.

5. Locke and other of his literary contemporaries have been recently studied by Christopher Fox, *Locke and the Scriblerians* (Berkeley and Los Angeles: University of California Press, 1988); there have, of course, been numerous studies of the influence of Locke's psychology on eighteenth-century intellectual and literary texts.

6. The encyclopedic commentary on *Absalom and Achitophel* in the California Dryden has but a single citation to Locke; see *The Works of John Dryden*, ed. H. T. Swedenberg, Jr., et al., 20 vols. (Berkeley and Los Angeles: University of California Press, 1956–), vol. 2, *Poems, 1681–1684*, ed. H. T. Swedenberg, Jr. (1972), 272. James Winn, however, notes the poem's response to "ideas of contractual monarchy now being developed by his old schoolfellow, Shaftesbury's secretary Locke" (*John Dryden and His World* [New Haven: Yale University Press, 1987], 359).

An exception in the case of Dryden is Richard Ashcraft, *Revolutionary Politics and Locke's "Two Treatises of Government"* (Princeton: Princeton University Press, 1986), though Ashcraft does not there analyze relations between *Ab-*

salom and Achitophel and *Two Treatises;* see also Richard Ashcraft, "The Language of Political Conflict in Restoration Literature," in *Politics as Reflected in Literature* (Los Angeles: William Andrews Clark Memorial Library, 1989), 1–28.

7. Macdonald notes (p. 20) that Narcissus Luttrell's copy of *Absalom and Achitophel* is dated November 17; there is, however, no indication in the Locke correspondence in the following days and months that Shaftesbury's secretary noted the appearance of Dryden's poem; see *The Correspondence of John Locke,* ed. E. S. de Beer, 8 vols. (Oxford: Clarendon Press, 1976–1989), 2:459ff. Richard Ashcraft, "John Locke's Library: Portrait of an Intellectual," in *A Locke Miscellany,* ed. Jean S. Yolton (Bristol: Thoemmes, 1990), 243, notes that Locke's literary holdings included poetry by Cleveland, Cowley, Donne, Jonson, Milton, and Shakespeare, and Marvell's *Rehearsal Transpros'd,* but nothing by Waller or Dryden.

8. On the relations between *Two Treatises* and *Patriarcha,* see *John Locke: Two Treatises of Government,* ed. Laslett, 67–78; John Dunn, *The Political Thought of John Locke* (Cambridge: Cambridge University Press, 1969), 58–76; and Ashcraft, *Revolutionary Politics,* 187–89. Gordon Schochet has studied Filmer's role in Restoration royalist political thought in *Patriarchalism in Political Thought* (New York: Basic Books, 1975), 179–91; and see, more recently, Mark Goldie, "John Locke and Anglican Royalism," *Political Studies* 31 (1983): 61–85; and *Sir Robert Filmer, "Patriarcha" and Other Writings,* ed. Johann P. Sommerville (Cambridge: Cambridge University Press, 1991), xv–xxiv.

9. Bruce King, "Dryden's Ark: The Influence of Filmer," *Studies in English Literature* 7 (1967): 403–14; and Anne T. Barbeau, *The Intellectual Design of John Dryden's Heroic Plays* (New Haven: Yale University Press, 1970), suggest ways in which Filmer's ideas may be reflected in Dryden's work. But Barbeau's reading of Filmer, whom she identifies as one of Dryden's contemporaries (40), is abstracted and naïve.

10. See, for example, William Assheton, *The Royal Apology* (London, 1684), or Sir George Mackenzie, *Jus Regium: Or, The Just and Solid Foundations of Monarchy in General* (Edinburgh, 1684); and see the commentary of Schochet, *Patriarchalism in Political Thought,* 192–209. On the continuing strength of patriarchalism after the Glorious Revolution, see Schochet, 209–24; J. P. Kenyon, *Revolution Principles: The Politics of Party, 1689–1720* (Cambridge: Cambridge University Press, 1977), 62–64; and James Daly, *Sir Robert Filmer and English Political Thought* (Toronto: University of Toronto Press, 1979), 158–71; but see Ashcraft's strictures on Daly (*Revolutionary Politics,* 187n16).

11. Cf. contemporary broadside verse linking paternalism and loyalty to the law: "The Parliament dissolv'd at Oxford, March 28. 1681" (London, 1681); and "Loyalty Triumphant; or a poem" (London, 1681).

12. *The Poems of John Dryden,* ed. James Kinsley, 4 vols. (Oxford: Clarendon Press, 1958), 1:218, lines 61–62; citations to the preface and text of *Absalom and Achitophel* are to volume 1 of the Kinsley edition and given parenthetically by line number in my text.

13. Dryden was not alone in seeing the paternal and political issues of patriarchy linked but differentiated; cf. [Mrs. Joan Philips], *Advice to His Grace* (London, 1681–82, Huntington Library copy, Bindley Pamphlets, dated June 6, 1681, and in hand, next to the title, "the Duke of Monmouth"): "When by the Rabbles fruitless Zeal You lost / Your Royal Fathers Love, Your growing Fortune cross'd; / Say, was Your Bargain, think ye, worth the Cost? / Remember what Relation, Sir, you bear / To Royal Charles; Subject and Son You are; / Two Names that strict Obedience does require."

14. An interesting variation on this presentation of Charles II can be found in Richard Duke, *Floriana. A Pastoral* (London, 1681), an elegy on the duchess of Southampton. Of Charles II, Duke writes: "Even mighty Pan, whose powerful Hand sustains / The Sovereign Crook that mildly awes the Plains, / Of's tendrest Cares made her the chiefest part: / And great Lovisa lodg'd her in her Heart." In manuscript, "Duchess of Portsmouth" appears next to the name "Lovisa."

15. Cf. Matthew Coppinger, "To the King's Majesty," *Poems, Songs and Love Verses* (London, 1682), B3^v–B4^r: "And you (Dread Sir,) more Great, we know / Have felt the power of Cupid's Bow. / And may you always in the Night, / Be fill'd with Venus's delight; / And in the day have choice of Pleasure, / Which may in sum outvie your Treasure." Cf. also Coppinger's dedicatory poem "To Her Grace the Duchess of Portsmouth": "Madam, it is but just, since you receive / All the Delights our Soveraigne can give, / That we, in gratitude unto our King, / Shou'd to your Highness bring an Offering. / For we by Duty are oblig'd to Prize / Those that are Gracious in our Princes Eyes."

16. Roy Porter provides a suggestive gloss for the program of sexual enlightenment hinted at in the opening lines of *Absalom and Achitophel;* see "The Exotic as Erotic: Captain Cook at Tahiti," in *Exoticism in the Enlightenment,* ed. G. S. Rousseau and Roy Porter (Manchester: Manchester University Press, 1990), 118: "Sexual liberation—the physical enjoyment of natural pleasures, to be sure, but no less mankind's emancipation from the mental bugbears and phobias of 'eros denied'—was a keynote of the *philosophes'* programme (*écrasez l'infâme!*) for general emancipation from ignorance, priestcraft and tyranny. . . . As the *Aufklärer* viewed it, looking back to Greek art and poetry, to Ovid, Catullus, Horace and Propertius—and even, perhaps, to Old Testament patriarchalism—before Christianity, sex had been enjoyed as a natural pleasure. Indeed, so it still was, beyond the holy geographical circle of Christendom. Exotic lands, past or present, real or imaginary, provided crusaders for sexual enlightenment with paradigms of the erotic, sex that was neither penalised, nor pathologised, nor exclusively procreative."

17. Cf. the Tory pamphlet [Thomas Baker], *The Head of Nile: Or the Turnings and Windings of the Factious* (London, 1681), 31–32, where "Whigg" reveals the rhetorical uses his party has made of the charge of tyranny: "Hold, no further, we shall stop you else, as we do others, we have a way, that if any but in the theoretick discourse runs the Crown of England up to its pitch, and tells how fine feather'd 'twas before 'twas stript, we presently ball they would

have it so again; and if they talk of any little Prerogatives, we run them to the extremities in every thing, what you would fain have him a King of France, or the Great Turk, send for what moneys he hears you have."

18. Dryden, of course, was not alone in thus presenting the king; cf. "The Parliament Dissolv'd at Oxford, March 28. 1681": "They shan't Cramp Justice with their Feigned Flaws; / For since I Govern only by the LAWS; / Why They should be Exempt, I see no Cause. / To the LAWS They must Submit; 'tis in vain / E're to Attempt to shake off those again; / For where CHARLES Commands, There must Justice Reign / When the Peoples Father does Espouse the LAW, / All those who Subjects from their Duty draw, / Do Viper-like, through Parents Bosom gnaw."

19. See, for example, [Christopher Nesse], *A Key (With the Whip) To open the Mystery & Iniquity Of The Poem Called, Absalom & Achitophel: Shewing its Scurrilous Reflections Upon both King and Kingdom* (London, 1682); or *Poetical Reflections on a late Poem Entituled, Absalom and Achitophel* (London, 1681), B^r–B^v: "To epitomize which scandalous Phamphlet (unworthy the denomination of Poesy) no eye can inspect it without a prodigious amazement; the abuses being so gross and deliberate, that it seems rather a Capital or National Libel, than personal exposures, in order to an infamous detraction. For how does he character the King, but as a broad figure of scandalous inclinations, or contriv'd unto such irregularities, as renders him rather the property of Parasites and Vice, than suitable to the accomplishment of so excellent a Prince? Nay, he forces on King David such a Royal resemblance, that he darkens his sanctity in spite of illuminations from Holy Writ."

20. Cf. *John Locke: Two Treatises of Government*, ed. Laslett, 87–89.

21. On this theme, see Richard Ashcraft, "Leviathan Triumphant: Thomas Hobbes and the Politics of Wild Men," in *The Wild Man Within*, ed. Edward Dudley and Maximillian E. Novak (Pittsburgh: University of Pittsburgh Press, 1972), 141–81; and Anthony Pagden, "Dispossessing the Barbarian: The Language of Spanish Thomism and the Debate over the Property Rights of the American Indians," in *The Languages of Political Theory in Early-Modern Europe*, ed. A. Pagden (Cambridge: Cambridge University Press, 1987), 79–98, esp. 83–85 on savagery and property rights.

22. See, for example, *The Saint turn'd Curtezan: Or, A New Plot discover'd by a precious Zealot, of an Assault and Battery design'd upon the Body of a Sanctify'd Sister, &c* (London, 1681); or *The Leacherous Anabaptist: Or, The Dipper Dipt* (London, 1681): "O Ye Roundheads and Whiggs, for ever be silent, / Cease to scandalize Tory, and honest Tantivy; / I'le tell you strange News that happened nigh Lent, / Which if you disprove, I swear I'le forgive ye: / Of Protestant Francis, / That tells us Romances, / Of horrible Plots more strange then Miles Prances; / For Frank twelve Geneva good Bibles did proffer, / To lie with his Maid, but she slighted his offer. / . . . / Then he offer'd one Bible if he might but Grope her, / But the resolute Quean still stoutly deny'd him; / Quoth she, Master Frank you a Leacherous Fop are, / And after that manner severely did chide him: / You're the Brethrens Teacher, / An Anabaptist

Preacher: / Reply'd he then to her, You a Papist and Bitch are; / For Frank twelve Geneva good Bibles did proffer, / To lie with his Maid, but she slighted his offer."

23. Like the work on Dryden and Filmer, the relations of Dryden and Hobbes have been the concern, mostly, of an older generation of scholars whose intellectual traditions were in the history of ideas rather than in politics and language; see, for example, Louis Teeter, "The Dramatic Use of Hobbes's Political Ideas," *ELH* 3 (1936): 140–69; and John A. Winterbottom, "The Place of Hobbesian Ideas in Dryden's Tragedies," *JEGP* 57 (1958): 665–83.

24. On the politics of gratitude, see John M. Wallace, "John Dryden's Plays and the Conception of a Heroic Society," in *Culture and Politics from Puritanism to the Enlightenment,* ed. Perez Zagorin (Berkeley and Los Angeles: University of California Press, 1980), 113–34.

25. Ashcraft, *Revolutionary Politics,* 331–37.

26. The phrase is C. B. Macpherson's; see *The Political Theory of Possessive Individualism: Hobbes to Locke* (Oxford: Clarendon Press, 1962).

27. Cf. *An Heroick Poem to His Royal Highness* (London, 1682): "Down, Down, Discoverers, who so long have plotted / With holy Shams to gull the Nation, / Both Peers and Prelacy they useless voted / By the old Babes of Reformation. / Property's all their cry, Rights and Freedom, / Law and Religion, they pull down, / With old intestine Lance to bleed 'em, / From Lawn-sleev'd Prelate to Purple Throne."

See also "Advice to His Grace" (June 6, 1681): "Believe those working Brains Your Name abuse; / You only for their Property doe use: / And when they're strong enough to stand alone; / You, as an useless Thing, away'l be thrown"; and "The True Presbyterian Without Disguise" (London, 1681): "They do not think it safe that any Lord / That has but sence, should sit at Council-Board; / Those that sit there should in their Foreheads have / Their Beast-ship Mark of either Fool or Knave; / Who lov'd the K. was Voted straight to be / Betrayer of the Subjects Liberty, / And their old long-lov'd Darling Property."

28. On the narrator's remarks as political theory, see Michael J. Conlon, "The Passage on Government in Dryden's *Absalom and Achitophel,*" *JEGP* 78 (1979): 17–32.

29. See Steven N. Zwicker, *Politics and Language in Dryden's Poetry: The Arts of Disguise* (Princeton: Princeton University Press, 1984), 85–122.

30. *Works of John Dryden,* 2:271, 274.

31. On the politics of Tory reaction, see J. R. Jones, *Country and Court: England, 1658–1714* (Cambridge, Mass.: Harvard University Press, 1978), 217–33; and Ronald Hutton, *Charles II* (Oxford: Clarendon Press, 1989), 404–45.

32. On the habits of reading contemporary with this poem, see above, Introduction, 3–7. John M. Wallace, " 'Examples Are Best Precepts': Readers and Meanings in Seventeenth-Century Poetry," *Critical Inquiry* 1, no. 2 (December 1974): 273–90; and Alan Roper, "Drawing Parallels and Making

Applications in Restoration Literature," in *Politics as Reflected in Literature* (Los Angeles: William Andrews Clark Memorial Library, 1989), 29–65, have argued for the limited and purely voluntary manner in which fables, allegories, and histories in seventeenth-century imaginative texts were applied to contemporary events. My own sense of the breadth and intensity of application is quite different from theirs, and I believe that the proper address to such habits of exegesis and application must include a fuller account of the evidence of marginalia and annotation than we have yet had. While such a project has been attempted for late sixteenth-century reading (see Lisa Jardine and Anthony Grafton, " 'Studied for Action': How Gabriel Harvey Read His Livy," *Past and Present* 129 [November 1990]: 30–78), little comparable work has been done for the late seventeenth century.

33. *Discourse Concerning Satire*, in *Poems of John Dryden*, 2:655.

34. See Conal Condren's shrewd remarks about Locke's philosophical manners in *The Status and Appraisal of Classic Texts* (Princeton: Princeton University Press, 1985), 245: "Locke was presenting an extraordinarily ambitious thesis under difficult circumstances, and much of its success, and its appeal, depended upon the room for interpretive movement allowed. How precisely and uncompromisingly the reader was prepared to relate it to concrete contemporary political issues was a matter which the level of abstraction left open to choice."

35. See, for example, the entries on Locke's style in Roland Hall and Roger Woolhouse, *Eighty Years of Locke Scholarship* (Edinburgh: Edinburgh University Press, 1983); exceptions are Condren, *Status and Appraisal of Classic Texts*, 243–51; and John J. Richetti, *Philosophical Writing: Locke, Berkeley, Hume* (Cambridge, Mass.: Harvard University Press, 1983), 67, 69–75.

36. *John Locke: Two Treatises of Government*, ed. Laslett, 155n. Citations to the Preface are to this edition; page numbers are given in my text in parentheses.

37. *John Locke: Two Treatises of Government*, ed. Laslett, 33.

38. Ashcraft, *Revolutionary Politics*, 214.

39. See Chapter 6, below, for a discussion of Williamite panegyric; and cf. Mark Goldie, "The Revolution of 1689 and the Structure of Political Argument: An Essay and an Annotated Bibliography of Pamphlets on the Allegiance Controversy," *Bulletin of Research in the Humanities* 83 (1980): 473–564.

40. Ashcraft, *Revolutionary Politics*, 128–80; though see Gordon Schochet on Ashcraft's reading of Locke's radicalism: "Radical Politics and Ashcraft's Treatise on Locke," *Journal of the History of Ideas* 50 (1989): 491–510.

41. As Laslett notes, however, H. R. Fox Bourne suggested in his *Life of John Locke* (1876) that the *First Treatise* was prepared in 1681 or 1682 (*John Locke: Two Treatises of Government*, 47).

42. *John Locke: Two Treatises of Government*, ed. Laslett, 156n.

43. *John Locke: Two Treatises of Government*, ed. Laslett, 156; cf. James Tyrrell, *Patriarcha non Monarcha* (London, 1681), unpaginated "Preface."

44. "The Preface" to *Religio Laici*, in *Poems of John Dryden*, 1:311.

45. *John Locke: Two Treatises of Government*, ed. Laslett, 78.

46. The linguistic character of the crisis is noted in contemporary literature; see, e.g., "True Loyalty in its Collours: Or, a Survey of the Laudable Addresses of the Young Men and Apprentices of the City of London, To His Majesty" (London, 1681), 1:

> No Name, because you can't Write well? A Fist
> Is a Good Hand, that can Writ Loyallist.
> Go on Brave Youths, and let your Paper show,
> What Love, what Service to your King you ow.
> How well, Now, London, must we judg of Thee,
> When in thy Sons we find such Loyalty?
> What? Though the Jesuits a-brooding lye,
> To Hatch for Us a Mortal Enemy;
> Loyal Addresses shall like Thunder Kill,
> The Poison-gathering Viper in the Shell.

47. *John Locke: Two Treatises of Government*, ed. Laslett, 299n.

48. See Ashcraft, *Revolutionary Politics*, 521–89.

49. The most famous of these was Count Anthony Hamilton, *Memoirs of Count Gramont* (London, 1714).

6. Representing the Revolution:
Don Sebastian and Williamite Panegyric

1. See J. P. Kenyon, *Revolution Principles* (Cambridge: Cambridge University Press, 1977), 1–4; J. R. Jones, *Country and Court* (Cambridge, Mass.: Harvard University Press, 1978), 252–53; J. G. A. Pocock, ed., *Three British Revolutions: 1641, 1688, 1776* (Princeton: Princeton University Press, 1980), 13, and Lawrence Stone, "The Results of the English Revolution of the Seventeenth Century," in the Pocock volume, 63–64; and Gary Stuart De Krey, *A Fractured Society: The Politics of London in the First Age of Party, 1688–1715* (Oxford: Clarendon Press, 1985), 45–47.

2. J. C. D. Clark, *English Society, 1688–1832* (Cambridge: Cambridge University Press, 1985), esp. section 3, "The Survival of the Dynastic Idiom," 119–89.

3. David Norbrook, "*Macbeth* and the Politics of Historiography," in *Politics of Discourse: The Literature and History of Seventeenth-Century England*, ed. Kevin Sharpe and Steven N. Zwicker (Berkeley and Los Angeles: University of California Press, 1987), 78–116.

4. The satiric verse in *Poems on Affairs of State*, ed. George deF. Lord et al., 7 vols. (New Haven: Yale University Press, 1963–1975), vol. 5, *1688–1697*, ed. William J. Cameron, gives some idea of the reception of the revolution.

5. See, for example, the verse in the Oxford volume *Britannia Rediviva*

(Oxford, 1660); R. Brathwait, *To His Majesty upon His Happy Arrivall* (London, 1660); or Waller's and Dryden's panegyrics.

6. I have addressed this topic in "Lines of Authority: Politics and Literary Culture in the Restoration," in *Politics of Discourse,* ed. Sharpe and Zwicker, 230–47.

7. The debates can be followed in volume 5 of William Cobbett's *Parliamentary History of England,* 36 vols. (London, 1806–1820); all the known sources for the debates in the Convention, including Lois Schwoerer's edition of "A Jornall of the Convention at Westminster begun the 22 of January 1688/89," can be found in David Lewis Jones, *A Parliamentary History of the Glorious Revolution* (London: HMSO, 1988).

8. See Thomas P. Slaughter, " 'Abdicate' and 'Contract' in the Glorious Revolution," *Historical Journal* 24 (1981): 323–37; John Miller, "The Glorious Revolution: 'Contract' and 'Abdication' Reconsidered," *Historical Journal* 25 (1982): 541–55; and Slaughter, " 'Abdicate' and 'Contract' Restored," *Historical Journal* 28 (1985): 399–403.

9. See *Poems on Affairs of State,* 5: 19–36; and such volumes as *The Design of Enslaving England Discovered* (1689); *London's Flames Reviv'd* (1689); and *Sidney Redivivus* (1689). The verse panegyrics on William are filled with references to bigotry, superstition, and Egyptian slavery.

10. The "amasing Concurrence of Providences, which have conspired to hatch and bring forth, and perfect this extraordinary Revolution" was a repeated theme in sermons and panegyrics on the revolution; see Gilbert Burnet, *A Sermon Preached . . . the 23rd of December, 1688* (London, 1689), B1^r; Simon Patrick, *A Sermon Preached . . . January 31, 1688* (London, 1689); William Sherlock, *A Sermon Preached before the Right Honorable The Lord Mayor* (London, 1689); and Simon Patrick, *A Sermon Preached in the Chappel of St. James* (London, 1689).

11. See Kenyon, *Revolution Principles,* 61–101.

12. Cf. the satire "Mall in her Majesty," in *Poems on Affairs of State,* 5:25–29.

13. Robert Smythies, "On the late Happy Revolution. A Pindarique Ode," *Musae Cantabrigienses* (Cambridge, 1689), a^v.

14. See Smythies, "On the late Happy Revolution," a3^r: "The Land with dire confusion thus o'respread, / Call'd the Great Nassau to its aid, / The peacefull Warriour quickly came, / And struck it not, but look't it into Frame; / He came and took a pittying view, / The Conscious heap his meaning knew, / And the unruly motions quickly drew / Into an Order regular and true."

15. [Thomas Rogers], "A Panegyric upon their Majesties King William and Queen Mary," in *Lux Occidentalis* (London, 1689), 12.

16. For examples (all drawn from *Musae Cantabrigienses*), see John Herbert, "To the King": "Great Prince, what Glories do's Thy Name deserve? / What Praise? who only Conquer'st to preserve" (b3^v); or the reference in Rich. Stone's panegyric to William's "kind Invasion" (c3^r); or B. Cudworth's verse: "No more the ancient Conquerour's splendid Name, / Shall fill alone the Glorious Rolls of Fame; / Whose Arms, Revenge, or vain ambition lead, / And

rais'd their bloody Trophies on the dead: / Your Pow'rfull Name the Mighty Work compleats, / And over willing minds an easier Conquest gets" (c4ᵛ).

17. Cf. Smythies, "On the late Happy Revolution," *Musae Cantabrigienses,* a2ᵛ; or W. Bisset, "Great Heroe!" *Musae Cantabrigienses,* d2ᵛ.

18. P. Sayve, "To the King," *Musae Cantabrigienses,* b2ᵛ.

19. John Guy, *On the Happy Accession of Their Majesties King William and Queen Mary . . . A Pindarique Ode* (London, 1699), C2ᵛ–D1ʳ.

20. *Poems on Affairs of State,* 5:vii.

21. *Poems on Affairs of State,* 5:xxv.

22. Steven N. Zwicker, *Politics and Language in Dryden's Poetry: The Arts of Disguise* (Princeton: Princeton University Press, 1984), 123–24.

23. See, especially, the commentary in volume 15 of *The Works of John Dryden,* ed. H. T. Swedenberg, Jr., et al., 20 vols. (Berkeley and Los Angeles: University of California Press, 1956–), vol. 15, *Plays,* ed. Earl Miner, 404–8.

24. See *Works of John Dryden,* 15:408–9.

25. See G. E. Cokayne, *The Complete Peerage,* ed. Vicary Gibbs et al., 13 vols. (London: St. Catherine Press, 1910–1959), 7:556–57.

26. The earl of Romney, a five-guinea subscriber to Dryden's *Virgil,* was given a particularly compromising plate for his subscription; see Zwicker, *Politics and Language,* 195–96.

27. *Works of John Dryden,* 15:60–61; all citations are to this edition. Citations to the dedication and preface are indicated in my text by volume and page number in parentheses, and citations to the text of the play are indicated by act, scene, and line number in parentheses.

28. For a full discussion of parallel and analogy in *Don Sebastian,* see David Bywaters, "Dryden and the Revolution of 1688: Political Parallel in *Don Sebastian,*" *JEGP* 85 (1986): 346–65.

29. *Works of John Dryden,* 15:72, 417n.

30. For a summary of the historical materials, see *Works of John Dryden,* 15:383–89.

31. *Works of John Dryden,* 15:385.

32. See Bywaters, "Dryden and the Revolution of 1688," 358–59.

33. See H. T. Swedenberg, Jr., "Dryden's Obsessive Concern with the Heroic," in *Essays in English Literature of the Classical Period Presented to Dougald MacMillan,* ed. Daniel W. Patterson and Albrecht B. Strauss (Chapel Hill: University of North Carolina Press, 1967), 12–26.

34. *The Poems of John Dryden,* ed. James Kinsley, 4 vols. (Oxford: Clarendon Press, 1958), 3:1424.

35. *The Poems and Letters of Andrew Marvell,* ed. H. M. Margoliouth, 3d ed. rev. Pierre Legouis with E. E. Duncan-Jones, 2 vols. (Oxford: Clarendon Press, 1971), 1:92, lines 37–40.

36. On this theme in Dryden's late poetry, see David Bywaters, *Dryden in Revolutionary England* (Berkeley and Los Angeles: University of California Press, 1991), esp. chap. 4, "The Poet, Not the Man: Poetry and Prose, 1692–1700," 104–62.

Index

absolutism: and Exclusion Crisis, 166,
170; and literary style, 159–60; and
patriarchalism, 132–33, 135, 138,
154–55; and property, 146–47
abundance: and Charles II, 134, 141–
42, 169; and commercial empire,
101–3, 107, 121; and the court, 111,
117, 119–20; in Milton's Eden, 123–
26, 128; and patriarchy, 149; and the
Restoration, 91–94, 114
Act against Unlicensed and Scandalous
Books (1649), 43, 220n39
Act of Indemnity and Oblivion (1660),
230n12, 232n24
"Advice to His Grace" (1681), 241n27
aesthetics: in *Eikonoklastes*, 45–46, 49,
51, 56, 59, 221n50; and polemic, 1–2,
30, 32, 34–35, 53, 211n16; as a
political subject, 10–11, 19, 20–21, 23,
24–25; and regicide, 37–40, 42–43
Albemarle, George Monck, duke of, 102
allegory, 4, 6–7, 18, 62, 118, 121, 124,
128, 165
Allestree, Richard, 229n8, 232n29
allusion, 12, 41, 46, 66, 67, 77, 195
Amphion, 15, 21, 76–77, 85, 87
analogy, 41, 47, 71, 76, 78, 105, 151,
180, 184–85, 191, 193, 197, 199,
228n45, 245n28
Anglesey, James: "Upon the Queens
Landing" (1662), 231n19
Anglicanism, 18, 52, 55, 66, 71, 72
Anglo-Dutch wars (1665–1667), 7–8,
94–119

animadversion, 16, 37, 47, 158, 160,
162
antiquity, 18, 19, 66, 70, 73, 74, 128,
133, 147, 149, 225n18
apocalypticism: and Cromwell, 76, 81–
83, 88, 227n41, 228n42; and poetry,
79, 88; and politics, 8, 72–73; and
retreat, 62, 75
appetite: and Charles II's court, 94,
102–4, 115–19; in Dryden's portrait
of Charles II, 134–36, 140, 168–70;
and the duchess of York, 96–98, 109–
11; and Henry Jermyn, 108; in
Milton's Eden, 123–24
Aristotle, 11, 14, 54, 70, 74, 152, 156
Ashcraft, Richard, 145, 157, 237n6,
238n7, 238n8, 238n10, 240n21
Atterbury, Francis, 4–5
Aylmer, G. E., 223n5

Bacchus, 90, 119, 120, 123
Bacon, Francis, 68, 70
Bagshaw, Edward, 232n22
Baker, Thomas: *The Head of Nile* (1681),
239n17
ballads, 43, 67, 71, 80, 83, 206n5
Barbeau, Anne T., 238n9
Barish, Jonas, 214n52
Barksdale, Clement: *Nympha libethris*
(1651), 223n4
Bennet, Henry, earl of Arlington, 118
Berkeley, George, earl of: *Historical
Applications* (1667), 230n11
Berkenhead, Sir John, 29

Library of Congress Cataloging-in-Publication Data

Zwicker, Steven N.
    Lines of authority : politics and English literary culture, 1649–1689 / Steven N.
Zwicker.
        p.   cm.
    Includes bibliographical references and index.
    ISBN 0-8014-2070-9
    1. English literature—Early modern, 1500–1700—History and criticism.   2. Politics
and literature—Great Britain—History—17th century.   3. Great Britain—Politics and
government—1649–1660.   4. Great Britain—Politics and government—1660–1688.
5. Authority in literature.   I. Title.
PR438.P65Z93 1993
820.9'358—dc20

                                                                    92-33995